Two week loan

WITHDRAWN

Please return on or before the last
date stamped below.
Charges are made for late return.

2 9 AUG 1997 CANCELLED		

The
INTERNATIONAL
Education Quotations
ENCYCLOPAEDIA

The INTERNATIONAL *Education Quotations* ENCYCLOPAEDIA

KEITH ALLAN NOBLE

Open University Press
Buckingham · Philadelphia

Open University Press
Celtic Court
22 Ballmoor
Buckingham
MK18 1XW

and

1900 Frost Road, Suite 101
Bristol, PA 19007, USA

First Published 1995

A catalogue record of this book is available from the British Library

ISBN 0 335 19394 3

Library of Congress Cataloging-in-Publication Data
The international education quotations encyclopaedia/[compiled] by
Keith Allan Noble.
     p.   cm.
  Includes bibliographical references and index.
  ISBN 0–335 19394 3 (hardback)
  1. Education–Quotations, maxims, etc.   I. Noble, Keith Allan, 1951
  LB7.I65   1995
  370–dc20   94–36312
                                       CIP

Printed on acid-free paper

Typeset by Type Study, Scarborough
Printed in Great Britain by St Edmundsbury Press Ltd,
Bury St Edmunds, Suffolk

to
the memory of a true educator,
Annie Jago (née Parry)

Contents

Summary

- intellectually stimulating, easy to read and useful;

- spans over 3000 years and contains nearly 2700 entries;

- compilation is international, objective and balanced;

- entries are taken from classic to contemporary sources;

- more than 1300 female and male authors are incorporated;

- abbreviations are minimal and simple to understand;

- well over 400 education related topics are listed;

- authors and sources are acknowledged alphabetically;

- explains the Quotation Quadrangle, a good memory aid;

- includes an index of the authors, and for each letter.

Acknowledgements

When you absolutely positively have to know ask a librarian.
American Library Association, 1986

Amerika Haus, Frankfurt aM, Deutschland
British Council, Köln, Deutschland
Catholic University, Washington, United States
Dalhousie University, Halifax, Canada
George Washington University, Washington, United States
Institut Français, Mainz, Deutschland
Institute of Education, London, United Kingdom
Japan Information and Cultural Centre, London, United Kingdom
Klaus-Kuhnke-Archiv für Populäre Musik, Bremen, Deutschland
Library of New South Wales, Sydney, Australia
Mount St Vincent University, Halifax, Canada
Newcomb College Center for Research on Women, Tulane University, New Orleans, United States
Ontario Institute for Studies in Education, Toronto, Canada
Sasakawa Peace Foundation, Washington, United States
Stadt- und Universitätsbibliothek, Frankfurt aM, Deutschland
Université d'Ottawa/University of Ottawa, Ottawa, Canada

Guidance from librarians in the above institutions helped greatly in the compilation of this work. Their contribution is gratefully acknowledged.

Prologue

Your involvement or interest in education means that you will find this encyclopaedia thought provoking and useful.

Spanning several millennia, it contains nearly 2700 education related quotations. They were carefully chosen from disparate sources and represent the thoughts of over 1300 people. These quotations come from ancient oriental philosophers; the sages of the Middle East; Greek and Roman scholars; thinkers from the Renaissance and Reformation; Napoleonic-era authors; 19th- and 20th-century writers; and those now pondering the next century.

There is no other compilation of similar quotations as varied as this volume. It is *the* first work, of this scope and size, dealing exclusively with the stated subject. As the reader will have already noted, the work also incorporates in its title the word *international*; this is due to the geographical range of national and individual sources from which the quotations were selected, not because international education is a focus of the work or because the volume is marketed internationally. W.O. Lester Smith wrote: "[E]ducation does not lend itself to definition, and certainly not to one that can endure as unalterably true". Consequently, you are advised to interpret *education* in its broadest sense, as this is how it was applied in this work; in no case was the word defined solely in relation to traditional schools or educational systems. Users and casual observers of recent works highlighting the words of others know that quotations are not just small, rare gems mined from more prosaic or poetic overburden. Overall, *quotations* are verbatim reproductions of thoughts which vary in clarity, shape and size, and which engage the emotional, intellectual, moral and/or spiritual senses. So here you will find various types of quotation ranging from one word to over 300 in length. Brevity was not a selection criterion, nor was fame of the author, for fame claims its fair share of fools. Collectively, the work has been called an *encyclopaedia* because it contains writings on numerous topics related to one specific subject, and it has been structured accordingly. The word encyclopaedia is most appropriate as etymologically it stems from the Greek roots for "general" and "education".

All of the quotations were chosen to illuminate education, be it past, present, or prognostic, and although the encyclopaedia contains many hundreds of topics it does not claim to be definitive. There were a number of purposes which prompted the preparation of this work, and each merits some elaboration.

Compilation: numerous volumes of epigrams, proverbs, and so on already exist. However, the common limitation of these works is the attempt to address all possible subjects. This reduces the significance of each individual subject, and it means that "education" is restricted and found somewhere between "ecstasy" and "effort". Education, which everyone in the world experiences either formally or informally, deserves better; therefore, compiling an encyclopaedia exclusively for education permits a much broader range of related quotations to be listed. Overall, you will find more than 400 topics here, which makes the encyclopaedia far more relevant and useful to those whose specific interest is education.

Revelation: it was anticipated that compiling such a large number and range of quotations would provide insight on education as it has been practised throughout the ages, and this belief has proved justified. Just as schools reflect the societies in which they are located, quotations can reveal much about the environment that existed when they came into being.

In my primary or, as they say in some countries, grade-school days, the chalkboards had proverbs in large letters printed across the top, and if we did not abide by them we were punished. Two of them remain in my mind to this day one was: EMPTY VESSELS MAKE THE MOST NOISE (an English proverb) and the other, SPEECH IS SILVER, SILENCE IS GOLDEN (a Persian proverb). This quickly tells you about the behaviour expected from the pupils, and it says a lot about the norms of the educational system that existed and the society that formed it. That children should be seen and not heard was an underlying belief in the society in which I was raised.

Contemplation: because education is generally considered to be a practical, doing profession, contemplation is a personal habit not commonly acquired or maintained by practitioners. All too frequently they (that is, educators, teachers and trainers) are caught up in a whirlwind of movement which at its centre has a complex and demanding set of rules set up by an all-powerful system. On a day-to-day basis, few of those who are physically involved in education have an inclination, or receive encouragement, to reflect either seriously or in great depth upon current educational circumstances and events, be they short- or long-term, local or national. Maintaining the status quo and the shortage of time simply militate against this.

Even after a cursory perusal of the quotations here, it is obvious that many educational issues have changed over the millennia. A few, however, are the same. For most readers this will not be a revelation, but it is still significant and should be kept in mind. This encyclopaedia reveals the insights of many thinkers – some wise, a few questioning, others challenging – and we are foolish if we ignore them. To spend time contemplating their words can provide answers to educational problems which might have puzzled us for some time.

Education: in our current world of specialization and specifics, education has become fragmented to the point where people who are involved or interested in the subject have difficulty communicating with each other: jargon abounds, selfish interests irritate and isolate, paradigms collide. Those who are curious about education or who are embarking on an educational career can be confused by the incessant pressure in the discipline to specialize and remain up-to-date with the latest trends and techniques. Small and simple monochrome sketches of reality are naively thrust forward as critical educational problems; the full palette of colours carelessly or deliberately unused. Overall, the big picture is rarely presented or understood well, and apart from some social critics and scholars of education, few people see the wide, multi-coloured reality of education: "Truth", as Oscar Wilde pointed out, "is rarely pure, and never simple".

With its many hundred points of view, this compilation provides those who want to know about education with a perspective which is not only broad and cosmopolitan, but also historic, hermeneutic, and heuristic. Such a perspective is seen best when the work is read like a novel or a work of non-fiction. To see it just as a compilation of quotable quotes, or to use it merely as a reference book, is to forfeit an opportunity of seeing education in a variety of its existing colours and shades.

To assist you in your reading, the encyclopaedia has been designed and published in a most reader-friendly manner. Unlike many works on quotations that are set in small, difficult-to-read type, the type and the page layout used here have been considered with your needs in mind, not the printer's. There is no laboriously long list to search through if you want to locate a specific quotation, as each letter of the alphabet has its own index page; and within the encyclopaedia itself, under each topic, the quotations are listed alphabetically by author, or by source if there is no known author. To locate a quotation from a known author, simply use the author index, as it lists all of her or his quotations included in the work.

In conjunction with each quotation, the common names of the author are given; additional or real names appear in parentheses (). All accompanying dates are from the Gregorian calendar; for those unfamiliar with this calendar, BC years decrease to zero and AD years increase from zero. The dates refer to the birth and death of the author or to the year of publication of the source, which is given in italics; note that the year of publication will vary according to the edition of the source. Books have the year of publication only, whereas journals, magazines, newspapers and other sources have additional day and/or month data, or volume and/or number data. Sufficient information is acknowledged and provided for the reader to further investigate the person, the period and/or the publication related to every quotation.

When reading this encyclopaedia it is important to keep in mind the following:

- the originator (usually referred to as the "author") of a quotation may not necessarily be responsible for the concept or thought upon which the quotation is based – it may stem from another person's mind;
- a quotation does not necessarily express the personal belief of the author(s) – it may be the belief of someone else, such as a character in a story;
- not every quotation is a perfect crystallization of an author's thoughts – the reader should refer to the whole source or milieu to put the quotation in its original context, because a few short words might not accurately reflect a lengthy phrase, a phrase might not capture the meaning of a complete sentence, a sentence might not describe a whole paragraph, and a paragraph cannot summarize an entire chapter of a book or an extensive period of time.

For readers whose first language is not English and who are unfamiliar with abbreviations used in the Western world, please note the following:

c.	means *circa*, Latin for "round about"; it indicates an approximation
né and née	mean the family/last name at birth, male and female respectively
no.	means number
pseud.	means pseudonym, which is the fictitious name the author has adopted, sometimes referred to as "pen name" or "nom de plume"; this name is not used for day-to-day living
pub.	means publisher
sic	is Latin for "thus", used in written texts to indicate that the preceding word or phrase is not a mistake and that it is meant to appear as given
vol.	means volume
?	means the exact date or item is not known.

Wherever an explanatory notation is required to assist you with your reading or understanding of a quotation or its context, the notation is given in brackets [].

With few exceptions, the quotations compiled in this work are from solitary authors. Abiding strictly by the tradition of singular authorship was thought to be too limiting, as it would have precluded several worthwhile quotations.

Considerable effort was taken to include quotations from female authors who, much to our loss, have been too frequently ignored over the last few thousand years. Numerous works by women were searched for quotations that could be considered relevant to education. There is a mass of works by and on Western men which far outweighs those by and on women. Consequently, there is an unbalanced emphasis on the thoughts of men, and the voice of women has been denied fair hearing. It is hoped that this compilation will help level the scales of equality. Quotations from non-Western authors were also sought to ensure that the encyclopaedia was truly international in its scope, not Eurocentric. Note that because most of the world's biggest and most prolific publishing houses are established in Western countries, and have been for hundreds of years, quotations revealing a non-European perspective are regrettably fewer in number.

When working with quotations there are four things requiring careful attention and consideration, and when brought together correctly these make up the figure I have labelled the Quotation Quadrangle. This four-sided mnemonic figure reflects and joins all of the critical aspects of quotations and their usage.

One side of the figure is *attribution*. Attributing a quotation to the correct person who said or wrote the words that are quoted can be difficult; determining the first person, however, can be exceedingly difficult. One scholar, George Seldes, spent 25 years full-time tracking down original sources in his efforts to produce compilations of quotations. Examples of quotations that are either similar or the same, and which have been recorded over the centuries, can be found in the literature. As the Latin playwright Terence astutely noted over 2000 years ago: "Nothing is ever said that has not been said before".

Partially, this problem is caused by the similarity between, and confusion over, names. For example, some female writers have had two names, their own and a male pseudonym they adopted to help them get published (see George Eliot and George Sand), or they were unacknowledged or concealed their own identities (Virginia Woolf points out: "I would venture to guess that Anon[ymous], who wrote so many poems without signing them, was often a woman"). There were four Greek philosophers called Zeno whose thoughts are still propounded; three Huxleys are regularly quoted; the words of two knighted authors with the name Walter

Raleigh appear in print; and people like Socrates the philosopher (not Socrates the early-Christian historian, or Socrates the Bithynian king, or Isocrates the Athenian orator), who it is claimed rarely wrote anything but had his utterances recorded by contemporaries and followers such as Plato, always deserve special consideration, for in these cases we rely on what someone else *said* was said. Obviously, the opportunity for error in such circumstances is great.

Inaccurate attribution is always a problem. What is not lost to antiquity is dimmed by failing memories, misrecorded by less-than-meticulous record keepers, distorted later by inaccurate transcription, and broadcast by erring users.

Inseparable from attribution is *accuracy*. Even after consulting several references, one can find conflicting wording for some quotations; and it must never be assumed that the oldest available reference source is most accurate. The problem is worsened when translation is involved, particularly when different translations exist. Here we should remember the words of Martin Joseph Routh: "Always verify your references". Understandably, this can be difficult when it comes to rare works, foreign languages and hard-to-locate sources. Similar words can be mistakenly transcribed, individual letters confused and punctuation used incorrectly, all of which will, unfortunately, distort the original.

It is essential to strive for accuracy, because when a quotation is not given accurately, the associated attribution is immediately rendered inaccurate.

The third side is *acknowledgement*. When using quotations, writers should acknowledge sufficient information for their readers – information that will assist them to locate and study the source of the quotation should they so desire. Providing this data is sometimes difficult, and when it is impossible, the quotation should not be used. Too frequently one reads a quotation unaccompanied by any form of attribution to the author or any acknowledgement of the source or the period of origin. When a source is acknowledged, it is important to note that the person from whose mind the words for the quotation have come, is not necessarily the author or editor of the source acknowledged. It can happen that the quotation does appear in the source cited, but the source can be a multi-authored work compiled by an editor, or the quotation can appear in a cited article authored by someone else, or the words can be, for example, those spoken by a character in a play.

It was Samuel Johnson who stated that "Every quotation contributes something to the stability or enlargement of the language", and of course he is correct, for a quotation given correctly. However, without an attribution and acknowledgement, an inaccurate quotation can remain uncorrected and be widely and even egregiously misused. In these situations there is no positive contribution to the language, only a negative diminution.

The final side of this memory-enhancing figure is *application*. Although Bertrand Russell urged us to "Have no respect for the authority of others, for there are always contrary authorities to be found", we tend to use the authority and the quotations of those who support our argument, case or stance. We must therefore be careful with application. It pays to investigate not only the source of the quotation, but also the author's character and the situation that existed when he or she produced the words that have become the quotation.

What would we think of Winston Churchill if we did not know his character and we read the following quotation from his pre-World War II work *Great Contemporaries*, in which he writes about Hitler: "If our country were defeated I hope we should find a champion as admirable to restore our courage and lead us back to our place among the nations". The attribution is correct and the quotation is given accurately, but applied in this form it could be used, mistakenly or deceitfully, to claim that Churchill supported Hitler. Those who are not familiar with the era (and millions of people around the world are not) could draw the conclusion that Churchill agreed with Hitler's activities. But when the preceding sentence, deceptively omitted, is added, the quotation conveys a different meaning, a meaning more in line with the real Churchill: "One may dislike Hitler's system and yet admire his patriotic achievement. If our country were defeated I hope we should find a champion as admirable to restore our courage and lead us back to our place among the nations".

Together, *attribution*, *accuracy*, *acknowledgement* and *application* make up the Quotation Quadrangle, and they are the essential considerations for quotations to be cited correctly. Each is a potential problem that can lead to distorted thinking and (subsequently) writing. When this occurs it detracts from or destroys the argument, case or stance for which the quotation is being used as support.

Overall, the quotations selected here were chosen using the following criteria:

- a quotation must have some relationship to education (remember that education was defined internationally and broadly, not parochially and narrowly);
- a quotation must have some relationship to education that is significant, or at least one that is not transient;
- a quotation must have an identifiable source for attribution and be accompanied by a minimum form of acknowledgement (proverbs by definition have no known author, so they are exempt);
- quotations from female and non-Western authors must be given equal consideration with those of male and Western authors respectively;

- most of the quotations must be from a range of significant sources that need not, however, be associated with education as it is or has been traditionally practised;
- titles and positions of authors must not be given any consideration.

This encyclopaedia arises from over two decades of intermittent researching, reading and recording. If you find any disagreement between quotations or feel tension develop within yourself, it demonstrates that this is an objective compilation, which is what was planned. Education is subjective and this inevitably creates bias, so evidence of conflict and tension demonstrates an objective balance, a polychrome perspective which is vital to gaining an understanding of the subject. No guarantee is given that the authors listed were the first to originate the quotations (this was not the intent of the work), nor that the quotations are without error. Of course, every effort has been made to ensure correct attribution, exact accuracy and acknowledgement, but any claim to complete lack of error would be arrogant and foolish.

You will find congruencies, contrasts and contradictions in this encyclopaedia which will disturb the narrow minds of traditionalists but stimulate free-thinkers. As quick examples: note the differences between **DROPOUT, STOPOUT** and **TUNEOUT**; compare BRADBURY (under **CLASSICS**), with SOUNDVIEW EXECUTIVE BOOK SUMMARIES (**BOOK**), EJIOGU & AJEYALEMI (**DEVELOPING COUNTRIES**) with KIDRON & SEGAL (**SYSTEM**), and EURICH (**COMPUTER**) with POSTMAN (**COMPUTER**); think about free expression on the campus after reading MUHAMMAD (**FREEDOM OF SPEECH**); contemplate the belief of GATTO (**CERTIFICATION**); reflect on the observations of BRAUSE (**SCHOOLING**), SEIKATSU (**TEACHER**), and SPENDER (**INEQUALITY**); and ask yourself why **VIOLENCE** is increasing at educational institutions.

To conclude, I am indebted to my publisher John Skelton for encouraging me to complete the manuscript, and for drawing my attention to the works of important Asian writers; I am most appreciative of the insights and encouragement from the anonymous reviewers who examined an earlier draft of this work; and I thank my colleagues at Open University Press, all of whom are true professionals and a pleasure to work with.

And finally, your interest in this work is appreciated and your comments are requested. Please see the Epilogue for details.

Keith Allan Noble, PhD

A

ABACUS

SCHOOL ROOM ABACI. These are intended for use only in teaching. In all abaci [plural of abacus], a bead above the cross-bar represents 5, while each of the five lower ones placed on a line stands for 1, thus making it possible to count 10 on every vertical line.

DEPARTMENT OF EDUCATION;
A Catalogue with Explanatory Notes of the Exhibits from the
Department of Education, Empire of Japan, in the International
Health and Education Exhibition Held in London, 1884

At an early date pebbles were added to fingers as an aid in counting; the survival of the *abacus*, and of the "little stone" (*calculus*) concealed in the word *calculate*, reveal to us how small, again, is the gap between the simplest and the latest man.

WILL(IAM) (JAMES) DURANT;
The Story of Civilization (vol. I), 1954

[A]n abacus is an adding machine, calculator, and computer. On second thoughts that's not quite true. The abacus is just a visual record of the computations going on in the mind of the person using it.

ROBERT FULGHUM;
All I Really Need to Know I Learned in Kindergarten, 1989

It is probable that calculations were made with beads and counters, either on a sand table, or strung on wires in an abacus (*abax* is Greek for "table").

JOHN MCLEISH; *Number,* 1992

ABC

. . . alienate, bore and control students (the ABCs of school). . . .

RITA S. BRAUSE; *Enduring Schools,* 1992

Learn the ABC of science before you try to ascend to its summit.

(IVAN PETROVICH) PAVLOV, 1849–1936

The merchant classes . . . wanted their children to know their ABC's so that they could handle the paper world of commerce.

NEIL POSTMAN; *The Disappearance of Childhood,* 1994

The ABCs are drummed into schoolchildren so early and in such a rigorous way that this system of organization sometimes seems as if it's God-given. But it isn't: only a cultural consensus put L before M instead of the other way around.

RICHARD SAUL WURMAN; *Information Anxiety*, 1991

ABD (All But Dissertation)

Do not make a mistake, A.B.D. is not a doctoral degree.

SAMUEL M.K ANYOMI;
*Traditional Students' Attitude Towards
Nontraditional Degree Programs*, 1986

If we are to rescue the ABD "at risk" population . . . we must deal with the issues of efficiency, excellence, and equity.

TRUDY L. HANSON;
a *paper* (Speech Communication Association), Oct. 1992

One of the more euphemistic phrases in higher education today is the expression *ABD*.

MICHAEL MONSOUR & STEVE CORMAN;
Communication Education, Apr. 1991

Upon finishing the required course work and surviving whatever examin ation ritual the department requires, students achieve the dubious status of A.B.D. . . . .

RICHARD W. MOORE; *Winning the Ph.D. Game*, 1985

Taking a *new* job before finishing is a way of not getting a PhD. At the very least it will put off completion for several years (in our experience six to eight years and more), until the intellectual learning curve of the new job allows it – or else you join the ranks of those whom the Americans call the "ABDs": the "all-but-dissertation" brigade.

ESTELLE M. PHILLIPS & D.S. PUGH; *How to Get a PhD*, 1994

ACADEME

The green retreats of Academus.

MARK AKENSIDE; *Pleasures of the Imagination*, 1744

And seek for truth in the groves of Academe.

(QUINTUS HORATIUS FLACCUS) HORACE, 65–8

The best Academe, a mother's knee.

JAMES RUSSELL LOWELL; *The Cathedral*, 1870

ACADEMIC FREEDOM

Although the principle of academic freedom clearly extends to scientific research, it does not give *carte blanche* to scientists to conduct their work in any way they please.

DEREK BOK; *Beyond the Ivory Tower*, 1982

Academic freedom is not merely the privilege of university teachers; students also have rights that need to be safe-guarded. An examiner has no right to penalize a candidate for reaching a conclusion different from that which he has reached himself, provided that the candidate gives sensible reasons in support of his view.

G(EORGE) LESLIE BROOK; *The Modern University*, 1965

But should students themselves enjoy academic freedom along with their professors? The answer is yes and no. The German universities make a useful distinction here between *Lernfreiheit* ("learning-freedom") and *Lehrfreiheit* ("teaching-freedom"). The former concerns the student: the freedom to choose what to study (elective curriculum), to decide when and how to study, and to make up one's own mind. The latter concerns the professor: the freedom to choose lecture subjects, to select problems for research, to draw one's own conclusions about truth. . . . Since students are only beginners, they are not mature enough scholars for full academic freedom.

JOHN S. BRUBACHER;
On the Philosophy of Higher Education, 1977

A university's essential character is that of being a center of free inquiry and criticism – a thing not to be sacrificed for anything else.

RICHARD HOFSTADTER; *Saturday Review*, 12 May 1979

Academic freedom has thus been transformed into *carte blanche* or academic licence, and it has protected not only intellectual independence but also personal failings and misconduct.

THOMAS SOWELL; *Inside American Education*, 1993

Education must not be compelled to submit to improper administrative control at the hands of the State. Education should be freely carried out by educators who themselves are free and independent.

KOTARO TANAKA; a *ministerial statement*, 1946

Academic freedom refers to the freedom of individual academics to study, teach, research and publish without being subject to or causing undue interference. Academic freedom is granted in the belief that it enhances the pursuit and application of worthwhile knowledge, and as such is supported by society through the funding of academics and their institutions. Academic freedom embodies an acceptance by academics of the need to encourage openness and flexibility in academic work, and of their accountability to each other and to society in general.

MALCOLM TIGHT;
Academic Freedom and Responsibility, 1988

ACADEMICS

Academic education is the act of memorizing things read in books, and things told by college professors who got their education mostly by memorizing things read in books.

GERALD KENNEDY; *Note Book*, 1927

That academics has become the path all children must pursue in order to meet their nonacademic aspirations – from engineer to lawyer to bookkeeper – is absurd.

DEBORAH MEIER; *Dissent*, Winter 1994

ADMINISTRATION

Administrators may exclude teachers from the decision process "because there's not enough time" or "because they're not around", or "because teachers don't understand these concerns".

RITA S. BRAUSE; *Enduring Schools*, 1992

So key academic and management decisions are forced on schools from above, with little regard for their effect on students and learning, or even for their consistency with other policies already in place. This is a prescription for failure.

MARVIN CETRON & MARGARET GAYLE;
Educational Renaissance, 1991

In 1965–85 the number of non-teaching staff in school administration in the United States grew by 102% while the number of students shrank by 8%.

The Economist, 8 Aug. 1992

There are many teachers who cannot really see why any other system than that of expertise is needed to run a school, and who therefore find the bureaucracy and conformity required by the other systems an insult to their profession and evidence of a reluctance to give up power by those at the top.

CHARLES HANDY & ROBERT AITKEN;
Understanding Schools as Organizations, 1986

As a general practice to please the city bureaus of education, school administrators tend to report only good news while covering up bad news in their schools.

JING LIN; *Education in Post-Mao China*, 1993

Many school administrators feel uncomfortable with theories. They prefer that social scientists provide them with practical prescriptions for administering their schools.

FRED C. LUNENBURG & ALLAN C. ORNSTEIN;
Educational Administration, 1991

Education is conducted within a bureaucratic structure.

SYBOUTS WARD; *Planning in School Administration*, 1992

ADULT EDUCATION

These three characteristics – full development, perspective and autonomy – are traits that mark off the adult from the non-adult in almost all societies. They carry profound implications for us as teachers.

ALAN ROGERS; *Teaching Adults*, 1986

The overall concept or umbrella term *adult education* is not always used. Some people prefer *continuing education* or, more recently, *life-long learning*.

ROBERT M. SMITH; *Learning How to Learn*, 1982

ADVERSITY

There is no education like adversity.

BENJAMIN DISRAELI, 1804–1881

AGE

Chronological age is not *necessarily* correlated with increased breadth and depth of experience.

STEPHEN D. BROOKFIELD;
Developing Critical Thinkers, 1987

What youth learns, age does not forget.

DANISH proverb

The earliest age is the most important one for education because the beginning decides the manner of progress and the end.

(FRIEDRICH) FROEBEL; *Reminiscences*, 1895

What you learn in youth you do not unlearn in old age.

GREEK proverb

Schools seem to have universally decided that age is the first factor to be separated out.

CHARLES HANDY & ROBERT AITKEN;
Understanding Schools as Organizations, 1986

[T]he tie between education and calendar age took some time to develop. The first attempts to establish classes or grades of students were based on the capacities of students to read, not on their calendar age. Differentiation by age came later.

NEIL POSTMAN; *The Disappearance of Childhood*, 1994

ALGEBRA

Stand firm in your refusal to remain conscious during algebra. In real life, I assure you, there is no such thing as algebra.

FRAN LEBOWITZ, 1950–

The study of algebra is alternately based on claims that (1) it's good training for the mind, (2) that we need it to survive in modern society, or (3) that like it or not it's an essential gateway for more highly skilled jobs. Meanwhile most of us can't remember the last time we solved a problem using an algebraic equation.

DEBORAH MEIER; *Dissent*, Winter 1994

ALPHABET

When you're a married man Samivel, you'll understand a good many things as you don't understand now; but vether it's worth going through so much, to learn so little, as the charity boy said ven he got to the end of the alphabet, is a matter o' taste. [*sic*]

CHARLES DICKENS; *Pickwick Papers*, 1836

The alphabet is a technique to record speech sounds in visible form.

IVAN ILLICH; *In the Mirror of the Past*, 1992

I often think how much easier life would have been for me and how much time I should have saved if I had known the alphabet. I can never tell where I and J stand without saying G, H to myself first. I don't know whether P comes before R or after, and where T comes in has to this day remained something that I have never been able to get into my head.

W(ILLIAM) SOMERSET MAUGHAM, 1874–1965

There are none worse than those who, as soon as they have progressed beyond a knowledge of the alphabet, delude themselves into the belief that they are the possessors of real knowledge.

(MARCUS FABIUS) QUINTILIAN(US), *c.*35–*c.*95

AMUSEMENT

People in general do not willingly read, if they can have something else to amuse them.

SAMUEL JOHNSON, 1709–1784

Amusement is the happiness of those who cannot think.

ALEXANDER POPE; *Thoughts on Various Subjects*, 1727

ANATOMY

Anatomy is to physiology as geography to history; it describes the theatre of events.

JEAN FRANÇOIS FERNEL, 1497?–1558

ANDRAGOGY

Although the word *andragogy* makes a neat contrast with the more familiar and traditional *pedagogy*, the contrast appears difficult to maintain.

K. PATRICIA CROSS; *Adults as Learners*, 1984

I believe that andragogy means more than just helping adults learn, and that it therefore has implications for the education of children and youth.

MALCOLM S. KNOWLES;
The Modern Practice of Adult Education, 1970

In essence, andragogy suggests a teacher role which is more responsive and less directive. The model encourages high levels of self-directed learning with the adult student having input regarding content, methodology, learning assessment techniques, and even program design.

THEODORE J. KOWALSKI;
The Organization and Planning of Adult Education, 1988

The word *andragogy* has entered the adult education lexicon, but its meaning has often remained elusive.

JOHN RACHAL; *Lifelong Learning*, May 1983

ANONYMOUS

The people you study have a right to remain anonymous.

EILEEN KANE; *Doing Your Own Research*, 1987

I would venture to guess that Anon[ymous], who wrote so many poems without signing them, was often a woman.

VIRGINIA WOOLF, 1882–1941

ANSWER

There are many who lust for the simple answer of doctrine or degree. They are on the left and right. They are not confined to a single part of the society. They are terrorists of the mind.

A. BARTLETT GIAMATTI; *The New York Times*, 6 Mar. 1983

The answer must lie in learning better ways of learning.

MARVIN MINSKY; *The Society of Mind*, 1985

The best student is the best answer-giver who says what the teacher wants to hear.

IRA SHOR; *Empowering Education*, 1992

The only interesting answers are those that destroy the questions.

SUSAN SONTAG; *Esquire*, Jul. 1968

ANTHROPOLOGIST

How briefly the anthropologists treat the Greek myths is noteworthy.

EDITH HAMILTON; *Mythology*, 1942

ANTHROPOLOGY

Anthropology provides no scientific basis for discrimination against any people on the ground of racial inferiority, religious affiliation, or linguistic heritage.

AMERICAN ANTHROPOLOGICAL ASSOCIATION;
a *resolution*, Dec. 1938

ARCHITECTURE

Architecture is frozen music.

(JOHANN WOLFGANG VON) GOETHE, 1749–1832

ARISTOTLE

Nothing is more ridiculous than to make an author a dictator, as the Schools have done Aristotle. The damage is infinite knowledge receives by it.

BEN JONSON; *Timber*, 1640

Aristotle invented science, but destroyed philosophy.

ALFRED NORTH WHITEHEAD, 1861–1947

ARITHMETIC

There is little point in girls of common extraction learning to read as well as young ladies or being taught as fine a pronunciation or knowing what a period is, etc. It is the same with writing. All they need is enough to keep their accounts and memoranda; you don't need to teach them fine hand-writing or talk to them of style: a little spelling will do. Arithmetic is different. They need it.

FRANÇOISE DE MAINTENON (née FRANÇOISE D'AUBIGNÉ);
Lettres sur l'éducation des filles, 1713

Arab numbers and algorithms made arithmetic so simple that one could throw away all auxiliary aids such as the abacus, and work directly with the numbers themselves.

JOHN McLEISH; *Number*, 1992

Arithmetic is where the answer is right and everything is nice and you can look out of the window and see the blue sky – or the answer is wrong and you have to start all over and try again and see how it comes out this time.

CARL SANDBURG; *Complete Poems*, 1950

ART

All art is concerned with coming into being.

ARISTOTLE, 384–322

Art is permanent revolution.

JEAN-LOUIS BARRAULT, 1910–

Art for art's sake is a philosophy of the well-fed.

CAO YU, 1910–

Art is either revolution or plagiarism; or
Art is either a revolutionist or a plagiarist.

PAUL GAUGUIN, 1848–1903

The reason that art is different from such disciplines as mathematics, mechanics, and chemistry is that art cannot be measured in terms of number and time, nor can it be handed down by instruction through textbooks.

EIICHI KIYOOKA; *Fukuzawa Yukichi on Education*, 1985

Art is the objectification of feeling, and the subjectification of nature.

SUSANNE K. LANGER, 1895–1985

Art is a form of catharsis.

DOROTHY PARKER, 1893–1967

ARTIST

The fundamental purpose of the artist is the same as that of a scientist: to state a fact.

HERBERT READ; *The Form of Things Unknown*, 1960

ASTROLOGY

Astrology is a disease, not a science.

MAIMONIDES (né MOSES BEN MAIMON);
Letter to Marseilles, 1195

ASTRONOMER

Astronomers work always with the past; because light takes time to move from one place to another, they see things as they were, not as they are.

NEALE E. HOWARD;
The Telescope Handbook and Star Atlas, 1967

ASTRONOMY

Astronomy teaches the correct use of the sun and the planets.
STEPHEN LEACOCK, 1869–1944

ATHLETE

I believe athletics is part of an education of a young person, as the Greeks and the English schoolmaster believed: and I believe athletics is part of an education because athletics teaches lessons valuable to the individual by stretching the human spirit in ways that nothing else can.
A. BARTLETT GIAMATTI; *A Free and Ordered Space*, 1988

If athletes rather than scholars are seen as representatives of educational institutions, the probable reason is that sports are a lowest common denominator, a signifier whose significance anyone can understand.
ALLEN GUTTMANN; *A Whole New Ball Game*, 1988

A college which is interested in producing professional athletes is not an educational institution.
ROBERT M. HUTCHINS, 1899–1977

The popular belief in [college] athletics is grounded upon the theory that violent exercise makes for bodily health, and that bodily health is necessary to mental vigor. Both halves of this theory are highly dubious. . . . The truth is that athletes, as a class, are not above the normal in health, but below it.
H(ENRY) L(OUIS) MENCKEN; *The American Mercury*, 1931

The mere athlete becomes too much of a savage.
PLATO (né ARISTOCLES), *c.*428–*c.*348

AUTHOR

The idea it is necessary to go to university in order to become a successful writer, or even a man or woman of letters (which is by no means the same thing), is one of those phantasies that surrounds authorship.
VERA BRITTAIN; *On Being an Author*, 1948

Choose an author as you choose a friend.

WENTWORTH DILLON, 1633–1685

We misquote authors so often because we have not understood them.

(JOHANN WOLFGANG VON) GOETHE, 1749–1832

It takes five books to make an author.

GEORGE GREENFIELD; *Scribblers for Bread*, 1989

AUTHORITY

The authority of them that teach hinders them that would learn.

(MARCUS TULLIUS) CICERO, 106–43

The strongest bulwark of authority is uniformity.

EMMA GOLDMAN; *My Further Disillusion*, 1924

Children must learn not just to behave in accordance with authority but to think critically about authority if they are to live up to the democratic idea of sharing political sovereignty as citizens.

AMY GUTMANN; *Democratic Education*, 1987

If the process of schooling is so dominated by adult authority, it is down-putting and rejectful of the individual and the group, and is likely to breed alienation and resentment, or dependency and conformity.

CHARLES HANDY & ROBERT AITKEN;
Understanding Schools as Organizations, 1986

Every great advance in natural knowledge has involved the absolute rejection of authority.

T(HOMAS) H(ENRY) HUXLEY, 1825–1895

Physical violence is the basis of authority.

(LEO NIKOLAYEVICH) TOLSTOY;
The Kingdom of God is Within You, 1893

AVERAGE

There must be such a thing as a child with average ability, but you can't find a parent who will admit that it is his child.

THOMAS BAILEY; *Wall Street Journal*, 17 Dec. 1961

A measure of central tendency, the arithmetical average of the scores.

JAMES H. McMILLAN & SALLY SCHUMACHER;
Research in Education, 1984

B

BACHELOR DEGREE (Baccalaureate Degree)

The bachelor's degree came into use somewhat later [than the Middle Ages] and at first indicated not the completion but the initiation of a course of study leading to the doctorate or mastership.... In many continental universities, however, it disappeared, becoming identical with [high school] matriculation.

WALTER CROSBY EELLS; *Degrees in Higher Education*, 1963

A bachelor's degree is increasingly being viewed as insufficient, according to a survey of college freshmen [first year students] for the American Council on Education.

International Herald Tribune, 24 Jan. 1994

In the eyes of some, the American baccalaureate degree is already virtually meaningless, in part because of its perversion by diploma mill operators.

DAVID W. STEWART & HENRY A. SPILLE;
Diploma Mills, 1988

For students, it has meant watered-down courses; unqualified instructors; a bachelor's degree of dubious value; and an outrageous bill for spending four or five years in a ghetto of appalling intellectual squalor and mediocrity.

CHARLES J. SYKES; *ProfScam*, 1988

[The bachelor or baccalaureate degree must not be confused with the Baccalauréat of France or the International Baccalaureate, which are high school matriculation programmes and diplomas.]

BACK TO BASICS

What it is that schools are supposed to return to is not always very clear.

ROBIN BARROW & GEOFFREY MILBURN;
A Critical Dictionary of Educational Concepts, 1986

The so-called "Back to Basics Movement" was the educational expression of that rightward shift which characterized American politics in the 1970s.

L. BECK; *The International Encyclopedia of Education* (vol. 1), 1985

Some back-to-basics advocates in the United States believe that our schools should be modeled after those in the industrialized nations of Europe and Asia. One of the arguments to support this view goes back to the test scores showing that students in ... Japan, West Germany, France, and England have higher academic achievement than American students.

KATHLYN GAY; *Crisis in Education*, 1986

BANKING

"Banking education" refers to the system whereby knowledge is seen as deposited by experts in the vaults that are learners' unformed minds. The educator retains total control over the goals, content, and evaluative criteria of the educational activity.

STEPHEN D. BROOKFIELD;
Understanding and Facilitating Adult Learning, 1986

In the banking concept of education, knowledge is a gift bestowed by those who consider themselves knowledgeable upon those whom they consider to know nothing.

PAULO FREIRE; *Pedagogy of the Oppressed*, 1972

The mind is not a receptacle that can be mechanically filled. It is alive and must be nourished.

ALDOUS HUXLEY, 1894–1963

Because it deposits information uncritically in students, the banking model is antidemocratic. It denies the students' indigenous culture and their potential for critical thought, subordinating them to the knowledge, values, and language of the status quo.

IRA SHOR; *Empowering Education*, 1992

BEAUTY

Beauty is truth, truth beauty, – that is all Ye know on earth, and all ye need to know.

JOHN KEATS; *Ode on a Grecian Urn*, 1819

Mathematics possesses not only truth, but some supreme beauty – a beauty cold and austere, like that of sculpture.

BERTRAND RUSSELL; *Mysticism and Logic*, 1925

BIOGRAPHY

The art of Biography
Is different from Geography.
Geography is about Maps,
But Biography is about Chaps.

EDMUND C. BENTLEY, 1875–1956

There is properly no history; only biography.

RALPH WALDO EMERSON, 1803–1882

Biography is to give a man some kind of shape after his death.

VIRGINIA WOOLF, 1882–1941

BIOLOGIST

For the biologist there are no classes – only individuals.

JEAN ROSTAND; *The Subsistence of Man*, 1962

BOARDING SCHOOL

Boarding schools differ.

ROYSTON LAMBERT; *The Hothouse Society*, 1968

Of the many unique features of our [UK] educational system, there is none which has attracted so much controversy, passion and fascination as our boarding schools.

ROYSTON LAMBERT; *The Hothouse Society*, 1968

It is even more striking that the worst aspect of boarding school life, for all types of schools and at all ages is *homesickness*.

ROGER MORGAN; *School Life*, 1993

BOOK

Few aspects of schooling currently have been subject to more intense scrutiny than the textbook.

MICHAEL W. APPLE & LINDA K. CHRISTIAN-SMITH;
The Politics of the Textbook, 1991

I am a man of one book [*The Bible*].

(THOMAS OF AQUIN) THOMAS AQUINAS, 1225–1274

Some books are undeservedly forgotten, none are undeservedly remembered.

W(YSTAN) H(UGH) AUDEN; *The Dyer's Hand*, 1963

Some books are to be tasted, others to be swallowed, and some few to be chewed and digested.

FRANCIS BACON, 1561–1626

[T]he books say *nothing*! Nothing you can teach or believe. They're about nonexistent people, if they're fiction. And if they're nonfiction, it's worse, one professor calling another an idiot, one philosopher screaming down another's gullet. All of them running about, putting out the stars and extinguishing the sun. You come away lost.

RAY BRADBURY; *Fahrenheit 451*, 1953

Books are a triviality. Life alone is great.

THOMAS CARLYLE; *Journal*, 1839

Textbooks have been so watered down that it is sometimes difficult to tell what subject they were intended to teach.

MARVIN CETRON & OWEN DAVIES; *Crystal Globe*, 1991

Most of today's books have an air of having been written in one day from books read the night before.

(NICOLAS SÉBASTIAN ROCH) CHAMFORT;
Maximes et Pensées, 1796

Damn the bright lights by which no one reads, damn the continuous music that no one hears, damn the grand pianos that no one can play, damn the white houses mortgaged up to their rain gutters, damn them for plundering the ocean for fish to feed the mink whose skins they wear, and damn their shelves on which there rests a single book – a copy of the telephone directory bound in brocade.

JOHN CHEEVER; *The New Yorker*, 25 Nov. 1967

Every book must be chewed to get out its juice.

CHINESE proverb

A room without books is as a body without a soul.

(MARCUS TULLIUS) CICERO, 106–43

We should choose our books as we would our companions, for their sterling and intrinsic merit.

C(HARLES) C(ALEB) COLTON; *Lacon*, 1825

Men must as far as possible be taught to become wise by studying the heavens, the earth, oaks, and beeches, but not by studying books.

(JOHN AMOS KOMENSKY) COMENIUS; *The Great Didactic*, 1657

Beware the man of one book.

ISAAC D'ISRAELI; *Curiosities of Literature, c.*1800

Books are fatal: they are the curse of the human race. Nine-tenths of existing books are nonsense, and the clever books are the refutation of the nonsense. The greatest misfortune that ever befell man was the invention of printing.

BENJAMIN DISRAELI, 1804–1881

God deliver me from a man of one book.

ENGLISH proverb

The way one reads a philosophy or history book is formed – or better, deformed – by education.

ERICH FROMM; *To Have or To Be?*, 1976

A book may be amusing with numerous errors, or it may be very dull without a single absurdity.

OLIVER GOLDSMITH, 1728–1774

Books teach us very little of the world.
> OLIVER GOLDSMITH; *Letters to Henry Goldsmith*, 1759

Some books are read in the parlour and some in the kitchen, but the test of a real genuine book is that it is read in both.
> T(HOMAS) C. HALIBURTON; *Wise Saws*, 1843

Woe be to him who reads but one book.
> GEORGE HERBERT, 1593–1633

The proper study of mankind is books.
> ALDOUS HUXLEY, 1894–1963

Borrowers of books – those mutilators of collections, spoilers of the symmetry of shelves, and creators of odd volumes.
> CHARLES LAMB; *Essays of Elia*, 1823

Books we want to have young people read should not be recommended to them but praised in their presence. Afterwards they will find them themselves.
> (GEORG CHRISTOPH) LICHTENBERG; *Aphorisms*, 1764–1799

Books are sepulchres of thought.
> HENRY WADSWORTH LONGFELLOW;
> *The Wind Over the Chimney*, 1864

We profit little by books we do not enjoy.
> JOHN LUBBOCK; *The Pleasures of Life*, 1887

The book you are reading has some good things, some indifferent, and many bad. There's no other way, Avitus, to make a book.
> (MARCUS VALERIUS) MARTIAL(IS), *c*.40–*c*.104

Books are, in one sense, the basis of all social progress.
> KARL MARX; *Das Kapital*, 1867

Books have their own destiny.

TERENTIANUS MAURUS, *c*.200–*c*.300

[I] do think, as a general rule, that teachers talk too much! A book is a very good institution! To read a book, to think it over, and to write out notes is a useful exercise; a book which will not repay some hard thought is not worth publishing.

MARIA MITCHELL, 1818–1889

All books are divisible into two classes, the books of the hour, and the books of all time.

JOHN RUSKIN, 1819–1900

For the last three thousand years and among civilized races, books have been the chief repositories of knowledge and the most powerful instrument of culture.

PRESERVED SMITH;
A History of Modern Culture (vol. I), 1962

Books are . . . funny little portable pieces of thought.

SUSAN SONTAG, 1933–

Every month, you receive quick-reading, time-saving summaries of the best new business books. Each contains *all the key points* in the original book. But instead of 200 to 500 pages, the summary is only *eight pages*. Instead of taking five or ten hours to read, it just takes *15 minutes*.

SOUNDVIEW EXECUTIVE BOOK SUMMARIES;
an *advertisement*, Feb. 1994

Books, the children of the brain.

JONATHAN SWIFT; *The Tale of a Tub*, 1704

I don't believe a committee can write a book. . . . It can, oh, govern a country, perhaps, but I don't believe it can write a book.

ARNOLD TOYNBEE;
a *statement* (NBC Television), 17 Apr. 1955

Books are the carrier of civilization. Without books, history is silent, literature dumb, science crippled, thought and speculation at a standstill.

BARBARA W. TUCHMAN;
Authors' League Bulletin, Nov.–Dec. 1979

A good book is the best of friends, the same today and for ever.

MARTIN TUPPER, 1810–1889

Much is written of the power of the Press, a power which may last but a day; by comparison, little is heard of the power of books, which may endure for generations.

STANLEY UNWIN, 1884–1968

The main fault of all books is that they are too long.

(LUC DE CLAPIERS, MARQUIS DE) VAUVENARGUES;
*Reflections and Maxims, c.*1747

Books rule the world.

VOLTAIRE (né FRANÇOIS MARIE AROUET), 1694–1778

The multitude of books is making us ignorant.

VOLTAIRE (né FRANÇOIS MARIE AROUET), 1694–1778

Beware you not be swallowed up in books! An ounce of love is worth a pound of knowledge.

JOHN WESLEY, 1703–1791

BOTANY

Botany has lately become fashionable amusement with the ladies. But how the study of the sexual systems of plants can accord with female modesty, I am not able to understand.

RICHARD POLWHELE; *The Unsex'd Females,* 1798

BRAIN

Brain, n[oun]. An apparatus with which we think that we think.

AMBROSE BIERCE; *The Devil's Dictionary,* 1911

The most wasteful "brain-drain" in America today is the drain in the kitchen sink.

ELIZABETH GOULD DAVIS; *The First Sex,* 1973

The realization that schools spend most of their time training students in what seem to be left [brain] hemisphere skills, and that most educators and taxpayers regard what seem to be right [brain] hemisphere skills as frills, has caused many people to wonder whether our educational system is unbalanced.

ROBERT ORNSTEIN; *Human Nature* (vol. 1), 1978

The left-brain based curriculum, with its inane true and false and multiple choice tests, would have to be scrapped.

NATHAN RUTSTEIN; *Education on Trial*, 1992

I have a brain and a uterus, and I use both.

PATRICIA SCHROEDER, 1940–

BULLYING

There is no end to the violations committed by children on children, quietly talking alone.

ELIZABETH BOWEN; *The House in Paris*, 1935

Surely you remember the boy in your own school class who was exceptionally "bright," did most of the reciting and answering while the others sat like so many leaden idols, hating him. And wasn't it this bright boy you selected for beatings and tortures after hours?

RAY BRADBURY; *Fahrenheit 451*, 1953

[A] teacher allowed a classroom to conduct a mock funeral for Hirofumi, including a procession. He was presented with a card, signed by most of the class, that said "Sayonara Hirofumi."

International Herald Tribune, 21–22 May 1994
[Hirofumi later killed himself; his suicide note read:
"This is life in hell and I can't go on".]

Bullying is, however, a very serious matter for pupils who are being bullied, and is one of the issues that must be assessed as an important welfare issue, even if relatively few pupils are seriously affected.

ROGER MORGAN; *School Life*, 1993

The Norwegian government's determination to tackle bullying in schools was prompted by the public outcry which ensued after three boys aged between ten and 14 committed suicide in a period of six months in 1982, partially as a result of severe bullying at school.

FIONA SMITH; *The European* (International Education), 4–10 Mar. 1994

Schools must not forget that they are *in loco parentis* and that it is their duty to protect vulnerable pupils. If schools don't address the problem seriously, victims are left vulnerable and bullies can regard such lack of response as covert messages of approval.

DELWYN TATTUM; *The Times*, 31 May 1994

BUSINESS

What is happening is that the taxpayer has had to fund the basic research, and is now having to buy this technology back from faculty members and corporations who are very busy making money and profit out of what essentially was taxpayer-funded research.

PAUL BAUMANN; in *The Academic-Industrial Complex* (Ideas-Canadian Broadcasting Corporation), 1982

To keep their mammoth plants financially solvent, many institutions have begun to use hard-sell Madison Avenue techniques to attract students. They sell college like soap.

CAROLINE BIRD; *The Case Against College*, 1975

As if T-shirts and coasters were not exciting enough, some souvenir shops are now offering custom-made colognes.... The new fragrance line features the University of Michigan's "Victors" and Michigan State University's "Spartan". Mr. Klama, who works with a fragrance designer, sold 100,000 two-ounce bottles last year for $24 each. Thirty college colognes are on the market or in production.

The Chronicle of Higher Education, 12 Jan. 1994

For people for whom alma mater is all that matters, something new is available: a custom-designed funeral casket. The caskets come in a variety of team colors. Special motifs, including athletic symbols are available.... [Oak Grove International] first produced a casket in the colors of Indiana University.... The company is now trying to come up with the designs for institutions in Texas and Tennessee as well as for Purdue University, but will not use specific trademarks of a college or university without permission.

The Chronicle of Higher Education, 30 Mar. 1994

The nation's grand central test-maker, the Educational Testing Service of Princeton, N.J., sells tests to the CIA, the Defense Department, the National Security Council, the Government of Trinidad and Tobago, the Institute of Nuclear Power Operations, the National Contact Lens Examiners, the International Council for Shopping Centers, the American Society for Heating, Refrigerating and Air-Conditioning Engineers, the Commission on Graduates of Foreign Nursing Schools, the Malaysian Ministry of Education, the National Board of Podiatry Examiners, and the Institute for the Advancement of Philosophy for Children.

PHILIP J. DAVIS & REUBEN HERSH; *Descartes' Dream*, 1986

No other country exports as many exams. Britain has captured the market in many countries that are expanding their education system.

The Economist, 28 Aug. 1993

Most Americans do value education as a business asset, but not as the entrance into the joy of intellectual experience or acquaintance with the best that has been said and done in the past. They value it not as an experience, but as a tool.

W(ILLIAM) H(ERBERT) P(ERCY) FAUNCE; in *Universities*, 1930

What makes a school profitable, or even economical, is not what makes it best academically.

KEITH GEIGER; *The Economist*, 4 Jun. 1994

A marketing orientation in an educational organization is, therefore, one in which the interests and needs of the pupil or student as customer are central.

LYNTON GRAY; *Marketing Education*, 1991

Cosmetic surgeries in Japan are reporting brisk business from students seeking to gain the sort of appearance they hope will give them the edge over rivals in the job market. Operations designed to provide "a striking and more intelligent look" include the reshaping of noses and the alteration of eyelids, according to advertising.

JOHN GREENLEES;
The Times Higher Education Supplement, 25 Mar. 1994

Texas A&M [University] . . . offered football coach Jackie Sherill $267,000 a year, plus perquisites. When interrogated about educational priorities, the chairman of the Board of Trustees was candid: "Higher education is a business, and I think Sherill's contract is part of that process."

ALLEN GUTTMANN; *A Whole New Ball Game*, 1988

The promarket forces have an ineradicable advantage in the years ahead. That advantage is the inherent futility of conventional school reform.

MYRON LIEBERMAN; *Public Education*, 1993

A market system of education would avoid the futile political effort to ascertain "the will of the people" on thousands of educational issues.

MYRON LIEBERMAN; *Public Education*, 1993

Education is the only business in which the consumer does the essential work.

LEWIS J. PERELMAN; *School's Out*, 1992

With all the millions of words written – and largely unread – about the educational crisis, people overlook the essential problem: public education is a $230-billion-a-year industry that badly needs the discipline of a market system to make it responsive to its customers.

WILLIAM TUCKER; *Forbes*, 2 Mar. 1992

Commerce is the school for cheating.

(LUC DE CLAPIERS, MARQUIS DE) VAUVENARGUES; *Reflections and Maxims, c.*1747

C

CAMPUS

I'm troubled that many now view the campus as a place where professors get tenured and students get credentialed; the overall efforts of the academy are not considered to be at the vital center of the nation's work.

ERNEST L. BOYER;
The Chronicle of Higher Education, 9 Mar. 1994

It used to be that the university campus was a kind of hermetically sealed-off area where the news of the day did not impinge upon your attention to the inner life and to the magnificent human heritage we have in our great tradition – Plato, Confucius, the Buddha, Goethe, and others who speak of the eternal values that have to do with the centering of our lives.

JOSEPH CAMPBELL; *The Power of Myth*, 1988

There are few places as serene and opulent as an American university campus.

DINESH D'SOUZA; *Illiberal Education*, 1992

I find that the three major administrative problems on a campus are sex for the students, athletics for the alumni, and parking for the faculty.

CLARK KERR; *Time*, 17 Nov. 1958

CENSORSHIP

A book is a loaded gun in the house next door. Burn it. Take the shot from the weapon. . . . Breach man's mind. Who knows who might be the target of the well-read man?

RAY BRADBURY; *Fahrenheit 451*, 1953

An electronic version of a ribald 18th century novel has been removed from a computer connected to the Internet, prompting a spirited debate about censoring computerized material. The book, *Fanny Hill; or Memoirs of a Woman of Pleasure*, was written by John Cleland in 1748 and 1749 and largely suppressed as pornography until late in the 20th century.

The Chronicle of Higher Education, 19 Jan. 1994

The learning too, of the censors and critics was often indeed remarkable. They condemned a recondite treatise on Trigonometry, because they imagined it contained heretical opinions concerning the doctrine of the Trinity; and another work which was devoted to the study of Insects was prohibited, because they concluded that it was a secret attack upon the Jesuits.

P.H. DITCHFIELD; *Books Fatal to Their Authors*, 1895

Don't join the book burners.

DWIGHT D. EISENHOWER, 1890–1969

Every burned book enlightens the world.

RALPH WALDO EMERSON, 1803–1882

And are these my judges?

GALILEO (GALILEI), 1564–1642

Decisions by local school boards to ban books from public-school libraries are among the most direct and open violations of the principle of nonrepression.

AMY GUTMANN; *Democratic Education*, 1987

The Texas State Textbook Committee controls such a large share of the national market in textbooks that the pressure it exerts on publishers to censor texts also changes the content of texts available for use in other states.

AMY GUTMANN; *Democratic Education*, 1987

A study by a group called People for the American Way, reporting on the rising censorship in American education, reveals that half of all biology texts treat evolution inadequately, one-sixth fail to mention it altogether.

ERICH HARTH; *Dawn of a Millennium*, 1990

Wherever they burn books they will also, in the end, burn human beings.

HEINRICH HEINE; *Almansor*, 1823

Holt, Rinehart & Winston Inc. has decided to pull its 700-page high school health text out of the Texas market rather than make hundreds of revisions demanded by state officials after the book drew criticism from anti-abortion and other groups upset by its discussion of condom use, homosexuality and other sexual issues.

International Herald Tribune, 18 Mar. 1994

Crankish attacks on the freedom to read are common at present. When backed and coordinated by organized groups, they become sinister.

URSULA K. LE GUIN; *Dancing at the Edge of the World*, 1989

Burn the libraries, for their value is in this one book [*The Koran*].

OMAR I, 581?–644

I believe it is vitally important that all those working in the academy in general, and in the field of language in particular, should express their thoughts and feelings about the many attempts in the modern world to silence those whose tongues speak in ways of which the powerful do not approve.

(AHMED) SALMAN RUSHDIE;
The Chronicle of Higher Education, 12 Jan. 1994
[currently in hiding after being condemned to death
by Iranian extremists for authoring *The Satanic Verses*]

I disapprove of what you say, but I will defend to the death your right to say it.

S.G. TALLENTYRE; *The Friends of Voltaire*, 1906

They carried their books and their statues and their paintings to the marketplace and celebrated a wild "carnival of the vanities" with holy singing and most unholy dancing, while Savonarola applied his torch to the accumulated treasure.

HENDRIK VAN LOON; *The Story of Mankind*, 1962

I detest what you write, but I would give my life to make it possible for you to continue to write.

VOLTAIRE (né FRANÇOIS MARIE AROUET), 1694–1778

God forbid that any book should be banned. The practice is as indefensible as infanticide.

REBECCA WEST (pseud. of CICELY ISABEL FAIRFIELD),
1892–1983

To admit authorities, however heavily furred and gowned, into our libraries and let them tell us how to read, what value to place upon what we read, is to destroy the spirit of freedom which is the breath of these sanctuaries.

VIRGINIA WOOLF, 1882–1941

CERTIFICATION

Most certification is pure "credentialism." It must begin to reflect our demands for excellence not our appreciation of parchment.
WILLIAM J. BENNETT; *The New York Times*, 3 Sep. 1986

Teaching must, I think, be decertified as quickly as possible.
JOHN TAYLOR GATTO; *Dumbing Us Down*, 1992

Instead of requiring the student to reach certain standards before she or he gets their certificate from school, we should require *the school* to ensure that the student has reached these standards before they let them go.
CHARLES HANDY; *The Empty Raincoat*, 1994

[Teacher] certification shouldn't be a requirement.
NATHAN RUTSTEIN; *Education on Trial*, 1992

The sine qua non of academic certification is that it represents the evaluation of a student's accomplishment by a competent and objective second party.
STEPHEN H. SPURR; *Academic Degree Structures*, 1970

CHARACTER

American education needs training for character.
SEYMOUR COHEN; *Affirming Life*, 1987

The end of learning is the formation of character.
KAIBARA EKKEN; *Ten Precepts*, 1710

Parents can only give good advice or put them on the right paths, but the final forming of a person's character lies in their own hands.
ANNE FRANK, 1929–1945

Education has for its object the formation of character.
HERBERT SPENCER, 1820–1903

CHEATING

I was thrown out of college for cheating on the metaphysical exam. I looked into the soul of another boy.
                    WOODY ALLEN (pseud. of ALLEN STEWART KONISBERG), 1935–

'Tis my opinion every man cheats in his way, and he is only honest who is not discovered.
                    SUSANNAH CENTLIVRE, c.1667–1723

Very often the lateral solution to a problem is regarded by vertical thinkers as a form of cheating.
                    EDWARD DE BONO; *The Use of Lateral Thinking*, 1971

Some students also complain that their professors are cheating *them* – spending more time consulting and publishing than teaching or preparing for classes. Those students see little reason why they should not cheat as well.
                    LESLIE FISHBEIN;
                    The Chronicle of Higher Education, 1 Dec. 1993

The cheating scandal [at the Naval Academy, Annapolis, Maryland] took months to uncover because the students refused to tell tales on their colleagues.
                    LUCY HODGES;
                    The Times Higher Education Supplement, 15 Apr. 1994

Young folks are sometimes very cunning in finding out contrivances to cheat themselves.
                    SAMUEL RICHARDSON, 1689–1761

CHILDHOOD

Childhood as a separate time of life developed first among the middle and upper classes, as did literacy. Boys were considered children long before girls, perhaps because boys were sent off to school to learn to read and write, while their sisters stayed home and immediately took on the dress and the tasks of adult women.... [T]he spread of childhood closely paralleled the growth of schools and education. Even as the schools began to redefine the notion of childhood, those children who remained outside of schools were still treated much like adults.

> JOSHUA MEYROWITZ; *No Sense of Place*, 1985

[W]e need to distinguish between the biological existence of children and the social construction of "childhood."

> JOSHUA MEYROWITZ; *No Sense of Place*, 1985

To children childhood holds no particular advantage.

> KATHLEEN NORRIS, 1931–

Where literacy was valued highly and persistently, there were schools, and where there were schools, the concept of childhood developed rapidly. That is why childhood emerged sooner and in sharper outline in the British Isles than anywhere else.

> NEIL POSTMAN; *The Disappearance of Childhood*, 1994

What is childhood but a series of happy delusions.

> SYDNEY SMITH, 1771–1845

CHILDREN

Everyone knows a great deal about one child – himself.

> DORA CHAPLIN; *The Privilege of Teaching*, 1962

One of the things we discovered in general about raising kids is that they really don't give a damn if you walked five miles to school.

> PATTY DUKE; *Call Me Anna*, 1979

How is it that little children are so intelligent and men so stupid? It must be education that does it.

> ALEXANDRE DUMAS (Fils), 1824–1895

As long as little children are allowed to suffer, there is no true love in this world.

> ISADORA DUNCAN; *This Quarter*, 1929

The finest inheritance you can give to a child is to allow it to make its own way, completely on its own feet.

> ISADORA DUNCAN; *My Life*, 1942

All the value of education rests in respect for the physical, intellectual and moral will of the child.

FRANCISCO FERRER, 1859–1909

Children are born true scientists.

R(ICHARD) BUCKMINSTER FULLER;
R. Buckminster Fuller on Education, 1979

Your children are not your children.
They are the sons and daughters of Life's longing for itself.
They came through you but not from you
And though they are with you yet they belong not to you.

KAHLIL GIBRAN; *The Prophet*, 1923

Children learn very early that this is a man's world.

ESTHER R. GREENGLASS; *A World of Difference*, 1982

The "profile" of children within the traditional school age range is also changing. There are more children in mainstream schools of different racial origins, with various disabilities or with different or difficult social backgrounds.

CHARLES HANDY & ROBERT AITKEN;
Understanding Schools as Organizations, 1986

Feel the dignity of a child. Do not feel superior to him, for you are not.

ROBERT HENRI, 1865–1929

As one of the biggest, unruliest, most dangerously contaminated places on earth, this is one tough city to live in, especially for kids. Some children in Mexico City are trained to tell the toxicity of the air by the red or black flags that fly over their schools.

International Herald Tribune, 20–21 Nov. 1993

A child miseducated is a child lost.

JOHN F. KENNEDY;
an *address* (State of the Union), 11 Jan. 1962

A destroyed home life, an idiotic school system, premature work in the factory, stupefying life in the streets, these are what the great city gives to the children of the under classes. It is more astonishing that the better instincts of human nature generally are victorious in the lower classes than the fact that this result is occasionally reversed.

ELLEN KEY (pseud. of KAROLINA SOFIA KEY);
The Century of the Child, 1909

Children are overwhelming, supercilious, passionate, envious, inquisitive, egotistical, idle, fickle, timid, intemperate, liars, and dissemblers; they laugh and weep easily, are excessive in their joys and sorrows, and that about the most trifling subject; they bear no pain, but like to inflict it on others; already they are men.

(JEAN DE) LA BRUYÈRE; *Les Charactères,* 1688

It would be worth the trouble to investigate whether it is not harmful to refine too much on the business of bringing up children. We do not know human beings well enough to take this whole process, so to speak, out of the hands of chance.

(GEORG CHRISTOPH) LICHTENBERG; *Aphorisms,* 1764–1799

Children ought to be able to accompany adults almost everywhere they go. In cultures like ours, where this is now largely impossible, schools and teachers might learn to take fuller advantage of the tendencies of children to imitate and practise skills on their own initiative rather than have them taught.

JEAN LIEDLOFF; *The Continuum Concept,* 1975

All that a child has right to claim from his father is nourishment and education, and the things nature furnishes for the support of life.

JOHN LOCKE, 1632–1704

The important thing is not so much that every child should be taught, as that every child should be given the wish to learn.

JOHN LUBBOCK, 1834–1913

I had learned to respect the intelligence, integrity, creativity and capacity for deep thought and hard work latent somewhere in every child; they had learned that I differed from them only in years and experience, and that as I, an ordinary human being, loved and respected them, I expected payment in kind.

SYBIL MARSHALL; *An Experiment in Education,* 1963

Free education for all children in public schools. Abolition of child labour.

KARL MARX & FRIEDRICH ENGELS;
The Communist Manifesto, 1848

Instead of being presented with stereotypes by age, sex, color, class, or religion, children must have the opportunity to learn that within each range, some people are loathsome and some are delightful.

MARGARET MEAD; *Twentieth Century Faith*, 1972

The child is confined to a [school] room with a large number of others of the same age. There is minimal interaction with children who are even one year older or younger.

JOSHUA MEYROWITZ; *No Sense of Place*, 1985

The child is the most avid learner of all living things on earth.

ASHLEY MONTAGU, 1905–

I will content myself with saying that children are helpless and easily victimized, and that therefore no one should be given unlimited power over them.

(MARCUS FABIUS) QUINTILIAN(US), *c*.35–*c*.95

When you inadvertently break the spirit of a child, it usually remains broken for the rest of his life.

NATHAN RUTSTEIN; *Education on Trial*, 1992

How sharper than a serpent's tooth it is
To have a thankless child.

WILLIAM SHAKESPEARE; *King Lear*, 1605–06

A government's responsibility to its young citizens does not magically begin at the age of six. It makes more sense to extend the free universal school system downward – with the necessary reforms and community control that child care should have from the start.

GLORIA STEINEM; *Ms*, Apr. 1974

Children become adults when they realize they have a right not only to be right but also to be wrong.

THOMAS STEPHEN SZASZ, 1920–

The kids offer the unbeatable combination of bigger size and strength, raging hormones, and incomplete socialization. In short, they are animals.

a TEACHER; *Giving Up on School*, 1991

Most "education" goes hand in hand with families in repressing children and guiding them towards their niche in society; school and college photos reflect this with their family-like groupings.

JUDITH WILLIAMSON; *Consuming Passions*, 1986

CHURCH

In its capacity as a secular church, the university can continue to be what the church has always been – the conscience of society....

JOHN S. BRUBACHER;
On the Philosophy of Higher Education, 1977

No man who worships education has got the best out of education... without a gentle contempt for education no man's education is complete.

G(ILBERT) K(EITH) CHESTERTON, 1874–1936

School has become the replacement for church in our secular society, and like church it requires that its teachings must be taken on faith.

JOHN TAYLOR GATTO; *Dumbing Us Down*, 1992

Universities are the cathedrals of the modern age. They shouldn't have to judge their existence by utilitarian criteria.

DAVID LODGE, 1935–

Education is the established church of the United States. It is one of the religions that Americans believe in. It has its own orthodoxy, its pontiffs and its noble buildings.

MICHAEL SADLER; *The New York Times*, 1 Sep. 1956

CLASSICS

Classics cut to fit fifteen-minute radio shows, then cut again to fill a two-minute book column, winding up at last as a ten- or twelve-line dictionary resume.

RAY BRADBURY; *Fahrenheit 451*, 1953

The classics are only primitive literature. They belong in the same class as primitive machinery and primitive music and primitive medicine.
STEPHEN LEACOCK, 1869–1944

Every man with a belly full of the classics is an enemy of the human race.
HENRY MILLER, 1891–1980

Books are always the better for not being read. Look at our classics.
GEORGE BERNARD SHAW, 1856–1950

A classic is something that everybody wants to have read and nobody wants to read.
MARK TWAIN (pseud. of SAMUEL LANGHORNE CLEMENS), 1835–1910

In art, the public accept what has been, because they cannot alter it, not because they appreciate it. They swallow their classics whole, and never taste them.
OSCAR WILDE; *The Soul of Man Under Socialism*, 1895

CLASSROOM

Learning is assumed to occur exclusively in the classroom, although there is little evidence to support this assumption (and much to refute it).
RITA S. BRAUSE; *Enduring Schools*, 1992

Despite much research suggesting better alternatives, classrooms still appeared to be dominated by textbooks, teacher lectures, and short-answer activity sheets.
EDUCATIONAL TESTING SERVICE;
America's Challenge, 1990

Africa is quite familiar with schools without walls, classrooms in the open.
ALI A. MAZRUI; *Uganda Now*, 1988

The least of the work of learning is done in classrooms.
THOMAS MERTON; *Love and Living*, 1980

Classrooms often stress individual competition.

ROBERT ORNSTEIN & PAUL EHRLICH;
New World New Mind, 1989

Teachers are in charge of classrooms.

LAWRENCE STENHOUSE;
British Journal of Educational Studies, Jun. 1981

CLEVER

He's very clever, but sometimes his brains go to his head.

MARGOT ASQUITH;
The Autobiography of Margot Asquith, 1923

What makes us so bitter against people who outwit us is that they think themselves cleverer than we are.

(FRANÇOIS DE) LA ROCHEFOUCAULD, 1613–1680

CO-EDUCATION

However, co-education, both ideologically and in practice, does seem to have failed to provide pupils of both sexes (as well as pupils of all social classes and ethnic groups) with even the semblance of equal opportunity.

ROSEMARY DEEM; *Co-education Reconsidered*, 1984

The questions of the equal and co-education of the sexes have drifted uppermost to-day, and seem forcing themselves to a solution. The present age cannot postpone action; it must take a definite and decided stand in the matter, and it remains to be seen whether it is to make an advance movement or put its seal of sanctions upon the dwarfed and inefficient systems of the past.

E(LIZA) B(ISBEE) DUFFEY; *No Sex in Education*, 1874

Co-education is favourable to reverence and respect for the opinions of others. . . .

CECIL GRANT & NORMAN HODGSON;
The Case for Co-Education, 1913

Is it too much to hope that the decision to build co-educational or single-sex schools shall be based on the needs of the child, and not merely the economy?

FRANK E. MORETON;
British Journal of Educational Psychology, vol. XVI, 1946

The so-called method of co-education is false in theory and harmful to Christian training.

PIUS XI (title of ACHILLE RATTI); *Divine illius magistri*, 1929

COLLEGE

At best, most college presidents are running something that is somewhere between a faltering corporation and a hotel.

LEON BOTSTEIN; *Center*, Mar. 1977

Only in quiet can you practice the abstraction and concentration that give you power as a thinker. I dare to say that education goes on with far too much chatter and sociability in all our colleges.

HELEN DAWES BROWN; *Talks to Freshman Girls*, 1914

I learned three important things in college – to use a library, to memorize quickly and visually, to drop asleep at any time given a horizontal surface and fifteen minutes. What I could not learn was to think creatively on schedule.

AGNES DE MILLE; *Dance to the Piper*, 1952

Colleges hate geniuses, just as convents hate saints.

RALPH WALDO EMERSON, 1803–1882

College is refuge from hasty judgement.

ROBERT FROST; *Quote*, 9 Jul. 1961

Upside-down thinking goes on to wonder why it is that everyone has to rush off to college at 18 when so much of what one needs to learn only becomes apparent at a much later age.

CHARLES HANDY; *The Age of Unreason*, 1989

Colleges are places where pebbles are polished and diamonds are dimmed.
ROBERT G. INGERSOLL; *Prose – Poems and Selections*, 1884

I cannot believe that a college education would be a good thing for everybody. I am convinced that too many, not too few, high school graduates go to college.
JOHN KEATS; *The Sheepskin Psychosis*, 1963

At college age, you can tell who is best at taking tests and going to school, but you can't tell who the best people are. That worries the hell out of me.
BARNABY C. KEENEY, 1914–1980

The scramble to get into college is going to be so terrible in the next few years that students are going to put up with almost anything, even an education.
BARNABY C. KEENEY; *Time*, 29 Aug. 1955

College is not a privilege, much less a right. It is a blessing, a golden moment in life in which the life of the mind and the spirit can be explored to the fullest. Many students fresh out of high school are not ready for such a "blessing".... We suggest that most seventeen-year-olds be *dis*couraged from going straight to college.
ROBERT SOLOMON & JON SOLOMON;
Up the University, 1993

COMMON SENSE

Common sense has availed many a man more than the seven arts, however liberal they might be.
BALTASAR GRACIÁN, 1601–1658

Everybody gets so much information all day long they lose their common sense.
GERTRUDE STEIN, 1874–1946

Common sense is the very antipodes of science.
EDWARD BRADFORD TITCHENER;
Systematic Psychology, 1929

Common sense is judgement without reflection.
GIOVANNI BATTISTA VICO, 1668–1744

COMMUNICATION

Economists and educators agree with certainty that children of the 21st century will have to know how to cope with change. And that means they will have to know how to learn. For this, they will have to know how to communicate.

LOUISE BROWN; *The Toronto Star*, 25 Apr. 1987

It seems to me that the form of many communications in academia, both written and verbal, is such as to not only obscure the influence of the personal or subjective, but also to give the impression of divine origin – a mystification composed of sybilline [*sic*] statements – from beings supposedly emptied of the "dross" of self.

in *On Lies, Secrets, and Silence*, 1980

COMPETITION

But competitive parents are damned if they are going to deny their children the opportunity of having English *and* reading homework at the age of four.

GERALDINE BEDELL; *The Independent*, 5 Feb. 1990

Whereas Singapore has been trying to heat up competition, most other Asian countries have been trying to cool it down, at least a little. In Japan, the Ministry of Education, embarrassed about the annual toll of teenage suicides, has tried to ban league tables and play down examinations.

The Economist, 20 Nov. 1993

Children love and want to be loved and they very much prefer the joy of accomplishment to the triumph of hateful failure. Do not mistake a child for his systems.

ERIK ERIKSON; *Childhood and Society*, 1950

A competitive culture endures by tearing people down.

JULES HENRY; *Culture Against Man*, 1963

The only stake others have in your performance under a competitive arrangement is a desire to see you fail.

ALFIE KOHN; *No Contest*, 1986

We are not asking our children to do their own best but to be the best. Education is in danger of becoming a religion based on fear; its doctrine is to compete. The majority of our children are being led to believe that they are doomed to failure in a world which has room only for those at the top.

EDA T. LE SHAN; *The Conspiracy Against Childhood*, 1967

Too much stress is laid upon competition in our society. Many essentially non-competitive activities are made competitive, for instance geography in schools.

LIBERTARIAN EDUCATION; *Freedom in Education*, 1992

So his mother was stunned when the prestigious New Delhi private school sent its icy rejection, declaring: "Your child was unable to perform according to the level of the school. Please do not make any further inquiries." Varun, at age 3, had flunked his nursery school entrance test, his first academic setback in a viciously competitive education system.

MOLLY MOORE; *International Herald Tribune*, 31 Oct. 1994

Who has the world's best schools?

Newsweek, 20 Dec. 1993

In education, the ideal of competition has had two kinds of bad effects. On the one hand, it has led to the teaching of respect for competition as opposed to co-operation, especially in international affairs; and on the other hand, it has led to a vast system of competitiveness in the class-room, and in the endeavour to secure scholarships, and subsequently in the search for jobs.

BERTRAND RUSSELL; *Education and the Social Order*, 1932

The typical classroom is framed by competition, marked by struggle between students (and often between teacher and students) riddled by indicators of comparative achievement and worth.

MARA SAPON-SCHEVIN & NANCY SCHNIEDEWIND,
Empowerment Through Multicultural Education, 1991

We throw all our attention on the utterly idle question whether A has done as well as B, when the only question is whether A has done as well as he could.

WILLIAM GRAHAM SUMNER, 1840–1910

COMPULSORINESS

Schooling is **not** compulsory in the United Kingdom – except by popular misconception. In the UK it is **education** that is compulsory for children. In law, parents have a basic choice: they can educate their children either by sending them to school or "otherwise", using a home-based programme.

in Compulsory Schooling Disease, 1993

Compulsory education was first introduced in 1819 in Prussia.

in The Guinness Book of Records, 1991

[In 1647 in New England] for the first time in history, a legislative body actually ordered that system of universal, compulsory, and state-supported education, which the more advanced spirits of the age had been demanding for a century.

PRESERVED SMITH; *A History of Modern Culture* (vol. I) 1962

COMPUTER

It therefore seems clear that the personal computer must be used as an adjunct, albeit a highly sophisticated one, to the lecture notes, laboratory exercise or tutorial notes.

BRIAN AUSTIN;
The Times Higher Education Supplement, 4 Feb. 1994

[T]here seems to be little agreement on what it [computer literacy] is.

ROBIN BARROW & GEOFFREY MILBURN;
A Critical Dictionary of Educational Concepts, 1986

Excessive computerization would lead to a life of formal actions devoid of meaning, for the computer lives by precise languages, precise recipes, abstract and general programs wherein the underlying significance of what is done becomes secondary. It fosters a spirit-sapping formalism.

PHILIP J. DAVIS & REUBEN HERSH; *Descartes' Dream*, 1986

Artificial intelligence is a powerful resource. . . . Such intelligent computer tools can not only take over and perform some jobs, quite independent of human help; they can also teach.

NELL P. EURICH; *The Learning Industry*, 1990

As more nursery schools invest in computers, some childhood educators say they see a variety of benefits to getting an early start on high technology.... Yet it is not all blue skies in the world of preschool computing. Some educators say they simply do not understand the rush.... Whatever concerns may exist, computing among the very young is clearly surging, pushed along by changes in hardware and software.

International Herald Tribune, 14 Feb. 1994

Anyone under age 18 has never known a world without personal computers.

JOHN MARKOFF; *International Herald Tribune,* 1 Sep. 1993

"People at school treat me like I'm nothing," he said. But on the Internet, the global network of networks accessible to anyone with a personal computer modem, he has found his place in a world that extends far beyond his home city.

JOHN MARKOFF; *International Herald Tribune,* 1 Sep. 1993

Computers are useless. They can only give you answers.

(PABLO RUIZ) PICASSO, 1881–1973

I believe the computer to be a vastly overrated technology.

NEIL POSTMAN; *Amusing Ourselves to Death,* 1985

The schools teach their children to operate computerized systems instead of teaching things that are more valuable to children. In a word, almost nothing that they need happens to the losers. Which is why they are losers.

NEIL POSTMAN; *Technopoly,* 1993

Although student apathy may have been as common as chalk dust in classrooms of the past, some believe that the increased use of computers in today's classrooms will help eradicate the problem. Classroom experience thus far, however, has failed to show that the availability of computers has had demonstrable impact on student attitudes toward learning.

JAMES P. RAFFINI; *Winners Without Losers,* 1993

That is the great mischief done by the data merchants, the futurologists, and those in the schools who believe that computer literacy is the educational wave of the future; they lose sight of the paramount truth that the mind thinks with ideas not with information.

THEODORE ROSZAK; *The Cult of Information,* 1986

[T]he modern world believes in computers and masses of facts, and it abhors simplicity.

E(RNST) F(RIEDRICH) SCHUMACHER; *Small is Beautiful*, 1973

It does not take a flaming Bolshevik, nor even a benighted neo-Luddite, to wonder whether all those computer companies, and their related textbook publishers, that are mounting media campaigns for computer literacy and supplying hundreds of thousands of computers to schools and colleges really have the interests of children and young people as their primary concern.

DOUGLAS SLOAN; *The Computer in Education*, 1984

I believe it's a mistake to spend so much money on computers. In fact, I think it's very, very destructive to put computers in elementary schools.

DAVID SUZUKI; *The Toronto Star*, 10 May 1987

Software dominates our working lives, but are designers of these unseen tools a remote élite who impose new ways of working on millions of people excluded by knowledge barriers from any say in the products they depend on?

The Times Higher Education Supplement, 4 Feb. 1994

CONCEPT

A concept is stronger than a fact.

CHARLOTTE PERKINS GILMAN; *Human Work*, 1904

CONDITIONING

Children come to school having been deeply conditioned by the biases of television.

NEIL POSTMAN; *Technopoly*, 1993

We cannot escape our childhood conditioning, and we cannot escape the consequence of narrow specialist training and education.

J(OSEPH) R(USSELL) ROYCE; *The Encapsulated Man*, 1964

CONFLICT

Conflicts in society spill over into education, and contentions in schooling spill over into the larger society.

IRA SHOR; *Empowering Education*, 1992

CONTINUING EDUCATION

Here in the United States, and to some extent in the United Kingdom, the term continuing education tends to be restricted to post-initial education in the vocational sphere.

PETER JARVIS; *Adult and Continuing Education*, 1983

Many continuing education activities are related to concurrent adult roles and responsibilities. This accumulating life experience both helps and hinders educational activity.

ALAN B. KNOX; *Helping Adults Learn*, 1986

CO-OPERATION

Children should be taught to co-operate rather than compete, and to develop a sense of self-worth that does not depend on being rated against others, whether in physical or academic competition.

The Independent, 9 Apr. 1994

The truth is that the vast majority of human interaction, in our society as well as in all other societies, is not competitive but cooperative interaction.

DAVID W. JOHNSON & ROGER T. JOHNSON;
Review of Educational Research, vol. 44, 1974

Competition also precludes the more efficient use of resources that cooperation allows.

ALFIE KOHN; *No Contest*, 1986

If they [children] experience co-operation, they can learn to share.

ROLAND MEIGHAN;
Theory and Practice of Regressive Education, 1993

What the world now needs is not competition but organisation and co-operation; all belief in the utility of competition has become an anachronism.

BERTRAND RUSSELL; *Education and the Social Order*, 1932

A prospective teacher should understand the significance of emphasizing cooperation and not competition in the classroom.

NATHAN RUTSTEIN; *Education on Trial*, 1992

COUNSELOR

[A] realistic high school counselor teaches kids to get ready for disappointment.

CAROL BLY; *Letters from the Country*, 1981

A guidance counselor who has made a fetish of security, or who has unwittingly surrendered his thinking to economic determinism, may steer a youth away from his dream of becoming a poet, an artist, a musician or any other of thousands of things, because it offers no security, it does not pay well, there are no vacancies, it has no "future".

HENRY M. WRISTON; *Wall Street Journal*, 1 Jun. 1960

CREATIVITY

A common barrier to creativity, the "right answer" syndrome, is locked into people's brains shortly after they start school.

WILLIAM J. ALTIER; *R&D Innovator*, 19--?
[pub. Winston J. Britt & Assocs, Madison WN, USA]

I see the mind of the 5-year-old as a volcano with two vents: destruction and creativeness.

SYLVIA ASHTON-WARNER; *Teacher*, 1963

The process of writing, any form of creativity, is a power intensifying life.

RITA MAE BROWN; *Starting from Scratch*, 1988

Normal means lack of imagination, lack of creativity.

JEAN DUBUFFET, 1901–1985

Creative minds always have been known to survive any kind of bad training.

ANNA FREUD; a *speech*, 1968

The invention of IQ did a great disservice to creativity in education.... Individuality, personality, originality, are too precious to be meddled with by amateur psychiatrists whose patterns for a "wholesome personality" are inevitably their own.

JOEL H. HILDEBRAND; *The New York Times*, 16 Jun. 1964

Creativity in science could be described as the act of putting two and two together to make five.

ARTHUR KOESTLER, 1905–1983

But it is better to fail in originality than to succeed in imitation.

HERMAN MELVILLE, 1819–1891

Modern education has made great strides in encouraging inventiveness, but it still has a long way to go before it can completely rid itself of the urge to suppress creativity.

DESMOND MORRIS; *The Human Zoo*, 1969

The Japanese university will be fully able to engage in the search for truth only as it makes a major transition from imitation to creativity.

MICHIO NAGAI; *Higher Education in Japan*, 1971

The bad teacher imposes his ideas and his methods on his pupils, and such originality as they may have is lost in the second-rate art of imitation.

STEPHEN NEILL; *A Genuinely Human Existence*, 1959

CRISIS

Consider also the crisis in our schools. Some students are successful, but far too many are educationally deficient, often dropping-out. What we're facing in education is not just academic failure, but also drugs, violence, and alienation – problems that cannot be solved by simply adding more requirements for graduation. Do colleges really believe they can ignore the social pathologies that surround schools and erode the educational foundations of our nation?

ERNEST L. BOYER;
The Chronicle of Higher Education, 9 Mar. 1994

Many schools and colleges are unable to make a major change until confronted by crisis – near bankruptcy or an exodus of staff or an explosive split among key personnel. Crisis is the common condition under which old enterprises are reborn, allowed once more to begin anew with a sense of starting down an uncharted road.

BURTON R. CLARK; *Educating the Expert Society*, 1962

Most of the recent raft of books and reports about the "educational crisis" perseverate on the difficulties students have in mastering the overt agenda of school.

HOWARD GARDNER; *The Unschooled Mind*, 1993

We are, I believe, very much in a cultural, political, and moral crisis and hence, ipso facto, in an educational crisis.

D. PURPEL; *The Moral and Spiritual Crisis in Education*, 1989

An acknowledged disaster area for America is its factory-style school system, devastated by drugs, violence, and alienation. Unfortunately, schools are in trouble outside the United States as well, especially in the inner cities. Does one find truly good inner-city schools anywhere? Brixton? Bijlmermeer? Berlin? The education crisis is not an American monopoly.

ALVIN TOFFLER; *Powershift*, 1990

CRITICAL THINKING

Critical thinkers can be parodied either as disgruntled and bitter subversives, or as elitist mockers of others' well-meant efforts. The pejorative associations surrounding the word critical have meant that advocating critical thinking is a form of social and educational bad taste.

STEPHEN D. BROOKFIELD; *Developing Critical Thinkers*, 1987

Street-smart children in the Bronx and elsewhere demonstrate outside school that they already possess higher-order thinking skills ... what these students lack is not critical thinking but academic knowledge.

E(RIC) D(ONALD) HIRSCH;
International Herald Tribune, 8 Sep. 1993

We do not ask why learning is defined in terms of a standardized test score, why obedience is valued above critical thinking – and we certainly do not

look at the institutions of our country whose existence depends on a passive, acceptant public of precisely the sort that our schools manufacture.

ALFIE KOHN; *No Contest*, 1986

Our public education system has not successfully made the shift from
teaching the memorization of facts to achieving the learning of critical
thinking skills.

JOHN SCULLEY, 1939–

Extolling the computer as a boon to critical thinking, professional educators by and large have been conspicuously uncritical about the computer
itself.

DOUGLAS SLOAN; *The Computer in Education*, 1984

CRITICISM

To criticize a particular subject, therefore, a man must have been trained
in that subject: to be a good critic generally, he must have an all round
education.

ARISTOTLE, 384–322

A teacher will not criticize a teacher, nor will a physician criticize a physician.

CHINESE proverb

CULTURE

Culture, the acquainting ourselves with the best that has been known and
said in the world, and thus with the history of the human spirit.

MATTHEW ARNOLD; *Literature and Dogma*, 1873

Culture is not racial but circumstantial.

JAMES DALE DAVIDSON & WILLIAM REES-MOGG;
The Great Reckoning, 1993

We have ignored cultural literacy in thinking about education.

E(RIC) D(ONALD) HIRSCH; *Cultural Literacy*, 1987

To be culturally literate is to possess the basic information needed to thrive in the modern world.

E(RIC) D(ONALD) HIRSCH; *Cultural Literacy*, 1987

The work of educating children and adolescents to become the upholders of a broadly based culture resting on firm foundations is possible only when they are respected as individuals who possess creative and inquisitive spirits.

TERUHISA HORIO;
Educational Thought and Ideology in Modern Japan, 1988

From a critical point of view, existing canons of knowledge and usage are not a common culture; they have ignored the multicultural themes, idioms, and achievements of nonelite groups such as women, minorities, homosexuals, and working people.

IRA SHOR; *Empowering Education*, 1992

Culture is an instrument wielded by professors to manufacture professors, who when their turn comes will manufacture professors.

SIMONE WEIL; *The Need for Roots*, 1949

If the majority culture knows so little about us, it must be *our* problem, they seem to be telling us; the burden of teaching is on us.

MITSUYE YAMADA; in *This Bridge Called My Back*, 1983

CURIOSITY

Why should we subsidize intellectual curiosity?

RONALD REAGAN, 1910–

Curiosity is a willing, a proud, an eager confession of ignorance.

LEONARD RUBINSTEIN; *Reader's Digest*, Oct. 1984

Disinterested intellectual curiosity is the lifeblood of real civilization.

G(EORGE) M(ACAULAY) TREVELYAN;
English Social History, 1942

CURRICULUM

[S]chool curriculum has become a major focus of popular contestation and a site for a kind of competitive struggle.
STANLEY ARONOWITZ & HENRY GIROUX;
Education under Siege, 1985

Is it educationally desirable that controversial issues should be included in the curriculum?
R(ICHARD) F(REDRICK) DEARDEN;
Theory and Practice in Education, 1984

One way of looking at the curriculum is through the trinity of tribal, national, and international subcultures.
HENRY D'SOUZA;
Kenyan Education in Its African Context, 1987

Our schools are centrally planned and already have a national curriculum in place mediated by the textbook industry and the standardized training of teachers.
JOHN TAYLOR GATTO; *Dumbing Us Down,* 1992

Central to the marketing of any educational service must be a concern for the nature and the quality of the curriculum.
LYNTON GRAY; *Marketing Education,* 1991

The Japanese curriculum since 1872 has been a modified form of the French encyclopedic curriculum.
ROBERT KING HALL; *Education for a New Japan,* 1949

The school curriculum tends to be embedded in the past, it is engaged in the present and, at least theoretically, is oriented towards the future.
LIBERTARIAN EDUCATION; *Freedom in Education,* 1992

Changes in the school curriculum are an immediate reflection of changes in the political and economic systems.
JING LIN; *Education in Post-Mao China,* 1993

Childrearing, which is probably the most important task that most human beings will ever undertake and one of vital importance for society, is ignored in our school curriculum.
MYRIAM MIEDZIAN; *Boys Will Be Boys,* 1991

The national curriculum is based on an unmerited regard for "traditional approaches" and a narrow perception of present needs. A shortage of people competent in mathematics, science and technology is thought to justify inclusion of these subjects in the "core", and everyone is to learn a foreign language. Yet the vast majority of children will use little of what they learn.... Qualities such as resilience, adaptability, creativity, tolerance and compassion are the real basics for employment and for general living.

JOHN MUNRO; *The Economist*, 8 May 1993

Many of the practices embedded in the masculine curriculum masquerade as essential to the maintenance of standards...[but in fact] they accomplish quite a different purpose: the systematic dehumanization of both female and male children through the loss of the feminine.

NEL NODDINGS; *Caring*, 1984

What is curriculum? Workers within the field of curriculum have sought for many years to determine a proper definition of the word curriculum. The end result of their endeavors always seems to be the addition of another new improved definition, more debate over the issue, and further criticism of other inadequate definitions.

MICHAEL SCHIRO; *Curriculum for Better Schools*, 1978

No curriculum can be neutral.

IRA SHOR; *Empowering Education*, 1992

Every day teachers face the moral conflict implicit in their contract of work. They must choose between responding to their children's real interests and getting through the curriculum.

CHRIS SHUTE; *Compulsory Schooling Disease*, 1993

The driving force behind the American school curriculum is not only the textbooks, but the standardized tests as well.

GEORGE H. WOOD; *Schools That Work*, 1993

CUSTODY

Schools have not necessarily much to do with education...they are mainly institutions of control where certain basic habits must be inculcated in the young. Education is quite different and has little place in school.

WINSTON (LEONARD SPENCER) CHURCHILL, 1874–1965

School is basically custodial rather than educational.
HOWARD GARDNER; *The Unschooled Mind*, 1993

in loco parentis (in place of a parent)
LATIN phrase

School is where you go between when your parents can't take you and industry can't take you.
JOHN UPDIKE; *The Centaur*, 1963

D

DANGER

There are no dangerous thoughts; thinking itself is dangerous.
HANNAH ARENDT, 1906–1975

The real danger is that students who are forced to undertake animal experiments as part of their studies will become so hardened by the suffering and the daily deaths they see that they become permanently desensitized to suffering. And there is real evidence to show that this does happen.
VERNON COLEMAN;
Why Animal Experiments Must Stop, 1991

Intellectual activity is a danger to the building of character.
(PAUL JOSEPH) GOEBBELS, 1897–1945

Education can be dangerous. It is very difficult to make it not dangerous. In fact, it is almost impossible.
ROBERT M. HUTCHINS, 1899–1977

If a little knowledge is dangerous, where is the man who has so much as to be out of danger?
T(HOMAS) H(ENRY) HUXLEY; *Science and Culture*, 1881

Nothing in the world is more dangerous than a sincere ignorance and conscientious stupidity.
MARTIN LUTHER KING; *Strength and Love*, 1963

The great danger of traditional education is that learning may remain purely verbal.
MIRRA KOMAROVSKY; *Women in the Modern World*, 1953

Long experience has taught us that it is dangerous in the interest of truth to suppress opinions and ideas; it has further taught us that it is foolish to imagine that we can do so.
JAWAHARLAL NEHRU; *The Unity of India*, 1937

The most dangerous thing about student riots is that adults take them seriously.
GEORGES POMPIDOU; *Life*, 20 Feb. 1970

A little learning is a dang'rous thing;
Drink deep, or taste not the Pierian spring:
There shallow draughts intoxicate the brain,
And drinking largely sobers us again.

ALEXANDER POPE; An Essay on Criticism, 1711

DEATH

To spend too much time in studies is death.

FRANCIS BACON; Essays, 1608

Furnish your mind with precepts, never stop learning; for life without learning is but an image of death.

CATO OF CÓRDOBA; Disticha moralia, c.200

University students are rarely able to cope with universals and death is the most embarrassing universal.

KATE CRUISE O'BRIEN; A Gift Horse, 1978

Animals learn death at the moment of death; ... man approaches death with the knowledge it is closer every hour, and this creates a feeling of uncertainty over his life, even for him who forgets in the business of life that annihilation is awaiting him. It is for this reason chiefly that we have philosophy and religion.

ARTHUR SCHOPENHAUER; The World as Will and Idea, 1819

Leisure without study is death.

(LUCIUS ANNAEUS) SENECA (the Younger), c.4BC–65

I'll learn him or kill him.

MARK TWAIN (pseud. of SAMUEL LANGHORNE CLEMENS);
Life on the Mississippi, 1883

DECIMAL

I could never make out what those damned dots [decimal points] meant.

RANDOLPH (HENRY SPENCER) CHURCHILL, 1849–1895

The decimal system, the place-value concept, the idea of zero and the symbol we use for it, the solution of indeterminate, quadratic and higher-order equations, modular arithmetic and the remainder theorem — all were taken up by European scholars millennia or centuries after they had been invented by the Chinese.

JOHN McLEISH; *Number*, 1992

Undergraduates are like decimals: they recur.

WARDEN SPOONER, 1844–1930

DEFINITION

Every definition is dangerous.

(DESIDERIUS) ERASMUS; *Adagia*, 1500

Man gives indifferent names to one and the same thing from the difference of their own passions.

THOMAS HOBBES, 1588–1679

Definition is that which refines the pure essence of things from the circumstances.

JOHN MILTON, 1608–1674

Define your terms!

VOLTAIRE (né FRANÇOIS MARIE AROUET), 1694–1778

DEGREE

Degrees is good things because they livils all ranks. [*sic*]

FINLEY PETER DUNNE; *Mr. Dooley's Opinions*, 1900

A degree is not an education, and the confusion on this point is perhaps the greatest weakness in American thinking about education.

ROCKEFELLER BROTHERS' FUND;
Prospect for America, 1961

DEMOCRACY

Education in character and in moral reasoning are therefore both necessary, neither sufficient, for creating democratic citizens.

AMY GUTMANN; *Democratic Education*, 1987

Democracy should offer teachers and students freedom to question their socialization, to rethink the status quo, and to act effectively on the critical knowledge. Traditional schools are not now enabling students or teachers to behave as reflective citizens in a multicultural democracy.

IRA SHOR; *Empowering Education*, 1992

The conversion of education into one more major national issue in democracies is a challenge to the mood of serenity in which education should be carried out.

HUGH THOMAS; *An Unfinished History of the World*, 1979

They are making it harder, daily, for the educators . . . to prepare students for democracy.

GEORGE H. WOOD; *Schools That Work*, 1993

DESCHOOLING

We need less school, not more.

JOHN TAYLOR GATTO; *Dumbing Us Down*, 1992

Everywhere not only education but society as a whole needs "deschooling."

IVAN ILLICH; *Deschooling Society*, 1971

To make this disestablishment effective, we need a law forbidding discrimination in hiring, voting or admission to centres of learning based on previous attendance at some curriculum.

IVAN ILLICH; *Deschooling Society*, 1971

DEVELOPING COUNTRIES

The third world is not a reality, but an ideology.

HANNAH ARENDT, 1906–1975

The fact that education at the tertiary level has been mainly academic and unsuitable to the needs of the economy, needs to be over-emphasized.

ALOY M. EJIOGU & DURO AJEYALEMI;
Emergent Issues in Nigerian Education, 1987

Where there are two PhDs in a developing country, one is Head of State and the other is in exile.

EDWIN HERBERT SAMUEL; *The New York Times*, 5 Jul. 1964

DICTIONARY

The perfect going-away gift for a college athlete – a dictionary.

DAVE ANDERSON; *The New York Times*, 20 May 1986

The trouble with the dictionary is that you have to know how a word is spelled before you can look it up to see how it is spelled.

WILL(IAM) (JACOB) CUPPY, 1884–1949

The responsibility of a dictionary is to record a language, set its style.

PHILIP BABCOCK GOVE, 1902–1972

No dictionary of a living tongue ever can be perfect, since while it is hastened to publication, some words are budding and some falling away.

SAMUEL JOHNSON; *Dictionary*, 1755

The dictionary is . . . only a rough draft.

MONIQUE WITTIG & SANDE ZEIG; *Lesbian Peoples*, 1976

DIFFERENCE

By nature all men are alike, but by education widely different.

CHINESE proverb

In education all the difference lies.

ANNE DOUGLAS HOWARD, ?–1760

DILETTANTE

A smattering of everything and a knowledge of nothing.
CHARLES DARWIN, 1809–1882

A dilettante is a product of where wealth and literature meet.
DOUGLAS DUNN; *The Listener*, 1977

Dilettante: a philanderer who seduces the several arts and deserts each in turn for another.
OLIVER HEREFORD, 1863–1935

DILIGENCE

Diligence is a great teacher.
ARABIC proverb

DIMINISHING RETURNS

The law of diminishing returns holds good in almost every part of our human universe.
ALDOUS HUXLEY, 1894–1963

DIPLOMA

I don't need no diploma to do what I do.
LOUIS "SATCHMO" ARMSTRONG, c. 1898–1971

It's an insane tragedy that 700,000 people get a diploma each year and can't read the damned diploma.
WILLIAM E. BROCK; *The New York Times*, 14 Jan. 1987

The fireworks begin today. Each diploma is a lighted match. Each one of you is a fuse.
EDWARD KOCH; *The New York Times*, 10 Jun. 1983

Diplomas and degrees were originally invented to make stages in a carefully planned educational sequence and were awarded not only for having reached the appropriate chronological point without academic mishap, but for having met some definite and definitively situated challenge, such as a series of examinations.

RICHARD F. STORR; *The Beginning of the Future*, 1973

Socrates gave no diplomas or degrees, and would have subjected any disciple who demanded one to a disconcerting catechism on the nature of true knowledge.

G(EORGE) M(ACAULAY) TREVELYAN, 1876–1962

DIPLOMA MILL

Basically a diploma mill is a person or an organization selling degrees or awarding degrees without an appropriate academic base and without requiring a sufficient degree of postsecondary level academic achievement.

DAVID W. STEWART & HENRY A. SPILLE;
Diploma Mills, 1988

DISABLED

I just don't understand why you don't have automatic doors that work. . . .

NATHASHA ALVAREZ;
The Chronicle of Higher Education, 20 Apr. 1994

Only a brief time ago, almost all students with severe disabilities were required to receive their education in segregated schools. It is now evident that when students complete segregated school programs their most probable life options are also segregated.

LOU BROWN;
Education of Learners with Severe Handicaps, 1986

They [University of Cambridge] haven't devoted any significant effort or funds to improving access or removing other obstacles to disabled students. They don't even know how many disabled people they employ.

STEPHEN W. HAWKING;
The Times Higher Education Supplement, 8 Jul. 1994

Sadly, many autistic children with severe learning difficulties are in settings where their needs are not understood and where they pose considerable management problems for the classroom teacher.

RITA JORDAN; in *Autism*, 1990

DYSLEXIA   An ambiguous word, never satisfactorily defined.

PETER LAWRENCE; *Is My Child Stupid?*, 1988

A curb is a wall to a handicapped person.

NATIONAL COUNCIL ON THE HANDICAPPED;
a *statement*, 1980s

It is probably reasonable to say that the problems involved in dealing with autistic children are more puzzling, varied and demanding than those of dealing with any other single category of handicap.

BRIAN ROBERTS; in *Autistic Children*, 1977

DISCIPLINE

I never reprimand a boy in the evening – darkness and a troubled mind are a poor combination.

FRANK L. BOYDEN; *Life*, 30 Nov. 1962

The discipline of the school should proceed from the life of the school as a whole and not directly from the teacher.

JOHN DEWEY; *Education Today*, 1940

Discipline must come through liberty.

MARIA MONTESSORI; *The Montessori Method*, 1912

The first idea that the child must acquire in order to be actively disciplined is that of the difference between good and evil; and the task of the educator lies in seeing that the child does not confound good with immobility, and evil with activity.

MARIA MONTESSORI, 1870–1952

In the 1940s a survey listed the top seven discipline problems in public schools: talking, chewing gum, making noise, running in the halls, getting out of turn in line, wearing improper clothes, not putting paper in wastebaskets. A 1980s survey lists these top seven: drug abuse, alcohol abuse, pregnancy, suicide, rape, robbery, assault. (Arson, gang warfare and venereal disease are also-rans.)

GEORGE F. WILL; *Newsweek*, 5 Jan. 1987

DISCONTENT

When textbooks are examined in terms of their presentation and reinforcement of a social order, women and minority groups are dissatisfied with the lack of reality in the presentation.

CAROL POLOWY; *Vital Speeches*, 1 Feb. 1975

As we approach the end of the century (and of the millennium) a deep discontent moves beneath the educational establishment, indeed, beneath the society.

BRUCE WILSHIRE; *The Moral Collapse of the University*, 1990

DISSERTATION

A frequent lament is that students finishing PhDs arc not suitably equipped to handle the demands of an academic career because their postgraduate qualification has involved only the very narrow task of writing a dissertation.

L.R. BARRETT; *Higher Education Review*, vol. 22, 1990

Dropping the dissertation requirement might allow most graduate students to get a life before they get a Ph.D. There are too many ten-year dissertations – projects whose only real consequence is the resolution on the part of the "doctor" never to write anything again. It is worth noting that most Ph.D.s junk their dissertation as soon as they get their degree. . . .

ROBERT SOLOMON & JON SOLOMON;
Up the University, 1993

The dissertation doctorate is certainly the least understood institution in American higher education.

DAVID STERNBERG;
How to Complete and Survive a Doctoral Dissertation, 1981

No one will ever total up the marriages ruined, the children neglected, the anguish suffered, and the years of fruitful work blighted by the curse of the unfinished dissertation.

> ROBERT PAUL WOLFF; *The Ideal of the University*, 1969

DISTANCE EDUCATION (Off-Campus Education)

Somewhat reluctantly the university left the calm of the world of scholarship to mingle with the hot and dusty turmoil without.

> A.L. HALL-QUEST; *The University Afield*, 1926

Distance education appears to be the wave of the future for many "non-traditional" students. For students with disabilities (and for those of us in academe who have a legal and ethical mandate to respond to them), distance education may be an especially important means to success.

> ESTHER H. PAIST;
> *The Chronicle of Higher Education*, 1 Jun. 1994

Within the last decade, governments and institutions around the world have embraced the concept of distance education. A remarkable array of courses and programs have been designed, developed and, depending on location, delivered by various means.

> ROBERT SWEET;
> in *Post-Secondary Distance Education in Canada*, 1989

Distance-education students tend to be more independent and auto-nomous.

> GORDON THOMPSON;
> in *Post-Secondary Distance Education in Canada*, 1989

[A] distance education course should have the intrinsic characteristics of being self-instructional. . . .

> ARMANDO ROCHA TRINDADE;
> *Distance Education in Europe*, 1992

The future of independent study is clearly entwined with the distance education movement.

> BARBARA L. WATKINS & STEPHEN J. WRIGHT;
> in *The Foundations of American Distance Education*, 1991

DOCTRINE

Civilized men have done their fiercest fighting for doctrines.
WILLIAM GRAHAM SUMNER, 1840–1910

A clash of doctrines is not a disaster it is an opportunity.
ALFRED NORTH WHITEHEAD;
Science and the Modern World, 1925

DOGMA

The bureaucratic organization which is intended to expedite the process of getting school moving and to respond to external demands, eventually becomes dogmatic. In place of improving educational practice by engaging all the available expertise, few people take responsibility for most decisions and generally perpetuate enduring traditions. The concern for excellence is displaced by the demand for immediate action and efficiency.
RITA S. BRAUSE; *Enduring Schools*, 1992

The death of dogma is the birth of reality.
(IMMANUEL) KANT, 1724–1804

The greater the ignorance the greater the dogmatism.
WILLIAM OSLER, 1849–1919

DOING

Life is doing things, not making things.
ARISTOTLE, 384–322

In doing we learn.
ENGLISH? proverb

DREAM

Wildest dreams are the necessary first steps toward scientific investigation.
CHARLES S. PIERCE, 1839–1914

Dare to be wrong and to dream.

(JOHANN CHRISTOPH FRIEDRICH VON) SCHILLER, 1759–1805

DROPOUT

The loneliness which leads to suicide is one of the many reasons why some students drop out of college.

CAROLINE BIRD; *The Case Against College*, 1975

Burger King, appalled that it had to train its employees with pictures instead of words, now helps to finance about 40 "Burger King Academies" for students at risk of dropping out.

The Economist, 4 Jun. 1994

Dropouts could be reconceptualized as critics of educational and labor market arrangements.

MICHELLE FINE; *Framing Dropouts*, 1991

[I]n many cities, fear of gangs in and around schools has become a primary reason for dropping out.

MARGARET DIANE LECOMPTE & ANTHONY GARY DWORKIN;
Giving Up on School, 1991

Wastage is not an attractive word when applied to human beings, but such substitutes as attrition, student mortality, and dropping out have the drawback of implying that all shortcomings reside in the student.

GORDON W. MILLER;
The International Encyclopedia of Higher Education, 1977

All, of course, did not reach this top of the ladder. The great masses never got further in their studies than the faculty of Arts, and indeed the majority left the university without obtaining any degree, even that of *Baccalarius Artium*.

FRIEDRICH PAULSEN;
German Education Past and Present, 1908

When asked why she dropped out, her answer is like an echo in a high school guidance counselor's ear: "I was very, very bored. I don't know how I felt really."

CRAIG A. POILE; *Ottawa Magazine*, Dec. 1987

Reformers and the establishment alike express alarm at whatever percentage of high school students fail to stay on to graduation. Yet, clearly, every single person in the whole society drops out of education at some point.

THOMAS SOWELL; *Inside American Education*, 1993

DRUGS

Especially worrisome are untold thousands of "crack babies" born each year to drug-addicted mothers. The first crack babies to reach school age in 1989 showed early signs of sociopathic behavior.

JAMES DALE DAVIDSON & WILLIAM REES-MOGG;
The Great Reckoning, 1993

When the crack children are separated out into special classrooms, the yearly cost of educating them averages $15,000 per year, versus the normal $3,500 per year.

WARREN FARRELL; *The Myth of Male Power*, 1993

An annual survey of 51,000 high school and eighth-grade youths found that more are now experimenting with cocaine and other illicit drugs. The study by University of Michigan researchers found that 9 percent of eighth graders (children about 13 years old), 19 percent of 10th graders and 26 percent of 12th graders reported using marijuana in the past year – increases of 2 to 4 percentage points from a year earlier. Eight percent of the eighth graders, 14 percent of 10th graders and 19 percent of the seniors said they smoked cigarettes daily – up by 1 to 2 percentage points.

International Herald Tribune, 1 Feb. 1994

DUNCE

How much a dunce that has been sent to roam
Excels a dunce that has been kept at home.

WILLIAM COWPER; *The Progress of Error*, c.1782

He [John Duns Scotus] devised the doctrine of the Immaculate Conception and was considered a near equal of Thomas Aquinas, yet the term "dunce" comes from his name. His followers, who were called "Dunses," resisted the Renaissance, and their name became associated with obstinate stupidity.

ED MORROW; *The Grim Reaper's Book of Days*, 1992

There is no dunce like a mature dunce.

(GEORGE) SANTAYANA;
Character and Opinion in the United States, 1921

I know a lot of people think I'm dumb. Well, at least I ain't no educated fool.

LEON SPINKS; *Los Angeles Times*, 28 Jun. 1978

E

ÉCOLE POLYTECHNIQUE

[T]he *école Polytechnique, a grande école* whose students (*Polytechnicians*) are trained for State administrative posts. ...
PIERRE BOURDIEU & JEAN-CLAUDE PASSERON;
Reproduction in Education, Society and Culture, 1977

[O]n February 25, 1794, the Convention began to establish those "écoles centrales" which were to be the departmental lycées, or high schools, of the future ... and on September 28, 1794, the école polytechnique began its prestigious career.
WILL(IAM) (JAMES) DURANT & ARIEL DURANT;
The Story of Civilization (vol. XI), 1975

ECONOMICS

Economics is what we might call, by way of eminence, the Dismal Science.
THOMAS CARLYLE, 1795–1881

ECONOMIST

If all economists were laid end to end, they would not reach a conclusion.
GEORGE BERNARD SHAW, 1856–1950

ECONOMY

Education is perhaps the most important tool to ensure that women become equal partners with men in society. Governments still don't seem to understand the tremendously positive effect this education can have on their societies' economic development.
MARCELA BALLARA;
International Herald Tribune, 8 Sep. 1993

The absurdity of defining education as an economic good becomes clear if we ask ourselves what is gained by perceiving education as a way to enhance even further the runaway consumption that threatens the earth, the air, and the water of our planet?
JOHN TAYLOR GATTO; *Dumbing Us Down,* 1992

More than half a million [UK] children, research indicates, are absent from class at least once a week without acceptable reason. At least 200,000 are skipping school every day. The figures are disturbing but their consequences offer cause for greater long-term concern. A work force that has been weaned on truancy is not best-placed to compete in the world economy.

The Guardian, 16 Oct. 1990

Educated girls become more economically productive women. They have healthier, better educated children, too, thus flattening population growth trends and lessening environmental pressure. Combined with better farming, fair prices and improved basic health services, education for [African] girls is a crucial and essential step away from the economic brink.

JOHN WILLIAM; *International Herald Tribune*, 15 Apr. 1994

Tampering with the schools will not solve our economic problems.

GEORGE H. WOOD; *Schools That Work*, 1993

EDUCATE

Every educated person is a future enemy.

MARTIN BORMANN, 1900–1945?

A number of people who are essentially ignorant now have degrees and diplomas to certify they are educated. These people either know how ignorant they are, and thus realize education is a fraud, or they go around saying they are just as good as everybody else. Ignorance is curable. Stupidity is not.

JOHN CIARDI; *Waco Tribune-Herald*, 18 Mar. 1976

Children have to be educated, but they have also to be left to educate themselves.

ERNEST DIMNET; *The Art of Thinking*, 1928

The self-educated are marked by stubborn peculiarities.

ISAAC D'ISRAELI; *The Literary Character*, 1795

You send your child to the schoolmaster, but 'tis the schoolboys who educate him.

RALPH WALDO EMERSON; *Conduct of Life*, 1860

To be able to be caught up into the world of thought – that is educated.

EDITH HAMILTON; *Saturday Evening Post*, 27 Sep. 1958

Whom, then, do I call educated? First, those who control circumstances instead of being mastered by them, those who meet all occasions manfully and act in accordance with intelligent thinking, those who are honourable in all dealings, who treat good-naturedly persons and things that are disagreeable, and, furthermore, those who hold their pleasures under control and are not overcome by misfortune, finally those who are not spoiled by success.

ISOCRATES, 436–338

The educated man tries to repress the inferior one in himself, without realizing that by this he forces the latter to become revolutionary.

(CARL GUSTAV) JUNG; *Psychology and Religion*, 1940

The more scholastically educated a man is generally, the more he is an emotional boor.

D(AVID) H(ERBERT) LAWRENCE; *John Galsworthy*, 1927

It is the educated barbarian who is the worst: he knows what to destroy.

HELEN MACINNES; *The Venetian Affair*, 1963

If you educate a man you educate a person, but if you educate a woman you educate a family.

RUBY MANIKAN; *The Observer*, 30 Mar. 1947

It is a woeful mistake to suppose that the educated are kinder or more tolerant: education creates vested interests, and renders the beneficiaries acutely jealous and very vocal.

LEWIS BERNSTEIN NAMIER; *Conflicts*, 1943

The educated man is a greater nuisance than the uneducated one.

GEORGE BERNARD SHAW, 1856–1950

An educated man should know everything about something, and something about everything.

C(ECILY) V(ERONICA) WEDGWOOD, 1910–

Men and women must be educated, in a greater degree, by the opinions and manners of the society they live in. In every age there has been a stream of popular opinion that has carried all before it, and given a familiar character, as it were, to the century. It may then fairly be inferred, that, till society be differently constituted, much cannot be expected from education.

MARY WOLLSTONECRAFT;
A Vindication of the Rights of Women, 1792

In our desire to educate, we've penalized imagination and rewarded conformity.

RICHARD SAUL WURMAN; *Information Anxiety*, 1991

EDUCATION

I consider a human soul without education, like marble in the quarry, which shows none of its inherent beauties till the skill of the polisher fetches out the colours, makes the surface shine and discovers every ornamental daub spot and vein that runs through the body of it.

JOSEPH ADDISON, 1672–1719

Education is to get where you can start to learn.

GEORGE AIKEN; *The New York Times*, 29 Jan. 1967

Real education should educate us out of self into something far finer — selflessness which links us with all humanity.

NANCY ASTOR; *My Two Countries*, 1923

Education, in its largest sense, is a thing of a great scope and intent. It includes the whole process by which a human being is formed to be what he is, in habits, principles, and cultivation of every kind. . . . You speak of beginning the education of your son. The moment he was able to form an idea his education was already begun.

ANNA LETITIA BARBAULD;
Miscellaneous Pieces in Prose, 1773

The test and the use of man's education is that he finds pleasure in the exercise of his mind.

JACQUES BARZUN; *Saturday Evening Post*, 3 May 1958

A good education is not so much one which prepares a man to succeed in the world, as one which enables him to sustain failure.

BERNARD IDDINGS BELL; *Life*, 16 Oct. 1950

Education, n[oun]. That which discloses to the wise and disguises from the foolish their lack of understanding.

AMBROSE BIERCE; *The Devil's Dictionary*, 1911

Our school education ignores, in a thousand ways, the rules of healthy development.

EMILY BLACKWELL, 1826–1910

Education is learning what you didn't know you didn't know.

GEORGE BOAS; *The American Scholar*, 1938

Education makes a people easy to lead, but difficult to drive; easy to govern but impossible to enslave.

HENRY PETER BROUGHAM, 1778–1868

Education is a wonderful thing. If you couldn't sign your name you'd have to pay cash.

RITA MAE BROWN; *Starting from Scratch*, 1988

To live for a time close to great minds is the best kind of education.

JOHN BUCHAN; *Memory Hold-the-Door*, 1940

Education is simply the soul of a society as it passes from one generation to another.

G(ILBERT) K(EITH) CHESTERTON, 1874–1936

The main fact about education is that there is no such thing. Education is a word like "transmission" or "inheritance"; it is not an object but a method.

G(ILBERT) K(EITH) CHESTERTON, 1874–1936

The forcing of Latin, geometry, and algebra in a certain kind of manner into a certain kind of head is not education; it is persecution.

FRANK MOORE COLBY; *The Colby Essays*, 1926

Education is the fundamental method of social process and reform.

JOHN DEWEY; *My Pedagogic Creed*, 1897

Education is a controlling grace to the young, consolation to the old, wealth to the poor, and ornament to the rich.

DIOGENES (the Cynic), *c*.400–*c*.325

Education has become too important to be left to educators.
PETER F. DRUCKER; *The Age of Discontinuity*, 1968

The wit was not wrong who defined education in this way: education is that which remains if one has forgotten everything he learned in school.
ALBERT EINSTEIN, 1879–1955

Crooked by nature, is never made straight by education.
ENGLISH? proverb

To accuse others for one's own misfortune is a sign of want of education; to accuse oneself shows that one's education has begun; to accuse neither oneself nor others shows that one's education is complete.
EPICTETUS, *c.*50–120

An education isn't how much you have committed to memory, or even how much you know. It's being able to differentiate between what you do know and what you don't. It's knowing where to go to find out what you need to know; and it's knowing how to use the information once you get it.
WILLIAM FEATHER, 1889–1981

When a man's education is finished, he is finished.
E.A. FILENE, 1860–1937

The prevailing philosophy of education tends to discredit hard work.
ABRAHAM FLEXNER; *Universities*, 1930

Education's purpose is to replace an empty mind with an open one.
MALCOLM S. FORBES, 1919–1990

Education – as the practice of freedom as opposed to education as the practice of domination – denies that man is abstract, isolated, independent, and unattached to the world; it also denies that the world exists as a reality from men.
PAULO FREIRE; *Pedagogy of the Oppressed*, 1972

Education is the ability to listen to almost anything without losing your temper or your self-confidence.
ROBERT FROST; *Reader's Digest*, Apr. 1960

Every man who rises above the common level has received two educations: the first from his teachers; the second, more personal and
important, from himself.

EDWARD GIBBON, 1737–1794

The ability to think straight, some knowledge of the past, some of the
future, some skill to do useful service, some urge to fit that service into the
well-being of the community – these are the most vital things education
must try to produce.

VIRGINIA GILDERSLEEVE; *Many a Good Crusade*, 1954

Education as an "investment," education as a way to beat the Russians and
best the Japanese, education as a way to get ahead of the fellow down the
street ... you really do not generate the educational values that count
when you stress only these external, comparative advantages.

MEG GREENFIELD; *Newsweek*, 16 May 1983

Education needs to be re-invented.

CHARLES HANDY; *The Age of Unreason*, 1989

Education made us what we are.

(CLAUDE-ADRIEN) HELVÉTIUS, 1715–1771

The first thing education teaches you to do is to walk alone.

ALFRED A. HORN, 1861–1931

Half of the little education people have is usually wrong.

E(DGAR) W(ATSON) HOWE, 1853–1937

Education is a kind of continuing dialogue, and a dialogue assumes ...
different points of view.

ROBERT M. HUTCHINS; *Time*, 8 Dec. 1952

The aim of education is the knowledge not of facts but of values.

WILLIAM RALPH INGE; *Cambridge Essays on Education*, 1917

Our education is a ceaseless compromise between the conservative and the
progressive factors.

WILLIAM JAMES; *The Principles of Psychology*, 1890

Education does not consist merely in adorning the memory and enlightening the understanding. Its main business should be to direct the will.

JOSEPH JOUBERT, 1754–1824

But I confess to a great misgiving as I watch the ceaseless stream of young men and women pour out of our educational establishments clutching their degrees, diplomas and certificates. Certainly we need all the doctors, engineers, lawyers, teachers we can produce, and even now must fill the gaps with expatriates who come to Zambia as our guests to help us out temporarily. What worries me is that we seem to take a functional view of education regarding its products as job fodder, to be fitted into some vocational slot as they emerge from the machine.

KENNETH KAUNDA; *Letters to My Children*, 1973

Education is a process that goes on from the cradle to the grave, in school and out, and in all the nuances of our lives.

AUGUST KERBER; *Quotable Quotes on Education*, 1968

Education is the inculcation of the incomprehensible into the indifferent by the incompetent.

JOHN MAYNARD KEYNES, 1883–1946

This kind of learning without real use should be left for another day, and one's best efforts should be given to an education that is relevant to everyday use.

EIICHI KIYOOKA; *Fukuzawa Yukichi on Education*, 1985

Very few people can stand the strain of education without getting superior about it.

STEPHEN LEACOCK, 1869–1944

Schooling is what happens inside the walls of the school, some of which is educational. Education happens everywhere, and it happens from the moment a child is born – and some say before – until a person dies.

SARA LAWRENCE LIGHTFOOT; *In a World of Ideas*, 1989

Education, then, beyond all other devices of human origin, is a great equalizer of conditions of men. . . .

HORACE MANN, 1796–1859

Education must have an end in view, for it is not an end in itself.

SYBIL MARSHALL; *An Experiment in Education,* 1963

It is in and through education that a culture, and polity, not only tries to perpetuate but enacts the kinds of thinking it welcomes, and discards and/or discredits the kind it fears.

ELIZABETH KAMARCK MINNICK;
Transforming Knowledge, 1990

We receive three educations, one from our parents, one from our schoolmasters, and one from the world. The third contradicts all that the first two teach us.

(CHARLES DE SECONDAT, BARON DE LA BRÈDE ET DE)
MONTESQUIEU, 1689–1755

And if education is always to be conceived along the same antiquated lines of mere transmission of knowledge, there is little to be hoped from it in the bettering of man's future. For what is the use of transmitting knowledge if the individual's total development lags behind.

MARIA MONTESSORI; *The Absorbent Mind,* 1967

If you think education is expensive, try ignorance.

BRYAN NICHOLSON, 1932–

Education is a transaction between teachers and learners.

MICHAEL OAKESHOTT;
Michael Oakeshott on Education, 1989

I am inclined to think that one's education has been in vain if one fails to learn that most school masters are idiots.

HESKETH PEARSON, 1887–1964

'Tis education forms the mind;
Just as the twig is bent, the tree's inclined.

ALEXANDER POPE, 1688–1744

Real education must ultimately be limited to one who insists on knowing, the rest is mere sheep-herding.

EZRA POUND; *The ABC of Reading,* 1934

It is impossible to withhold education from the receptive, as it is impossible to force it upon the unreasoning.

AGNES REPPLIER; *Times and Tendencies,* 1931

Both class and race survived education, and neither should. What is education then? If it doesn't help a human being to recognize that humanity is humanity, what is it for? So you can make a bigger salary than other people?

BEAH RICHARDS, 1926–

Education, properly understood, is that which teaches discernment.

JOSEPH ROUX; *Meditations of a Parish Priest,* 1886

Education does not mean teaching people to know what they do not know; it means teaching them to behave as they do not behave.

JOHN RUSKIN, 1819–1900

Education, therefore, tends to prevent societies from adapting to new ideas as quickly as they ought, and causes many adult men and women to feel a horror derived from their early training, in regard to things which it would be well to accept as a matter of course.

BERTRAND RUSSELL; *Education and the Social Order,* 1932

Education which was at first made universal in order that all might be able to read and write has been found capable of serving quite other purposes. By instilling nonsense it unifies populations and generates collective enthusiasm.

BERTRAND RUSSELL; *Unpopular Essays,* 1950

Education is light, lack of it darkness.

RUSSIAN proverb

You can't impose education on anyone.

(GEORGE) SANTAYANA, 1863–1952

Education is what remains when we have forgotten all that we have been taught.

GEORGE SAVILE, 1633–1695

If western civilisation is in a state of permanent crisis, it is not far-fetched to suggest that there may be something wrong with its education. No civilisation, I am sure, has ever devoted more energy and resources to organise education, and if we believe in nothing else, we certainly believe that education is, or should be, the key to everything. In fact, the belief in education is so strong that we treat it as the residual legatee of all our problems.

E(RNST) F(RIEDRICH) SCHUMACHER; *Small is Beautiful*, 1973

The problems of education are merely reflections of the deepest problems of our age. They cannot be solved by organisation, administration, or the expenditure of money, even though the importance of all these is not denied. We are suffering from a metaphysical disease, and the cure must therefore be metaphysical. Education which fails to clarify our central convictions is mere training or indulgence. For it is our central convictions that are in disorder, and, as long as the present anti-metaphysical temper persists, the disorder will grow worse. Education, far from ranking as man's greatest resource, will then be an agent of destruction, in accordance with the principle *corruptio optimi pessima* [corruption of what is best is worst].

E(RNST) F(RIEDRICH) SCHUMACHER; *Small is Beautiful*, 1973

After three decades, education in many African countries is worse than before independence ... teachers are looking for second and third jobs to feed their own children.

ANDERSON SHANKAGA;
International Herald Tribune, 15 Apr. 1994

Education is what survives when what has been learnt has been forgotten.

B(URRHUS) F(REDERIC) SKINNER; *New Scientist*, May 1964

Education is a private matter between the person and the world of knowledge and experience, and has little to do with school or college.

LILLIAN SMITH; *Redbook*, Sep. 1969

For education does not lend itself to definition, and certainly not to one that can endure as unalterably true.

W.O. LESTER SMITH; *Education*, 1957

To me education is a leading out of what is already there in the pupil's soul. To Miss Mackay it is putting in of something that is not there, and that is not what I call education, I call it intrusion....

MURIEL SPARK; *The Prime of Miss Jean Brodie*, 1961

Education is a weapon whose effects depend on who holds it in his hands and at whom it is aimed.

> (JOSEPH) STALIN (né IOSIF VISSARIONOVICH DZHUGASHVILI),
> 1879–1953

What does education often do? It makes a straight-cut ditch of a free, meandering brook.

> H(ENRY) D(AVID) THOREAU; *Journal*, Oct. 1850

Education ... has produced a vast population able to read and write but unable to distinguish what is worth reading.

> G(EORGE) M(ACAULAY) TREVELYAN, 1876–1962

It is possible to impart a certain amount of knowledge at one time to a large class, but in true education, each one ought to be dealt with as a separate individual, for we know that one's mental and moral characteristics vary as do the faces of each one of us.

> UME(KO) TSUDA, 1865–1929

Education is what you must acquire without any interference from your schooling.

> MARK TWAIN (pseud. of SAMUEL LANGHORNE CLEMENS),
> 1835–1910

In some institutions education is reduced almost to a daily struggle to maintain order and prevent chaos.

> ROBERT VAN DE WEYER; *The Health of Nations*, 1991

We don't need no education
We don't need no thought control
No dark sarcasm in the classroom
Teachers leave those kids alone,
Hey teacher leave us kids alone
All in all it's just another brick in the wall
All in all you're just another brick in the wall.

> ROGER WATERS;
> *Another Brick in the Wall – Part 2* (pub. Pink Floyd Music), 1979

Education isn't only books and music – it's asking questions, all the time. There are millions of us, all over the country and no one, not one of us, is asking questions, we're all taking the easiest way out. Everyone I ever worked with took the easiest way out. We don't fight for anything, we're so mentally lazy we might as well be dead.

ARNOLD WESKER; *Roots*, 1959–60

Education is a wonderful thing, but it is well to remember from time to time that nothing that is worth knowing can be taught.

OSCAR WILDE; *The Critic as Artist*, 1891

Education ministries often are bloated with time-servers.

JOHN WILLIAM; *International Herald Tribune*, 15 Apr. 1994

Education has really only one basic factor, a sine qua non – one must want it.

GEORGE EDWARD WOODBURY, 1855–1930

Knowye, Our subjects:
Our Imperial Ancestors have founded Our Empire on a basis broad and everlasting and have deeply and firmly implanted virtue; Our subjects ever united in loyalty and filial piety have from generation to generation illustrated the beauty thereof. This is the glory of the fundamental character of Our Empire, and herein also lies the source of Our education. . . .
The 30th day of the 10th month of the 23rd year of Meiji.
(Imperial Sign Manual, Imperial Seal)

K. YOSHIDA & T. KAIGO; *Japanese Education*, 1937

EDUCATOR

He who can't remember clearly his own childhood, is a poor educator.

MARIE VON EBNER-ESCHENBACH; *Aphorisms*, 1905

As educators, we live in a fool's paradise, or worse in a knave's, if we are unaware that when we are teaching *something* to anyone we are also teaching *everything* to that same anyone.

FLORENCE HOWE; *Myths of Coeducation*, 1984

Like all great educators, she [Montessori] extended our sense of educability.

BRIAN JACKSON, 1933–1983

[O]ne's job as an educator is not only to implant new ideas but also to dispose of or modify old ones.

DAVID A. KOLB; *Experiential Learning*, 1984

There is a need for educators who are themselves educated; superior, noble spirits who prove themselves every moment by what they say and by what they do not say . . . and not the learned boors which grammar school and university offer youth today as "higher nurses".

(FRIEDRICH WILHELM) NIETZSCHE;
Die Götzen-Dämmerung, 1889

The truth is the profession of educator has not yet attained, in our societies, the normal status to which it has the right in the scale of intellectual values.

JEAN PIAGET;
Science of Education and the Psychology of the Child, 1970

To be effective educators we [teachers] have to help one another.

MAURICE TUGWELL;
University Affairs/Affaires Universitaires, Nov. 1993

EMOTION

Human beings are full of emotion, and the teacher who knows how to use it will have dedicated learners. It means sending dominant signals instead of submissive ones with your eyes, body and voice.

LEON LESSINGER; *Newsweek*, 8 Mar. 1976

EMPLOYMENT

A lot of fellows nowadays have a BA, MA, or PhD. Unfortunately, they don't have a JOB.

(ANTOINE) "FATS" DOMINO, 1928–

To the babyboomers, that meant the now familar [underemployment] specter of a physicist working as a cab driver, an economist waiting on tables, or an English Ph.D. repairing driveways.

LANDON Y. JONES; *Great Expectations*, 1980

I do not know how many of Australia's taxi drivers have degrees but a dozen of those who whisked me about Melbourne and Sydney recently were graduates. Some had PhDs.

GEOFF MASLEN;
Australian Campus Review Weekly, 30 Jan. 1992

ENCYCLOPAEDIA

Those who consult an encyclopaedia will find the information they require plus much they do not.

G(ILBERT) K(EITH) CHESTERTON, 1874–1936

Language is an encyclopaedia of ignorance.

EDWARD DE BONO, 1933–

ENGLISH

English is weak in describing emotional states or intensities of interpersonal relationships.

RITA MAE BROWN; *Starting from Scratch*, 1988

American English is the greatest influence of English everywhere.

ROBERT M. BURCHFIELD; *Newsweek*, 2 Jun. 1986

My personal opinion is that English should not be a school subject.

A(LEXANDER) S(UTHERLAND) NEILL;
Talking on Summerhill, 1971

Once, speaking only English was good enough. Today it is a handicap.

JEAN-MARK RECOUR; *The European*, 25–31 Mar. 1994

English is a very male-oriented language because of its evolution in a patriarchal society, but times, values, norms, and conditions change – perhaps at a greater pace than the rules of language have.

MANJU SAH & CATHERINE RANCY;
Guidelines for Non-sexist Writing, 1986
[pub. Canadian Advisory Council on the Status of Women]

What has been termed 'correct' English is nothing other than the blatant legitimation of the white middle-class code.

DALE SPENDER; *Man Made Language*, 1980

Is there any word in English quite so useful, so hopeful, so truly pregnant as "yet"?

GORE VIDAL (né EUGENE LUTHER VIDAL), 1925–

ENLIGHTENMENT

It is not the answer that enlightens, but the question.

EUGÈNE IONESCO, 1912–1994

ENVIRONMENT

Our own method of education is characterised by the central importance that we attribute to the question of environment.

MARIA MONTESSORI; *The Secret of Childhood*, 1936

EQUALITY

And yet, in the schoolroom more than any other place, does the difference of sex, if there is any, need to be forgotten.

SUSAN B. ANTHONY, 1820–1906

For there is to be no sex barrier of any kind in this [Plato's] community; least of all education – the girl shall have the same intellectual opportunities as the boy, the same chance to rise to the highest positions in the state.

WILL(IAM) (JAMES) DURANT; *The Story of Philosophy*, 1926

On the other hand, I flattered myself that I am not the first lady to have had something published; that minds have no sex and that if the minds of women were cultivated like those of men, and if as much time and energy were used to instruct the minds of the former, they would equal those of the latter.

MARIE MEURDAC;
La Chymie charitable et facile en faveur des dames, 1680

Equality is not when a female Einstein gets promoted to assistant professor: equality is when a female schlemiel moves ahead as fast as a male schlemiel.

EWALD B. NYQUIST; *The New York Times*, 9 Oct. 1975

If it were customary to send litle girls to school and to teach them the same subjects as are taught boys, they would learn just as fully and would understand the subtleties of all arts and sciences. Indeed, maybe they would understand them better ... for just as women's bodies are softer than men's so their understanding is sharper.

CHRISTINE DE PISAN; *La Cité des dames*, 1404

The girls must be trained in precisely the same way, and I'd like to make this proposal without any reservations whatever about horseriding or athletics being suitable activities for males but not for females.

PLATO (né ARISTOCLES), *c*.428–*c*.348

We conclude that in the field of public education the doctrine of "separate but equal" has no place.

EARL WARREN;
Brown vs. Board of Education of Topeka, 17 May 1954

Parents need to be made aware of situations where homophobic comments and so on are made by children. Just as anti-racist and anti-sexist policies depend upon the involvement of parents and not merely the targeting of pupils, so too does the implementation of an equal opportunity statement and code that includes sexuality.

NEIL WILSON; in *Education Equality*, 1992

ERROR

Any man can make mistakes, but only an idiot persists in his error.

(MARCUS TULLIUS) CICERO, 106–43

If errors were wisdom there'd be no need for schools ....

CORNELIA & BILLY (MACLEOD);
If Wishes Were Horses (pub. MacLeod Music), 1986

Many a truth sprang from an error.

MARIE VON EBNER-ESCHENBACH; *Aphorisms*, 1905

Error is always in haste.

ENGLISH? proverb

Nothing is more vital than error.
BERGEN EVANS; *The Natural History of Nonsense*, 1946

The most learned among us differ only from the ignorant by their faculty of finding amusement in multifarious and complicated errors.
ANATOLE FRANCE (pseud. of ANATOLE FRANÇOIS THIBAULT), 1844–1924

The most powerful cause of error is the war existing between senses and reason.
(BLAISE) PASCAL; *Pensées*, 1669

Love truth, but pardon error.
VOLTAIRE (né FRANÇOIS-MARIE AROUET), 1694–1778

Learning preserves the errors of the past as well as its wisdom.
ALFRED NORTH WHITEHEAD, 1861–1947

ERUDITION

Erudition, n[oun]. Dust shaken out of a book into an empty skull.
AMBROSE BIERCE; *The Devil's Dictionary*, 1911

Erudition, like a bloodhound, is a charming thing when held firmly in leash, but it is not so attractive when turned loose upon a defenseless unerudite public.
AGNES REPPLIER; *Points of View*, 1891

ESTHETICS

Esthetics is the study of ideal form; it is the philosophy of art.
WILL(IAM) (JAMES) DURANT; *The Story of Philosophy*, 1926

ETHICS

Ethics and science need to shake hands.
RICHARD CLARKE CABOT, 1868–1939

There cannot be two sets of ethical principles, one for life in the schools, and the other for life outside of the school.
JOHN DEWEY; *Moral Principles in Education*, 1909

Ethics is the study of ideal conduct; the highest knowledge, said Socrates, is the highest knowledge of good and evil, the knowledge of the wisdom of life.
WILL(IAM) (JAMES) DURANT; *The Story of Philosophy*, 1926

A man's ethical behavior should be based effectually on sympathy, education, and social ties; no religious base is necessary. Man would indeed be in a poor way if he had to be restrained by fear of punishment and hope of reward after death.
ALBERT EINSTEIN, 1879–1955

A keen sense of ethical responsibility is essential if you are going to do research in any field involving people.
MIRIAM LEWIS; *Understanding Psychological Research*, 1979

Science cannot stop while ethics catches up. . . .
ELVIN STACKMAN; *Life*, 9 Jan. 1950

EXAMINATION

This year Georgia became the first state to require a standardized written exam as part of a "readiness assessment" that determines who passes and who fails kindergarten.
EZRA BOWEN; *Time*, 25 Apr. 1988

[I]t was now to bear my testimony to the truth, and to be put to the torture of their examination.
CHARLOTTE BRONTË; *Villette*, 1853

In many schools, few teachers could pass the final exam in the courses they are supposed to teach.

MARVIN CETRON & MARGARET GAYLE;
Educational Renaissance, 1991

Examinations are formidable even to the best prepared, for the greatest fool may ask more than the wisest man can answer.

C(HARLES) C(ALEB) COLTON, 1780?–1832

To create an education system without examinations is to fail to prepare children and students for the realities of adult life.

C. B(RIAN) COX; in *The Black Papers on Education*, 1971

Many studies have found that because of test-oriented teaching, American students' classroom activities consist of listening, reading textbook sections, responding briefly to questions, and taking short-answer and multiple-choice quizzes. They rarely plan or initiate anything, create their own products, read or write something substantial, or engage in analytic discussions or in projects requiring research, invention, or problem solving.

LINDA DARLING-HAMMOND & ANN LIEBERMAN;
The Chronicle of Higher Education, 29 Jan. 1992

Exams in India ... are like the old-fashioned British sort: they test the ability to memorize rather than to reason. Flying squads of invigilators move from one exam hall to another to check that no students take cribs into the exam with them. Even so, in many places ... friends and relations flock outside exam halls, tossing books or slips of paper to students to help them answer questions. The tougher students put daggers on their desks to discourage invigilators from being nosey. In some areas invigilators – for a modest fee – help promote this egalitarian cause.

The Economist, 7 May 1994

On the day of marking the scripts, the imperial revisers, the chief assistant examiner, the invigilating censor and keeper of scripts all stayed in the two wings of the Wen-hua Hall, with its doors tightly shut. The guard duty would be taken over by Imperial Guards under the supervision of the commander of the guards of the Ching-yün gate. The watch over the closed doors was extremely strict.

HUANG FU-CH'ING;
Chinese Students in Japan in the Late Ch'ing Period, 1982

Final examinations, too, like entrance examinations, can be used for one of two different aims. Either they certify the attainment of normal proficiency in a given field, all but the incompetent being allowed make-up exams in case of failure, or they can be used to screen out all but the top students — possibly even a fixed number.

KARL JASPERS; *The Idea of the University*, 1959

At twenty-five, thirty-five, forty, grown men are still visiting hell upon themselves and their families, subordinating all other concerns in the endless struggle to pass accountancy exams and bar finals, to obtain medical or surgical qualifications or to get a PhD.

ROSALIND MILES; *The Rites of Man*, 1992

[T]his veritable plague on education at all levels continues to poison – such terminology is not too strong here – normal relations between the teacher and the student by jeopardizing for both parties the joy in work as well as mutual confidence. The two basic faults of the examination are that generally it does not give objective results, and it becomes, fatally, an end in itself (for even admission examinations are always, first of all, final examinations: the admission examination to high school becomes an end for primary education, etc.).

JEAN PIAGET; *To Understand is to Invent*, 1974

In an examination those who do not wish to know ask questions of those who cannot tell.

WALTER RALEIGH, 1861–1922

No instrument smaller than the world is fit to measure men and women: examinations measure examinees.

WALTER RALEIGH; *Laughter Through a Cloud*, 1923

Many of our current testing practices, particularly final exams, encourage the development of academic bulimia: binge-and-purge learning. If we were to graph the time that students spend studying, we would find a disappointingly low level of effort until the week or two before a major exam.

KARL L. SCHILLING;
The Chronicle of Higher Education, 2 Feb. 1994

Vacation was approaching. The schoolmaster, always severe, grew severer and more exacting than ever, for he wanted the school to make a good showing on "Examination" day. His rod and ferule were seldom idle now — at least among the smaller pupils. Only the biggest boys, and young ladies of eighteen and twenty, escaped lashing.

> MARK TWAIN (pseud. of SAMUEL LANGHORNE CLEMENS);
> *The Adventures of Tom Sawyer*, 1876

Moreover in a highly competitive society parents are naturally anxious that their offspring should be well armed for life's battles; and for want of any other tangible criteria, they are apt to judge schools by examination results.

> ROBERT VAN DE WEYER; *The Health of Nations*, 1991

In an educational situation where the yardstick for success is not exam achievement, the responsibility for establishing credibility still lies with the staff.

> ROGER WHITE; *Absent with Cause*, 1980

In examinations the foolish ask questions that the wise cannot answer.

> OSCAR WILDE;
> *Phrases and Philosophies for the Use of the Young*, 1894

EXAMPLE

Example is the school of mankind, and they will learn at no other.

> EDMUND BURKE, 1729–1797

EXPERIENCE

Experience is a good teacher, but she sends in terrific bills.

> MINNA ANTRIM: *Naked Truth and Veiled Allusions*, 1902

Experience, the universal mother of the sciences.

> (MIGUEL DE) CERVANTES (SAAVEDRA), 1547–1616

Experience and education cannot be directly equated to each other. For some experiences are mis-educative.

> JOHN DEWEY; *Experience and Education*, 1938

Any experience that does not violate expectations is not worthy of the name experience.

(GEORG WILHELM FRIEDRICH) HEGEL, 1770–1831

Most of the important experiences that truly educate cannot be arranged ahead of time with any precision.

HAROLD TAYLOR; *Saturday Review*, 7 Jan. 1961

EXPERT

Since everyone has been to school, everyone is an "expert" on education.

PHILIP G. ALTBACH; *Excellence in Education*, 1985

F

FACT

There is a whole world of difference between truth and facts. Facts can obscure the truth.
                                    MAYA ANGELOU (née MARGUERITE JOHNSON), 1928–

I grow to honour facts more and more, and theory less and less.
                                    THOMAS CARLYLE, 1795–1881

No facts are to me sacred; none are profane; I simply experiment, an endless seeker with no past at my back.
                                    RALPH WALDO EMERSON, 1803–1882

The facts speak for themselves.
                                    EURIPIDES, 485–406

Facts do not cease to exist because they are ignored.
                                    ALDOUS HUXLEY, 1894–1963

The fatal futility of fact.
                                    HENRY JAMES, 1843–1916

There are no external facts, as there are no absolute truths.
                                    (FRIEDRICH WILHELM) NIETZSCHE, 1844–1900

Facts are the air of science. Without them you never can fly.
                                    (IVAN PETROVICH) PAVLOV, 1849–1936

Facts explain nothing. On the contrary, it is fact that requires explanation.
                                    MARILYNNE ROBINSON; *Housekeeping*, 1980

Comment is free but facts are sacred.
                                    CHARLES PRESTWICH SCOTT;
                                    Manchester Guardian, 6 May 1926

Facts are stubborn things.
                                    TOBIAS SMOLLETT, 1721–1771

FAILURE

One reason for the failure of America's schools is that the educational system is designed more for organizational and political convenience than for learning.

MARVIN CETRON & MARGARET GAYLE;
Educational Renaissance, 1991

The main failure of education is that it has not prepared people to comprehend matters concerning human destiny.

NORMAN COUSINS; *Saturday Review*, 15 Apr. 1978

Behind the failure of a child often lies the failure of a home....

R.R. DALE & S. GRIFFITHS; *Down Stream*, 1965

One of the many reasons that many people are able to avoid facing the population problem is that they remain ignorant of the functioning of those most critical parts of the human inheritance – the ecological systems that support civilization.... This lack of understanding represents a colossal failure of education, a failure that goes unrecognized by most "educated" people.

PAUL EHRLICH & ANNE EHRLICH;
The Population Explosion, 1990

The line between those who will be winners and those who will be losers seems sharper than ever, and the line is the product of education.

DAVID HALBERSTAM; *The Next Century*, 1991

The UK education system is based on failure and not achievement, designed to weed out the majority of pupils from the prestigious academic A level track.

INSTITUTE FOR PUBLIC POLICY RESEARCH;
Social Justice in a Changing World, 1993

What we need not do is to "flunk out" those who fail. Why put an indelible stigma on those who may simply not be ready? Rather, send them away for a few years.

ROBERT SOLOMON & JON SOLOMON;
Up the University, 1993

FEAR

Fear of learning is endemic in our culture.

RICHARD SAUL WURMAN; *Information Anxiety,* 1991

FOLK HIGH SCHOOL

The folk high school system is uniquely Danish. Inspired by the ideas of the poet-clergyman Grundtvig in the mid-nineteenth century, they were developed initially to prepare the common people for the transition from absolute monarchy to universal suffrage.

ROGER WHITE; *Absent with Cause,* 1980

FOOL

He who makes himself his own teacher, makes himself pupil to a fool.

BERNARD OF CLAIRVAUX, 1090–1153

A learned fool is one who has read everything and remembers it.

JOSH BILLINGS (pseud. of HENRY WHEELER SHAW),
1818–1885

Fools have been and always will be the majority.

DENIS DIDEROT; *A Philosophical Conversation,* 1777

Fools must be rejected not by arguments, but by facts.

FLAVIUS JOSEPHUS (né JOSEPH BEN MATTHIAS), 37–105?

Who loves not wine, women and song,
Remains a fool his whole life long.

MARTIN LUTHER, 1483–1546

For fools rush in where angels fear to tread.

ALEXANDER POPE; *An Essay on Criticism,* 1711

The fool doth think he is wise, but then a wise man knows himself to be a fool.

WILLIAM SHAKESPEARE; *As You Like It,* 1599–1600

'Tis an old maxim in the schools,
That flatter's the food of fools;
Yet now and then your men of wit
Will condescend to take a bit.

> JONATHAN SWIFT, 1667–1745

Be wise with speed,
A fool at forty is a fool indeed.

> EDWARD YOUNG, 1683–1765

FRAUD

Taken as a whole, academic research and writing is the greatest intellectual fraud of the twentieth century.

> MARTIN ANDERSON; *Imposters in the Temple*, 1992

FREEDOM

Some books leave us free and some books make us free.

> RALPH WALDO EMERSON; *Journals*, 22 Dec. 1839

Only the educated are free.

> EPICTETUS, *c*.50–120

Education is delivery from bondage.

> ANDRÉ GIDE, 1869–1951

Your freedom and mine cannot be separated.

> NELSON MANDELA; *Time*, 25 Feb. 1985

You can't separate peace from freedom because no one can be at peace unless he has his freedom.

> MALCOLM X (né MALCOLM LITTLE); *Malcolm X Speaks*, 1965

Moreover, according to them [the Stoics] not only are the wise free, but they are also kings.

> ZENO (the Stoic), *c*.335–*c*.263

FREEDOM OF SPEECH

The most beautiful thing in the world is freedom of speech.
DIOGENES (the Cynic), c.400–c.325

[H]ostility to free expression in the name of race and gender sensitivities is now the norm, not the exception, on the American campus.
DINESH D'SOUZA; Illiberal Education, 1992

We don't put as many restrictions on freedom of speech as we should.
CANETTA IVY; The New York Times, 25 Apr. 1989

[F]reedom of expression is no more sacred than freedom from intolerance or bigotry.
JOHN JEFFRIES; The New York Times, 6 Dec. 1989

We don't owe the white man nothin' in South Africa. He's killed millions of our women, our children, our babies, our elders. We don't owe him nothing in South Africa. If we want to be merciful at all, when we gain enough power from God Almighty to take our freedom and independence from him, we give him twenty-hour hours to get out of town by sundown. That's all. If he won't get out of town by sundown, we will kill everything white that ain't right [inaudible] in South Africa. We kill the women, we kill the children, we kill the babies. We kill the blind, we kill the crippled [inaudible] we kill 'em all. We kill the faggot, we kill the lesbian, we kill them all. You say why kill the babies in South Africa? Because they gonna grow up one day to oppress our babies, so we kill the babies. Why kill the women? They, they – because they lay on their back and reinforcements roll out from between their legs. So we kill the women too. You'll kill the elders too? Kill the old ones too. Goddamit, if they in a wheelchair, push 'em off a cliff in Capetown, or Johannesburg, or [inaudible], or Port Shepstone or Durban, how the hell you think they got old. They old oppressing black people. I said kill the blind, kill the crippled, kill the lazy. Goddamit, and when you get through killing 'em all, go to the goddamn graveyard and dig up the grave and kill 'em, goddamn, again. 'Cause they didn't die hard enough. And if you've killed 'em all and don't have the strength to dig 'em up, then take your gun and shoot in the goddamn grave. Kill 'em again, 'cause they didn't die hard enough.
KHALID ABDUL MUHAMMAD;
a speech (Kean College, New Jersey), 29 Nov. 1993
[also spelt MOHAMMAD and MOHAMMED]

During the past few years scores of visiting speakers to our universities have been abused, shouted down or otherwise ill-treated and prevented from speaking on the grounds that they canvassed fascist, racist and other types of morally offensive doctrines.

BHIKHU PAREKH;
in *Academic Freedom and Responsibility*, 1988

Nobody should suffer victimization in their professional or private life on account of their political opinions; everyone should be allowed free expression.

MALCOLM TIGHT;
in *Academic Freedom and Responsibility*, 1988

The university recognizes and respects the fundamental right to free speech. But freedom of speech does not include the right to harass or injure others.

UNIVERSITY OF MICHIGAN; in *Illiberal Education*, 1992

FULBRIGHT

[James W.] Fulbright is responsible for the greatest movement of scholars across the face of the earth since the fall of Constantinople in 1453.

R.M. MCCALLUM; *Saturday Evening Post*, 23 Mar. 1963

FULL-TIME

The notion of the "full-time" student has penalized both women and the poor. The student with a full-time job and a full-time academic program is obviously more handicapped than the student who can afford to go to college without working. Many women – married, divorced, or single mothers – have the equivalent of an unpaid full-time job at home and are discouraged from considering advanced study.

ADRIENNE RICH; *On Lies, Secrets, and Silence*, 1980

In a sense, there is really no such thing as a full-time student. All students are effectively part-time, more or less.

MALCOLM TIGHT; *Higher Education*, 1991

FUTURE

Schools will be less important in future. Individuals will learn more often on their own, the "places" of learning will be more dispersed, and the age at which subjects are learned will depend on the individual, not tradition.
MARVIN CETRON & OWEN DAVIES; *Crystal Globe*, 1991

[T]he educational foundations of our society are presently being eroded by a rising tide of mediocrity that threatens our very future as a Nation and a people.
DAVID P. GARDNER; in *A Nation at Risk*, 1983

Education for the future is likely to be less about subjects and gathering knowledge and more about learning to live as an independently functioning being who is both self-regarding and regardful of others. That is, education will be more concerned with the growth of the whole person and the building of self-esteem based on Rogerian psychological ideas. The teacher's role is likely to be less didactic, less judgemental and more enabling and facilitating.
CHARLES HANDY & ROBERT AITKEN;
Understanding Schools as Organizations, 1986

I touch the future, I teach.
(SHARON) CHRISTA (CORRIGAN) MCAULIFFE, 1948–1986

The direction in which education starts a man, will determine his future life.
PLATO (né ARISTOCLES); *The Republic (Politeia)*, c.400BC

G

GENERALIZE

To generalize is to be an idiot.

WILLIAM BLAKE, 1757–1827

We defend ourselves with descriptions and tame the world by generalizing.

IRIS MURDOCH; *The Black Prince*, 1975

GENIUS

There was never a genius without a tincture of madness.

ARISTOTLE, 384–322

I have known no man of genius who had not to pay, in some affliction of defect either physical or spiritual, for what the gods had given him.

(HENRY) MAX(IMILIAN) BEERBOHM, 1872–1956

Execution is the chariot of genius.

WILLIAM BLAKE, 1757–1827

Since when was genius found respectable.

ELIZABETH BARRETT BROWNING; *Aurora Leigh*, 1856

Genius is a nuisance, and it is the duty of schools and colleges to abate it by setting genius-traps in its way.

SAMUEL BUTLER, 1835–1902

No power of genius has ever had the smallest success in explaining existence.

THOMAS CARLYLE, 1795–1881

Intelligence recognizes what has happened. Genius recognizes what will happen.

JOHN CIARDI; *Quote*, 30 Oct. 1966

Genius is one percent inspiration and ninety-nine percent perspiration.

THOMAS ALVA EDISON, 1847–1931

Universities are of course hostile to geniuses.

RALPH WALDO EMERSON; *English Traits*, 1856

A genius is just somebody who has the will to try harder and stretch himself more than the next guy.

(JOE) "FOLEY" (McCREARY);
International Herald Tribune, 11 Nov. 1993

Let schoolmasters puzzle their brain,
With grammar, and nonsense, and learning,
Good liquor, I stoutly maintain,
Gives genius a better discerning.

OLIVER GOLDSMITH, 1728–1774

Genius . . . means little more than the faculty of perceiving in an unhabitual way.

WILLIAM JAMES; *The Principles of Psychology*, 1890

The principal mark of genius is not perfection but originality, the opening of new frontiers.

ARTHUR KOESTLER, 1905–1983

Genius is one of the many forms of insanity.

CESARE L. LOMBROSO; *The Man of Genius*, 1891

The genius of Einstein leads to Hiroshima.

(PABLO RUIZ) PICASSO, 1881–1973

The concept of genius as akin to madness has been carefully fostered by the inferiority complex of the public.

EZRA POUND; *The ABC of Reading*, 1934

We have come to regard direct and natural speech as incompatible with genius, while all that is any way abnormal is admired as exquisite.

(MARCUS FABIUS) QUINTILIAN(US), *c*.35–*c*.95

It takes a lot of time to be a genius, you have to sit around so much doing nothing, really doing nothing.

GERTRUDE STEIN; *Everybody's Autobiography*, 1937

When a true genius appears in the world, you may know him by this sign, that the dunces are all in confederacy against him.

JONATHAN SWIFT, 1667–1745

Knowledge is no proof of genius.

(LUC DE CLAPIERS, MARQUIS DE) VAUVENARGUES;
*Reflections, c.*1747

The genius which runs to madness is no longer genius.

OTTO WEININGER, 1880–1903

Genius is born, not paid.

OSCAR WILDE, 1854–1900

Genius lasts longer than Beauty. That accounts for the fact that we all take such pains to over educate ourselves.

OSCAR WILDE: *The Picture of Dorian Gray*, 1891

To the neglect of learning, genius sometimes owes its greatest glory.

EDWARD YOUNG, 1683–1765

GEOGRAPHY

In one recent study, only a minority of junior-high school students could find the United States on a world map!

MARVIN CETRON & MARGARET GAYLE;
Educational Renaissance, 1991

The unity of all the sciences is found in geography.

JOHN DEWEY; *The School and Society*, 1899

GEOLOGY

The importance of geology is that, without geology, geography would have no place to put itself.

ART LINKLETTER; *A Child's Garden of Misinformation*, 1965

GEOMETRY

There is no royal road to geometry.

EUCLID; *Elements, c.*300BC

Let no one without geometry enter here.

an *inscription* (over the Academy portal), *c.*400BC
[To the Greeks geometry was mathematics, so the
word mathematics appears in some translations;
the original is *medeis ageometretos eisito.*]

There are no sects in geometry.

VOLTAIRE (né FRANÇOIS MARIE AROUET), 1694–1778

GRADUATE SCHOOL (School for Doctoral and/or Master Students)

Another criticism of the graduate school is based on the fact that so few doctoral graduates continue productive research after the dissertation is approved and the degree granted.

OLIVER C. CARMICHAEL; *Graduate Education,* 1961

The most pressing area of reform in graduate education is to guarantee prompt recognition of genuine student innovation.

WILFRED CUDE; *The Ph.D. Trap,* 1987

GRADUATE STUDENT (Doctoral and Master Students)

[T]he students may be more interested in graduate degrees because they feel that advanced training will give them a competitive edge in their quest for jobs and financial security.

ALEXANDER W. ASTIN;
The Chronicle of Higher Education, 26 Jan. 1994

Graduate students report terrible dilemmas with respect to figuring out the rules for virtually every phase of their work.

PAULA J. CAPLAN; *Lifting a Ton of Feathers*, 1993

Graduate students are encouraged to choose their fields early and, by the time they get to their dissertations, to have laid claim to a molehill with mountainous pretensions.

ROBERT SOLOMON & JON SOLOMON;
Up the University, 1993

GRADUATION

In the United States admission to a university is no guarantee of graduation ... in Japan, however, entrance is tantamount to graduation.

MICHIO NAGAI; *Higher Education in Japan*, 1971

GRAMMAR

"Whom are you?" said he, for he had been to night school.

GEORGE ADE, 1866–1944

The notion "grammatical" cannot be identified with "meaningful" or "significant" in any semantic sense.

NOAM (AVRIL) CHOMSKY; *Syntactic Structures*, 1957

Ghetto dialects do not employ tense as an essential feature of grammar.

JAMES DALE DAVIDSON & WILLIAM REES-MOGG;
The Great Reckoning, 1993

Everything yields to success, even grammar.

VICTOR HUGO, 1802–1885

To grammar even kings bow.

MOLIÈRE (né JEAN-BAPTISTE POQUELIN);
Les Femmes savantes, 1672

Why care for grammar as long as we are good?

ARTEMUS WARD (pseud. of CHARLES FARRAR BROWNE),
1834–1867

GRAMMAR SCHOOL

Varied as these grammar schools must have been in their external organisation throughout the Middle Ages, there was, besides, considerable difference in the importance attached to the relative position of "grammar" in the curriculum at various periods.

FOSTER WATSON; *The Old Grammar Schools,* 1916

At the time when the English Grammar Schools were most flourishing, namely the 17th century, they subserved a practical national aim. Puritan England, by no means concerned with the teachings of the Classics *per se,* looked to the Grammar Schools for that subsidiary help which the study of Latin, Greek and Hebrew afforded to the intensive study of the Scriptures and *pietas literata* [devotional literature].

FOSTER WATSON; *The Old Grammar Schools,* 1916

GREEK

Nothing we learn about them [the Greeks] is alien to ourselves.

EDITH HAMILTON; *Mythology,* 1942

[T]he classical Greeks recognized as true men only those citizens who let themselves be fitted by *paideia* (education) into the institutions their elders had planned.

IVAN ILLICH; *Deschooling Society,* 1971

Except the blind forces of Nature, nothing moves which is not Greek in its origin.

HENRY MAINE; *Village Communities,* 1871

Greek ideas – that mathematics was geometry, that arithmetic was the theory of divine numbers and that science was abstract reasoning – crippled Western science and mathematics for centuries.

JOHN McLEISH; *Number,* 1992

Don't appear so scholarly, pray. Humanize your talk, and speak to be understood. Do you think a Greek name gives more weight to your reasons?

MOLIÈRE (né JEAN-BAPTISTE POQUELIN), 1622–1673

Where the Greeks had modesty, we have cant; where they had poetry, we have cant; where they had patriotism, we have cant; where they had anything that exalts, delights, or adorns humanity, we have nothing but cant, cant, cant.

T(HOMAS) L(OVE) PEACOCK, 1785–1866

The chief strength of the ancient Greeks lay in their freedom from hampering intellectual tradition. They had no venerated classics, no holy books, no dead languages to master, no authorities to check their free speculation.

JAMES HARVEY ROBINSON, 1863–1936

Nobody can say a word against Greek: it stamps a man at once as an educated gentleman.

GEORGE BERNARD SHAW; *Major Barbara*, 1907

H

HALF-TRUTH

The thing from which the world suffers just now more than from any other evil is not the assertion of falsehood, but the endless and irresponsible repetition of half-truths.

G(ILBERT) K(EITH) CHESTERTON, 1874–1936

Two half-truths do not make a truth, and two half-truths do not make a culture.

ARTHUR KOESTLER; *The Ghost in the Machine*, 1967

Science is always simple and profound. It is only the half-truths that are dangerous.

GEORGE BERNARD SHAW; *The Doctor's Dilemma*, 1906

There are no whole truths; all truths are half-truths. It is trying to treat them as whole truths that plays the devil.

ALFRED NORTH WHITEHEAD; *Dialogues*, 1954

HAPPINESS

A good education is another name for happiness.

ANN PLATO; *Essays*, 1841

HEALTH EDUCATION

Health education is a process which effects changes in the health practices of people and in the knowledge and attitudes related to such changes. Education is an internal process for the individual concerned.

ASSOCIATION OF SCHOOLS OF PUBLIC HEALTH;
Professional Preparation in Health Education in
Schools of Public Health, 1965

A good health educator does not frighten people to death. He frightens them to life.

HENRY COHEN; *The Wit of Medicine*, 1972

You can't talk of the dangers of snake poisoning and not mention snakes.
C. EVERETT KOOP; *Time*, 24 Nov. 1986
[comment on AIDS and health education in schools]

Health education is an unexciting subject of marginal intellectual content.
JAMES LE FANU; in *Preventionitis*, 1994

HIGHER EDUCATION (Post-Secondary or Tertiary Education)

Most higher education is devoted to affirming the traditions and origins of an existing elite and transmitting them to new members.
MARY CATHERINE BATESON; *Composing a Life*, 1989

Equalizing opportunity through universal higher education subjects the whole population to the intellectual mode natural only to a few. It violates the fundamental egalitarian principle of respect for the differences between people.
CAROLINE BIRD; *The Case Against College*, 1975

Higher education is booming in the United States; the Gross National Mind is mounting along with the Gross National Product.
MALCOLM MUGGERIDGE;
The Most of Malcolm Muggeridge, 1966

Tenure and its partner in crime, the PhD, have inflicted what may turn out to be fatal wounds on higher education.
PAGE SMITH; *Killing the Spirit*, 1990

The whole course of evolution in industry, and in the achievement of higher education and exceptional talent, has shown man's invariable tendency to shut women out when their activities have reached a highly specialized period of growth.
ANNA GARLIN SPENCER, 1851–1931

An institution of higher learning has two broad functions: one is the education of its members, and the other is their certification.
STEPHEN H. SPURR; *Academic Degree Structures*, 1970

Higher education does not actively discriminate against women; rather, through an acceptance of particular values and beliefs, it makes it difficult for women to succeed.

KIM THOMAS; *Gender and Subject in Higher Education*, 1990

HIPPOCRATIC OATH

I swear by Apollo Physician, by Asclepius, by Hygiaea, by Panacea, and by all the gods and goddesses, making them my witness, that I will carry out, according to my ability and judgement, this oath and this indenture. To hold my teacher in this art equal to my own parents; to make him partner in my livelihood; when he is in need of money to share mine with him; to consider his family as my own brothers, and to teach them this art, if they want to learn it, without fee or indenture; to impart precept, oral instruction, and all other instruction to my sons, to the sons of my teacher, and to indentured pupils who have taken the physician's oath, but to nobody else. I will use treatment to help the sick according to my ability and judgement, but never with a view to injury and wrongdoing. Neither will I administer a poison to anyone when asked to do so, nor will I suggest such a course. Similarly I will not give to a woman a pessary to cause abortion. But I will keep pure and holy both my life and my art. I will not use the knife, not even, verily, on sufferers from stone, but I will give place to such as are craftsmen therein. Into whatsoever houses I enter I will enter to help the sick, and I will abstain from all intentional wrongdoing and harm, especially from abusing the bodies of man or woman, bond or free. And whatsoever I shall see or hear in the course of my profession, as well as outside my profession in my intercourse with men, if it be what should not be published abroad, I will never divulge, holding such things to be holy secrets. Now if I carry out this oath, and break it not, may I gain forever reputation among all men for my life and for my art; but if I transgress it and forswear myself, may the opposite befall me.

HIPPOCRATES (or HIPPOCRATIC SCHOOL), *c.*460–*c.*370

HISTORIAN

No honest historian can take part with – or against – the forces he has to study.

HENRY (BROOKS) ADAMS;
The Education of Henry Adams, 1907

Historian: an unsuccessful novelist.

H(ENRY) L(OUIS) MENCKEN, 1880–1956

The historian looks backward. In the end he also believes backward.

(FRIEDRICH WILHELM) NIETZSCHE, 1844–1900

HISTORY

History is the sum total of the things that could have been avoided.

KONRAD ADENAUER, 1876–1967

Even the gods cannot change history.

AGATHON, 448–400

History, n[oun]. An account, mostly false, of events, mostly unimportant, which are brought about by rulers mostly knaves, and soldiers mostly fools.

AMBROSE BIERCE; *The Devil's Dictionary*, 1911

That great dust-heap called "history".

AUGUSTINE BIRRELL, 1850–1933

History is more or less bunk. It's tradition. We don't want tradition.

HENRY FORD, 1863–1947

History punishes those who come late to it.

MIKHAIL (SERGEEVICH) GORBACHEV, 1931–

History never finishes.

PJOTR HESSELING; *Frontiers of Learning*, 1986

The essential matter of history is not what happened but what people thought or said about it.

FREDERICK W. MAITLAND, 1850–1906

History is but a chain of incidents and absurdities.

(FRIEDRICH WILHELM) NIETZSCHE, 1844–1900

117

We have need of history in its entirety, not to fall back on it, but to escape from it.
(JOSÉ) ORTEGA Y GASSET, 1883–1955

Those who cannot remember the past are condemned to repeat it.
(GEORGE) SANTAYANA; *The Life of Reason*, 1905–6

We learn from history that we learn nothing from history.
GEORGE BERNARD SHAW, 1856–1950

History is only a confused heap of facts.
PHILIP DORMER STANHOPE, 1694–1773

History as a discipline can be characterized as having a collective forgetfulness about women.
CLARICE STASZ STOLL; *Female and Male*, 1974

History is the propaganda of the victors.
ERNST TOLLER, 1893–1939

History is the register of human crimes and misfortunes.
VOLTAIRE (né FRANÇOIS MARIE AROUET), 1694–1778

History is after all nothing but a pack of tricks which we play on the dead.
VOLTAIRE (né FRANÇOIS MARIE AROUET), 1694–1778

Historical research of the truly scholastic kind is not concerned with human beings at all. It is a pure study, like higher mathematics.
C(ICELY) V(ERONICA) WEDGWOOD; *Velvet Studies*, 1946

Human history becomes more and more a race between education and catastrophe.
H(ERBERT) G(EORGE) WELLS, 1866–1946

HOME SCHOOLING

Ten years ago, choosing to educate your child at home was a sure sign of crankiness. Today it is a growing fashion.
The Economist, 11 Jun. 1994

The question of home versus school is difficult to argue in the abstract. If ideal homes are contrasted with actual schools, the balance tips one way; if ideal schools are contrasted with actual homes, the balance tips the other way.

> BERTRAND RUSSELL; *Education and the Social Order,* 1932

Education, like neurosis, begins at home.

> MILTON R. SAPIRSTEIN; *Parodoxes of Everyday Life,* 1955

All home schoolers seem to share a belief that education is integral to family life.

> THOMAS TOCH; *US News & World Report,* 9 Dec. 1991

Studies suggest that home-schooled kids do as well or better than their public school peers on national standardized tests. Perhaps more important, anecdotal evidence suggests that many children schooled at home are independent and inquisitive learners.

> THOMAS TOCH; *US News & World Report,* 9 Dec. 1991

Opponents of home schooling frequently argue that common schooling is necessary for the common good, that schools should serve public, not merely private purposes.

> JANE VAN GALEN; in *Home Schooling,* 1991

[T]he Ideologues pattern their home schools closely after traditional schools, but they are highly suspicious of the motives of school officials and vehemently resist any regulation of home education. The Pedagogues strive to provide an educational environment for their children that is distinctly different from school, while they dismiss opposition from public educators with an almost patronizing indifference.

> JANE VAN GALEN; in *Home Schooling,* 1991

HOMEWORK

Schools, however, are still structured as if students have at least several hours each day to devote to homework, which is assumed as a normal extension of the school day.

> MARGARET DIANE LECOMPTE & ANTHONY GARY DWORKIN;
> *Giving Up on School,* 1991

Homework provides the necessary time for thoughtful writing and serious reading, time that is rarely available during school hours.

DIANE RAVITCH; *The Schools We Deserve*, 1985

HONESTY

[T]o make your children *capable of honesty* is the beginning of education.

JOHN RUSKIN, 1819–1900

HONORARY DEGREE

The institution [Alfred University, New York] recently awarded honorary doctorates to the long-time owners of a local diner that serves the university community. Alfred officials presented the degrees to John and Angela Ninos, who have operated the Collegiate Restaurant here for 40 years. The university says that in addition to filling orders, the couple ... have helped hundreds of students pay tuition by hiring them for part-time work. Alfred typically awards such degrees only to well known professionals or academics.

The Chronicle of Higher Education, 19 Jan. 1994

The Greeks had their laurel wreaths. The English have their honors list. The French are always wearing ribbons in their lapels. In this country honorary degrees from universities serve that function.

JACK W. PELTASON; *The New York Times*, 27 May 1984

People with honorary awards are looked upon with disfavor. Would you let an honorary mechanic fix your brand-new Mercedes?

PAUL SIMON; *The New York Times*, 4 Jun. 1984

HUBRIS

The driving sin of our academic intellectuals is hubris – unchecked intellectual arrogance.

MARTIN ANDERSON; *Imposters in the Temple*, 1992

HUMANISM

The young men were deserting the lecture halls of the established universities to go and listen to some wild-eyed "humanist"* with his new-fangled notions about a "reborn civilization."

HENDRIK VAN LOON; *The Story of Mankind*, 1962
[*EMMANUEL CHRYSOLERAS, C.1355–1415]

HUNGER

What good is school when you're hungry?

LEILA ABOUZEID;
in *Women and the Family in the Middle East*, 1985

Hungry people cannot be good at learning or producing anything, except perhaps violence.

HAN SUYIN; *Pearl's Kitchen*, 1973

HYPOCRISY

Hypocrisy is one of the least appealing human traits. The modern university is knee-deep in it.

PAGE SMITH; *Killing the Spirit*, 1990

I

ICONOCLASM

Rough work, iconoclasm, but the only way to get at truth.

OLIVER WENDELL HOLMES;
The Professor at the Breakfast Table, 1860

IDEA

One of the greatest pains to human nature is the pain of a new idea.

WALTER BAGEHOT, 1826–1877

One can live in the shadow of an idea without grasping it.

ELIZABETH BOWEN; *The Heat of the Day*, 1949

Ideas are indeed the most dangerous weapons in the world.

WILLIAM O. DOUGLAS; *An Almanac of Liberty*, 1954

Ideas move rapidly when their time comes.

CAROLYN HEILBURN;
Toward a Recognition of Androgyny, 1973

Many ideas grow better when transplanted into another mind than in the one where they sprang up.

OLIVER WENDELL HOLMES, 1841–1935

A stand can be made against invasion by an army; no stand can be made against invasion by an idea.

VICTOR HUGO, 1802–1885

It is ideas, not vested interests, which are dangerous for good or evil.

JOHN MAYNARD KEYNES, 1883–1946

The best ideas are common property.

(LUCIUS ANNAEUS) SENECA (the Younger), *c.*4BC–65

The man with a new idea is a crank until the idea succeeds.

MARK TWAIN (pseud. of SAMUEL LANGHORNE CLEMENS),
1835–1910

An idea does not pass from one language to another without change.

(MIGUEL DE) UNAMUNO (Y JUGO);
The Tragic Sense of Life, 1913

An unexamined idea, to paraphrase Socrates, is not worth having; and a society whose ideas are never explored for possible error may eventually find its foundations insecure.

MARK VAN DOREN; *Man's Right to Knowledge*, 1954

Almost all really new ideas have a certain aspect of foolishness when they are first produced.

ALFRED NORTH WHITEHEAD, 1861–1947

All great ideas are dangerous.

OSCAR WILDE; *De Profundis*, 1905

IDEOLOGY

Every day the old ideologies become more ridiculous.

ERICH FROMM; *To Have or To Be?*, 1976

Education gets sacrificed to ideology, and the students become pawns in the process.

ROBERT SOLOMON & JON SOLOMON;
Up the University, 1993

IGNORAMUS

Ignoramus, n[oun]. A person unacquainted with certain kinds of knowledge familiar to yourself, and having certain other kinds that you know nothing about.

AMBROSE BIERCE; *The Devil's Dictionary*, 1911

IGNORANCE

Nothing in education is as astonishing as the amount of ignorance it accumulates in the form of inert facts.

HENRY (BROOKS) ADAMS;
The Education of Henry Adams, 1907

Ignorance is a right! Education is eroding one of the few democratic freedoms remaining to us.

CHRISTOPHER ANDREAE;
Christian Science Monitor, 21 Feb. 1980

Too many of our countrymen rejoice in stupidity, look upon ignorance as a badge of honor. They condemn everything they don't understand.

TALLULAH BANKHEAD; *Tallulah*, 1952

The ignorant classes are the dangerous classes. Ignorance is the womb of monsters.

HENRY WARD BEECHER;
Proverbs from Plymouth Pulpit, 1867

Ignorance of good and evil is the most upsetting fact of human life.

(MARCUS TULLIUS) CICERO, 106–43

Ignorance and superstition even bear a close and mathematical relation to each other.

J(AMES) F(ENIMORE) COOPER, 1789–1851

Education is a progressive discovery of our own ignorance.

WILL(IAM) (JAMES) DURANT, 1885–1981

Ignorance gives one a large range of probabilities.

GEORGE ELIOT (pseud. of MARY ANN EVANS);
Daniel Deronda, 1874

Ignorance is the necessary condition of life itself. If we knew everything, we could not endure existence for a single hour.

ANATOLE FRANCE (pseud. of ANATOLE FRANÇOIS THIBAULT);
The Gardens of Epicurus, 1894

Nothing is more terrible than ignorance in action.

(JOHANN WOLFGANG VON) GOETHE, 1749–1832

The most violent element in societies is ignorance.

EMMA GOLDMAN; *Anarchism*, 1910

Most ignorance is vincible ignorance. We don't know because we don't want to know.

ALDOUS HUXLEY, 1894–1963

There is no slavery but ignorance.

ROBERT G. INGERSOLL;
The Liberty of Man, Woman and Child, 1877

The greatest vested interest is not property but ignorance.

WILLIAM JOVANOVICH; *Now, Barrabas*, 1964

Ignorance does not excuse.

WILLIAM LANGLAND, *c.*1330–*c.*1400

He who would be cured of ignorance must confess it.

(MICHEL EYQUEM DE) MONTAIGNE, 1533–1592

The first observation – a surprising one – that comes to mind after the passage of thirty years is the ignorance in which we still remain with regard to the results achieved by our educational techniques.

JEAN PIAGET;
Science of Education and the Psychology of the Child, 1970

For as there are misanthropists or haters of men, there are misologists, or haters of ideas, and both spring from the same cause, which is ignorance of the world.

PLATO (né ARISTOCLES), *c.*428–*c.*348

Only ignorance! only *ignorance*! how can you talk about *only* ignorance? Don't you know that it is the worst thing in the world, next to wickedness?

ANNA SEWELL; *Black Beauty*, 1877

Our lives are universally shortened by ignorance.

HERBERT SPENCER; *Principles of Biology*, 1864–7

The bliss that comes from ignorance should seldom be encouraged for it is likely to do one out of a more satisfying bliss.

RUTH STOUT;
How to Have a Green Thumb Without an Aching Back, 1955

Ignorance is not bliss – it is oblivion.

PHILIP WYLIE; *Generation of Vipers*, 1942

IGNORANT

The ignorant in comparison of the learned, are worse than dead.
STEFANO GUAZZO; *Civil Conversations*, 1574

[T]here are things about which we would prefer to remain ignorant.
WILLIAM PROXMIRE; in *Love and Limerance*, 1989

Everybody is ignorant, only on different subjects.
WILL(IAM PENN ADAIR) ROGERS, 1879–1935

The day will yet come when posterity will be amazed that we remained ignorant of things that will to them seem so plain.
(LUCIUS ANNAEUS) SENECA (the Younger), *c.*4BC–65

It is only the ignorant who despise education.
(PUBLILIUS) SYRUS, *c.*85–43

ILLIBERAL EDUCATION

Instead of liberal education, what American students are getting is its diametrical opposite, an education in closed-mindedness and intolerance, which is to say, illiberal education.
DINESH D'SOUZA; *Illiberal Education*, 1992

ILLITERACY

She said that I must always be intolerant of ignorance but understanding of illiteracy. That some people unable to go to school, were more educated and even more intelligent than college professors. She encouraged me to listen carefully to what country people called mother wit. That in the homely sayings was couched the wisdom of generations.
MAYA ANGELOU (née MARGUERITE JOHNSON);
I Know Why the Caged Bird Sings, 1969

With one or two exceptions, colleges expect their players of games to be reasonably literate.
MAURICE BOWRA, 1898–1971

The great mass of humanity should never learn to read or write.

D(AVID) H(ERBERT) LAWRENCE, 1885–1930

Television is the literature of the illiterate, the culture of the lowbrow, the wealth of the poor, the privilege of the underprivileged, the exclusive club of the excluded masses.

LEE LOEVINGER; *National Observer*, 17 Oct. 1966

I . . . can't read a book but I can read de people. [*sic*]

SOJOURNER TRUTH, 1797–1883

IMAGINATION

Every great advance in science has issued from a new audacity of imagination.

JOHN DEWEY; *The Quest for Certainty*, 1929

Japan and the Asian tigers have outperformed the West at mass-producing educated workers. Their next task is to mix in more imagination.

The Economist, 21 Nov. 1992

We especially need imagination in science. It is not all mathematics, nor all logic, but is somewhat beauty and poetry.

MARIA MITCHELL, 1818–1889

The first thing the average educator sets to work to kill in the young is imagination.

BERTRAND RUSSELL; *Education and the Social Order*, 1932

INDIVIDUAL

Whatever an education is, it should make you a unique individual, not a conformist.

JOHN TAYLOR GATTO; *Dumbing Us Down*, 1992

I have always regarded the development of the individual as the only legitimate goal of education.

SUSAN JACOBY; *Inside Soviet Schools*, 1974

INEQUALITY

Children come into the education system already unequal. Then the educative process adds proportionately less value to students from marginalised groups. Finally, young adults are released into an unequal society in which bias is rife, such as in the job market.

PAUL BARASI; *Education Equality*, 1992

When only one sex wins, both sexes lose.

WARREN FARRELL; *The Myth of Male Power*, 1993

[A] teacher who slaps a *girl* with a ruler fears a parent will slap the teacher with a lawsuit. And a male teacher who spanks a girl with his hand can forget about tenure or retirement pay. In practice, corporal punishment is boy punishment. Many schools protest the propensity to hit black boys more than white boys, but no schools protest the propensity to hit exclusively boys.

WARREN FARRELL; *The Myth of Male Power*, 1993

True education makes for inequality; the inequality of individuality, the inequality of success; the glorious inequality of talent, of genius; for inequality, not mediocrity, individual superiority, not standardization, is the measure of the progress of the world.

FELIX E. SCHELLING, 1858–1945

In education as in other institutions, sex can dictate the allocation of resources, and there can be no doubt about the basic belief that boys are entitled to more of them.

DALE SPENDER; *The Writing or the Sex?*, 1989

Separate educational facilities are inherently unequal.

EARL WARREN;
Brown vs. Board of Education of Topeka, 17 May 1954

INFORMATION

The age-graded school not only gives children in each age group certain information, it also consciously holds back information.

JOSHUA MEYROWITZ; *No Sense of Place*, 1985

We now mass-produce information the way we used to mass-produce cars.
JOHN NAISBITT; *Megatrends*, 1982

The new source of power is not money in the hands of a few but information in the hands of many.
JOHN NAISBITT; *Megatrends*, 1982

Americans' appetite for information is increasing, but their attention span is decreasing.
RICHARD SAUL WURMAN; *Information Anxiety*, 1991

[W]e learn reading, writing, and arithmetic, but what we need to learn in the information age are seeing, hearing, and expressing.
RICHARD SAUL WURMAN; *Information Anxiety*, 1991

INNOCENCE

Once you start asking questions, innocence is gone.
MARY ASTOR (pseud. of LUCILLE LANGHANKE);
A Life on Film, 1971

The apple cannot be stuck back on the Tree of Knowledge; once we begin to see, we are doomed and challenged to seek the strength to see more, not less.
ARTHUR MILLER; *Saturday Evening Post*, 1 Feb. 1964

INSTRUCTION

Instruction must be comprehensible and yet difficult rather than easy, otherwise it causes ennui.
(JOHANN FRIEDRICH) HERBART; *The Science of Education*, 1904

INSUBORDINATION

If they give you ruled paper, write the other way.
JUAN RAMÓN JIMÉNEZ, 1881–1958

Too much rigidity on the part of teachers should be followed by a brisk spirit of insubordination on the part of the taught.

AGNES REPPLIER; *Points of View*, 1891

INTELLECTUAL

An intellectual is a man who doesn't know how to park a bike.

SPIRO AGNEW, 1918–

There is a wide streak of snobbery in almost everyone who considers himself or herself an academic intellectual.

MARTIN ANDERSON; *Imposters in the Temple*, 1992

With school turning out more runners, jumpers, racers, tinkerers, grabbers, snatchers, fliers, and swimmers instead of examiners, critics, knowers, and imaginative creators, the word "intellectual," of course, became the swear word it deserves to be.

RAY BRADBURY; *Fahrenheit 451*, 1953

Intellectual activity anywhere is the same, whether at the frontier of knowledge or in a third-grade classroom.

JEROME S. BRUNER; *The Process of Education*, 1965

Intellectuals are the most intolerant of all people.

PAUL DURCAN, 1944–

[T]he greatest intellect ever to come out of Australia ... the wandering Einstein of Queensland they called him.

RAY GALTON & ALAN SIMPSON; *The Poetry Society*, 1959

A highbrow is a person educated beyond his intelligence.

J. BRANDER MATTHEWS, 1852–1929

Anti-intellectualism has long been the anti-semitism of the businessman.

ARTHUR M. SCHLESINGER; *Partisan Review*, 4 Mar. 1953

I believe the intellectual life of the whole of western society is increasingly being split into two groups ... literary intellectuals at one pole – at the other scientists, and as the most representative, the physical scientists. Between the two a gulf of mutual incomprehension.

C(HARLES) P(ERCY) SNOW;
The Two Cultures and the Scientific Revolution, 1961

Marxism is the opium of the intellectuals.

EDMUND WILSON; *Memoirs of Hecate County*, 1949

INTELLIGENCE

A great deal of intelligence can be invested in ignorance when the need for illusion is deep.

SAUL BELLOW, 1915–

Intelligence is characterized by a natural incomprehension of life.

HENRI BERGSON; *Creative Evolution*, 1907

Intelligence is not to make no mistakes, but quickly to see how to make them good.

BERTOLT BRECHT; *The Measures Taken*, 1930

Intelligence consists of recognizing opportunity.

CHINESE proverb

The test of a first rate intelligence is the ability to hold two opposed ideas in the mind at the same time and still retain the ability to function.

F(RANCIS) SCOTT FITZGERALD, 1896–1940

Where there is intelligence there is knowledge.

GREEK proverb

The difference between intelligence and education is this: intelligence will make you a good living.

CHARLES F. KETTERING, 1876–1958

Intelligence is not an innate internal characteristic of the individual but arises as a product of the interaction between the person and his or her environment.

DAVID A. KOLB; *Experiential Learning*, 1984

To perceive things in the germ is intelligence.

LÂO-TZU (né LI URH), *c.*600–*c.*500

If the aim of intellectual training is to form the intelligence rather than stock the memory, and to produce intellectual explorers rather than mere erudition, then traditional education is manifestly guilty of a grave deficiency.

JEAN PIAGET;
Science of Education and the Psychology of the Child, 1970

A great many people think polysyllables are a sign of intelligence.

BARBARA WALTERS;
How to Talk with Practically Anybody about Practically Anything, 1970

Intelligence appears to be the thing that enables a man to get along without education. Education appears to be the thing that enables a man to get along without the use of his intelligence.

A(LBERT) E(DWARD) WIGGAN; *New Decalogue of Science,* 1923

Where you need intelligence, strength will not do.

YIDDISH proverb

INTERNATIONAL BACCALAUREATE

Now that the idea of the International Baccalaureate has established its validity as a university entrance qualification it is beginning to be used as an international yardstick to measure the comparability of other such qualifications.

INTERNATIONAL BACCALAUREATE OFFICE;
General Guide to the International Baccalaureate, 1972

The idea of an internationally accepted school-leaving qualification based on a unified programme of studies grew from the concern of teachers in international and multinational schools throughout the world for the special problems of their mobile students.

INTERNATIONAL BACCALAUREATE OFFICE;
General Guide to the International Baccalaureate, 1972

[The International Baccalaureate must not be confused with the Baccalauréat of France, which is also a high school matriculation programme, or with the Bachelor or Baccalaureate university degree.]

133

INTERNATIONAL EDUCATION

Ideological strains such as isolationism, jingoism, and chauvinism militate not only against much of what is being taught in global education but against teaching it at all.

JAMES M. BECKER; *Schooling for a Global Age*, 1979

The effects of internationalization should be felt in what is taught in the classroom, in how students learn, in the make-up of the student body and the teaching staff, in the research activities undertaken, the reading lists and case studies used, the opportunities offered to students and in the activities and services offered to the wider community.

TIM LOUGHEED & ANIA WASILEWSKI;
University Affairs/Affaires Universitaires, Mar. 1994

IQ TEST

This intelligence testing business reminds me of the way they used to weigh hogs in Texas. They would get a long plank, put it over a cross-bar, and somehow tie the hog on one end of the plank. They'd search all around till they found a stone that would balance the weight of the hog and they'd put that on the other end of the plank. Then they'd guess the weight of the stone.

JOHN DEWEY, 1859–1952

The mere fact that the IQ test provides quantifiable information does not rescue it from the dustbin of fads and quackeries.

GEORGE H. DOUGLAS; *Education Without Impact*, 1992

The IQ tests do not measure *native* intelligence, but something that depends strongly on the environment, and the hierarchic ranking of races according to intellectual characteristics is flawed.

ERICH HARTH; *Dawn of a Millennium*, 1990

There is no testing instrument better known, nor more misunderstood, than the intelligence test.

DARLENE L. STEWART; *Creating the Teachable Moment*, 1993

IVORY TOWER

After World War II, therefore, the image of the ivory tower [university] grew obsolete.

DEREK BOK; *Beyond the Ivory Tower*, 1982

For the educator, complacent in his ivory tower, to scorn affiliation with a cause he considers to be noble, to refuse to attempt to win disciples from the ranks of students he is in a position to influence, is unmistakably to foreswear a democratic responsibility, and to earn for himself the contemptible title of dilettante and solipsist.

WILLIAM F. BUCKLEY; *God and Man at Yale*, 1951

Our troubled planet can no longer afford the luxury of pursuits confined to an ivory tower. Scholarship has to prove its worth, not on its own terms, but by service to the nation and the world.

OSCAR HANDLIN, 1915–

In American society, the university is traditionally considered to be a psychological moratorium, an ivory tower where you withdraw from the problems of society and the world around you to work on important things like your career and your marriage.

ABBIE HOFFMAN;
a *speech* (University of South Carolina), 16 Sep. 1987

The idea of retiring to a tower, getting away from the world and its temptations, has been frequently expressed since the Syrian hermit Simeon Stylites, who died about 459[AD], spent thirty-five years on top of a tall pillar to escape mankind.

F.N. MAGILL; *Magill's Quotations in Context*, 1969

One of the commonest misconceptions about research is that it is an "ivory tower" activity, far removed from reality and from social contact with others.

ESTELLE M. PHILLIPS & D.S. PUGH; *How to Get a PhD*, 1994

J

JESUIT

To the Jesuits must be given the credit of providing education with a uniform and universal method.

ROBERT R. RUSK; *Doctrines of the Great Educators*, 1918

[16th century] education was further subjugated by the church when the Jesuits came to compete with and finally to vanquish the universities.

PRESERVED SMITH;
A History of Modern Culture (vol. I), 1962

JUDGEMENT

The seat of knowledge is in the head; of wisdom in the heart. We are sure to judge wrong if we do not feel right.

WILLIAM HAZLITT; *Characteristics*, 1823

Everyone complains of his memory, but no one complains of his judgement.

(FRANÇOIS DE) LA ROCHEFOUCAULD, 1613–1680

A strong memory is commonly coupled with infirm judgement.

(MICHEL EYQUEM DE) MONTAIGNE, 1533–1592

K

KINDERGARTEN

The first kindergarten in Japan was thus established by the Department of Education, in connection with the Tokyo Female Normal School in 1876. The organization (after the Froebel method) was as follows: Children under school age were trained with the object of fostering moral virtues, promoting physical development, unfolding the intellectual faculties, accustoming them to social interaction, and training them in good habits. . . .

> DEPARTMENT OF EDUCATION;
> *Outlines of the Modern Education in Japan*, 1893

In the kindergarten the children are guided to bring out their plays in such a manner as really to reach the aim desired by nature, that is, to serve for their development.

> (FRIEDRICH) FROEBEL, 1782–1852

Those preschools that emphasize *curiosity* and *self-motivation*, such as the Montessori schools, produce the greatest long-term gains.

> ROBERT ORNSTEIN & PAUL EHRLICH;
> *New World New Mind*, 1989

The infant school, from birth to six years of age, is comparable with the mother school of *The Great Didactic* to which Comenius refers us.

> ROBERT R. RUSK; *Doctrines of the Great Educators*, 1918

His [Friedrich Froebel's] last great educational achievement was the foundation, at Blankenburg in 1837, of the first "garden of children," the Kindergarten.

> ROBERT R. RUSK; *Doctrines of the Great Educators*, 1918

KNOW

The knower is one with the thing known.

> ARISTOTLE, 384–322

All men by nature desire to know.

> ARISTOTLE, 384–322

Nobody knows enough, but many too much.
MARIE VON EBNER-ESCHENBACH; *Aphorisms*, 1905

They that think they know everything know nothing.
ENGLISH proverb

He that knows little often repeats it.
ENGLISH proverb

Who knows most says least.
FRENCH proverb

We know what we have, but not what we shall get.
GERMAN proverb

To know everything is to know nothing.
ITALIAN proverb

The further one pursues knowledge, the less one knows.
LÂO-TZU (né LI URH), *c*.600–*c*.500

Teach thy tongue to say "I do not know".
MAIMONIDES (né MOSES BEN MAIMON), 1135–1204

To know by rote is not to know.
(MICHEL EYQUEM DE) MONTAIGNE; *Essays*, 1580–1595

The more you know the less you will sleep.
RUSSIAN proverb

I think we have a need to know what we do not need to know.
WILLIAM SAFIRE; *The New York Times*, 1 Sep. 1956

It is only when we forget all our learning that we begin to know.
H(ENRY) D(AVID) THOREAU, 1817–1862

KNOWLEDGE

Emancipation from error is the condition of real knowledge.
HENRI FREDERIC AMIEL, 1821–1881

Knowledge can only be obtained by sacrifice.
Babylonian Talmud, c.450

There are two modes of acquiring knowledge, namely by reasoning and experience. Reasoning draws a conclusion and makes us grant the conclusion, but does not make the conclusion certain, nor does it remove doubt so that the mind may rest on the intuition of truth, unless the mind discovers it by the path of experience.
ROGER BACON; *Opus Majus,* 1266–7

Human life is limited, but knowledge is limitless. To drive the limited in pursuit of the limitless is fatal; and to presume that one really knows is fatal indeed.
CHAUANG-TZU, *c.300–c.200*

Love of knowledge is akin to wisdom.
CONFUCIUS (Latin for K'UNG FU-TZU), 551–479

When you know a thing, to recognize that you know it, and when you do not know a thing, to recognize that you do not know it. That is knowledge.
CONFUCIUS (Latin for K'UNG FU-TZU), 551–479

The only good is knowledge, and the only evil is ignorance.
DIOGENES LÄERTIUS, *c.*100–*c.*200

Knowledge has already become the primary industry, the industry that supplies the economy the essential and central resources of production.
PETER F. DRUCKER, 1909–

Knowledge has outstripped character development, and the young today are given an education rather than an upbringing.
ILYA EHRENBURG; *Saturday Review,* 30 Sep. 1967

Knowledge is the knowing that we cannot know.
RALPH WALDO EMERSON; *Representative Men,* 1850

Knowledge has no enemy but ignorance.

ENGLISH proverb

Our education generally tries to train people to have knowledge as a possession.

ERICH FROMM; *To Have or To Be?*, 1976

In order to widen one's knowledge and experience, one must listen to the words of others, read books, and form one's own ideas.

YUKICHI FUKUZAWA; *An Encouragement of Learning*, 1969

Without knowledge, without sin.

GERMAN proverb

Knowledge acquired in childhood is not soon forgotten.

HEBREW proverb

Knowledge is ruin to my young men.

(ADOLF) HITLER, 1889–1945

Among all things, knowledge is truly the best thing: from not being liable ever to be stolen, from its not being purchasable and from its being imperishable.

*The Hitopadesa, c.*500

Knowledge is of two kinds. We know a subject ourselves, or we know where we can find information upon it.

SAMUEL JOHNSON, 1709–1784

Knowledge unused is like a torch in the hand of a blind man.

KASHMIRI proverb

[W]e must remember that while you can inform people, you can't knowledge them, and this has always helped me distinguish these terms, particularly with respect to the difference between a passive process and an active one.

JULES B. LAPIDUS;
Trevor N.S. Lenham Memorial Lecture in Graduate Education
(University of Calgary), 19 Mar. 1990

A study of history shows that civilizations that abandon the quest for knowledge are doomed to disintegration.

BERNARD LOVELL; *The Observer*, 14 May 1972

Knowledge advances by steps, and not by leaps.

THOMAS BABINGTON MACAULAY; *Essays*, 1844

The grand achievement of the present age is the diffusion of superficial knowledge.

JOHN STUART MILL, 1806–1873

Because of the way knowledge has developed in separate disciplines, children come to learn about themselves and their world piecemeal. If they get through college, most are introduced to mathematics, chemistry, physics, biology, geography, history, sociology, anthropology, economics, psychology, art, music, literature, languages, and more. But they rarely learn to relate one area to another.

ROBERT ORNSTEIN & PAUL EHRLICH;
New World New Mind, 1989

It is important to use all knowledge ethically, humanely, and lovingly.

CAROL PEARSON; *The Hero Within*, 1986

Knowledge is light, ignorance is a cloud.

PHILIPPINE proverb

Knowledge which is acquired under compulsion obtains no hold on the mind.

PLATO (né ARISTOCLES); *The Republic (Politeia)*, c.400BC

Knowledge, if it does not determine action, is dead to us.

PLOTINUS, 205–270

Consider: what Thamus* called the "conceit of wisdom" – the unreal knowledge acquired through the written word – eventually became the pre-eminent form of knowledge valued by the schools.

NEIL POSTMAN; *Technopoly*, 1993
[*a king in ancient Egypt]

If knowledge hangs around your neck like pearls instead of chains you are a lucky man.

ALAN PRICE; *O Lucky Man!* (pub. Warner Brothers), 1973

143

Knowledge alone effects emancipation.

SHANKARA, *c.*800–*c.*900

His knowledge of books had in some degree diminished his knowledge of the world.

WILLIAM SHENSTONE, 1714–1763

Our knowledge is a little island in a great ocean of non knowledge.

ISAAC BASHEVIS SINGER; *The New York Times*, 3 Dec. 1978

We are creating and using up ideas and images at a faster and faster pace. Knowledge, like people, places, things and organizational forms, is becoming disposable.

ALVIN TOFFLER; *Future Shock*, 1970

Knowledge is in every country the surest basis of public happiness.

GEORGE WASHINGTON, 1732–1799

With knowledge you are nowhere lost.

YIDDISH proverb

KNOW YOURSELF

You never find yourself until you face the truth.

PEARL BAILEY; *The Raw Pearl*, 1968

"Know myself?" If I knew myself, I'd run away.

(JOHANN WOLFGANG VON) GOETHE, 1749–1832

If people can be educated to see the lowly side of their own natures, it may be hoped that they will also learn to understand and to love their fellow men better.

(CARL GUSTAV) JUNG, 1875–1961

He knows the universe and does not know himself.

(JEAN DE) LA FONTAINE, 1621–1695

The greatest thing in the world is for a man to know how to be himself.

(MICHEL EYQUEM DE) MONTAIGNE, 1533–1592

Know Thyself.

THALES OF MILETUS, *c*.640–*c*.546

Only the shallow know themselves.

OSCAR WILDE, 1854–1900

L

LANGUAGE

Language is the road map of a culture. It tells you where its people come from and where they are going.

RITA MAE BROWN; *Starting from Scratch*, 1988

Language is a uniquely human characteristic. Each person has programmed into his genes a faculty called universal grammar.

NOAM (AVRIL) CHOMSKY, 1928–

In language clarity is everything.

CONFUCIUS (Latin for K'UNG FU-TZU), 551–479

If names are not correct, language is not in accordance with the truth of things.

CONFUCIUS (Latin for K'UNG FU-TZU), 551–479

Where there is no written language anything which must be remembered must be said.

MARGARET CRAVEN; *I Heard the Owl Call My Name*, 1973

The liberation of language is rooted in the liberation of ourselves.

MARY DALY; *The Church and the Second Sex*, 1975

Who does not know another language knows not his own.

(JOHANN WOLFGANG VON) GOETHE, 1749–1832

Because everybody can talk, everybody thinks he can talk about language.

(JOHANN WOLFGANG VON) GOETHE, 1749–1832

There is no common language or medium of understanding between people of education and those without it – between those who judge of things from books or from their senses.

WILLIAM HAZLITT, 1778–1830

There is no tracing the connection of ancient nations, but by language.

SAMUEL JOHNSON, 1709–1784

I am always sorry when any language is lost, because languages are the pedigree of nations.

SAMUEL JOHNSON, 1709–1784

Language is human reason, which has its internal logic of which man knows nothing.

(CLAUDE) LÉVI-STRAUSS; La Pensée sauvage, 1962

Language has always been held to be man's richest art form, that which distinguishes him from the animal creation.

MARSHALL McLUHAN; Understanding Media, 1964

But if thought corrupts language, language can also corrupt thought.

GEORGE ORWELL (pseud. of ERIC BLAIR);
Politics and the English Language, 1946

Life is too short to learn German

RICHARD PORSON, 1759–1808

Language is the soul of intellect, and reading is the essential process by which that intellect is cultivated beyond the commonplace experience of everyday life.

CHARLES SCRIBNER; Publishers Weekly, 30 Mar. 1984

This monopoly over language is one of the means by which males have ensured their own primacy, and consequently have ensured the invisibility or "other" nature of females.

DALE SPENDER; Man Made Language, 1980

All speech, written or spoken, is a dead language, until it finds a willing and prepared hearer.

ROBERT LOUIS STEVENSON, 1850–1894

It is only in Indo-European languages that distinctions between past, present, and future have been fully devloped.

G.J. WHITROW; Time in History, 1988

Everything that can be said can be said clearly.

(LUDWIG JOSEF JOHANN) WITTGENSTEIN, 1889–1951

LATERAL THINKING

The difference between lateral thinking and vertical thinking is that with vertical thinking logic is in control of the mind, whereas with lateral thinking logic is at the service of the mind.

EDWARD DE BONO; *The Use of Lateral Thinking*, 1971

LATIN

A mass-market Latin radio show is a dream fulfillable perhaps only in Finland, where half the population have studied Latin in school.

DIANA BEN-AARON;
The Times Higher Education Supplement, 18 Mar. 1994

There is a negative proof of the value of Latin. No one seems to boast of not knowing it.

PETER BRODIE; *The New York Times*, 18 Jul. 1984

A silly remark can be made in Latin as well as in Spanish.

(MIGUEL DE) CERVANTES (SAAVEDRA);
The Dialogues of the Dogs, 1613

The more one thinks about Latin the easier it is to see why the Roman Empire fell.

EDWARD JOHN STANLEY DERBY, 1918–

The Romans would never have found time to conquer the world if they had been obliged first to learn Latin.

HEINRICH HEINE, 1797–1856

There is no universal language of learning comparable to Latin in the Middle Ages.

BRUCE R. JOYCE & ALEXANDER M. NICHOLSON;
Schooling for a Global Age, 1979

[K]nowledge of Latin and some knowledge of Greek became the mark of a gentleman, and was forced upon boys, with the result that men lost the taste for it.

BERTRAND RUSSELL; *Education and the Social Order*, 1932

LAW

Law is a bottomless pit.
                    JOHN ARBUTHNOT; *The History of John Bull*, 1712

The law is reason unaffected by desire.
                                        ARISTOTLE, 384–322

Lawyers are the only person in whom ignorance of the law is not punished.
                              JEREMY BENTHAM, 1748–1832

Law in general is human reason.
                    (CHARLES SECONDAT, BARON DE LA BRÈDE ET DE)
                    MONTESQUIEU; *The Spirit of Laws*, 1748

LEARN

We cannot learn without pain.
                                        ARISTOTLE, 384–322

What we have to learn to do, we learn by doing.
                    ARISTOTLE, *Nicomachean Ethics*, c.350BC

If you would have your son to walk honourably through the world, you must not attempt to clear the stones from his path, but teach him to walk firmly over them – not insist upon leading him. . . .
                    ANNE BRONTË; *The Tenant of Wildfell Hall*, 1848

There are some things you learn best in calm, and some in storm.
                    WILLA CATHER; *The Song of the Lark*, 1915

He who learns but does not think, is lost! He who thinks but does not learn is in great danger.
                    CONFUCIUS (Latin for K'UNG FU-TZU), 551–479

It is impossible for a man to learn what he thinks he already knows.
                                        EPICTETUS, c.50–120

One learns by failing.

FRENCH proverb

Once you learn something it is hard to unlearn.

GREEK proverb

We learn by teaching.

ITALIAN proverb

The important thing is not so much that every child should be taught, as that every child should be given the wish to learn.

JOHN LUBBOCK, 1834–1913

School yourself to demureness and patience. Learn to inure yourself to drudgery in science. Learn, compare, collect the facts!

(IVAN PETROVICH) PAVLOV, 1849–1936

LEARNED

Nobody is born learned. Nobody is born ready taught.

(MIGUEL DE) CERVANTES (SAAVEDRA); *Don Quixote*, 1605–15

The most learned are not the wisest.

DUTCH proverb

I hate a learned woman.

EURIPIDES; *Hippolytus*, 428BC

There is nothing more displeasant to the learned than the companie [*sic*] of the ignorant.

STEFANO GUAZZO; *Civil Conversations*, 1574

It does not make much difference what a person studies – all knowledge is related, and the man who studies anything, if he keeps at it, will become learned.

HYPATIA, *c.*370–415

Learned ladies are not to my taste.

MOLIÈRE (né JEAN-BAPTISTE POQUELIN), 1622–1673

A learned girl is one of the most intolerable monsters of creation.
WILLIAM MAKEPEACE THACKERAY, 1811–1863

The learned tradition is not concerned with truth, but with the learned adjustment of learned statements of antecedent learned people.
ALFRED NORTH WHITEHEAD, 1861–1947

LEARNER

Learners should not be forced to submit to an obligatory curriculum, or to discrimination based on whether they possess a certificate or a diploma.
IVAN ILLICH; *Deschooling Society*, 1971

People are naturally curious. They are born learners. Education can either develop or stifle their inclination to ask why and to learn.
IRA SHOR; *Empowering Education*, 1992

LEARNING

The most useful piece of learning for the uses of life is to unlearn what is untrue.
ANTISTHENES, *c*.445–*c*.360

I have heard the most of that which bears the name of learning, and which has abused such quantities of ink and paper, and continually employs so many ignorant, unhappy souls, for ten, twelve, twenty years in a university (who yet poor wretches think they are doing something all the while) as logic, etc. and several other things (that shall be nameless lest I misspell them) are much more absolutely nothing than the errantist play that e'er was writ.
APHRA BEHN; *The Dutch Lover*, 1673

Learning, n[oun]. The kind of ignorance distinguishing the studious.
AMBROSE BIERCE; *The Devil's Dictionary*, 1911

Learning which does not advance each day will daily decrease.
CHINESE proverb

Learning is like rowing upstream; not to advance is to drop back.

CHINESE proverb

Learning without thought is labour lost; thought without learning is perilous.

CONFUCIUS (Latin for K'UNG FU-TZU), 551–479

Learning to read is different ... from learning by reading.

ELIZABETH EISENSTEIN;
The Printing Press as an Agent of Change, 1979

[M]emorizing a fixed sequence of discrete letters represented by meaning-less symbols and sounds has been the gateway to book learning for all children in the West.

ELIZABETH EISENSTEIN;
The Printing Press As an Agent of Change, 1979

If we norish not Larning both church & commonwealth will sinke. [*sic*]

JOHN ELIOT, 1604–1690

Who so neglects learning in his youth, loses the past and is dead for the future.

EURIPIDES, 485–406

[N]o matter how important and distinctive our role as researchers may be, the most significant mandate universities are perceived to perform is that of education. The primary value that universities are expected to add to the social and economic progress of our country is the development of our human resources through learning. And there is a widespread feeling, whether fully justified or not, that we are undervaluing that function in the priorities we reflect through our allocation of resources, reward structures, and foci of attention.

ROBIN H. FARQUAR;
University Affairs/Affaires Universitaires, Feb 1994

Anyone who stops learning is old, whether at twenty or eighty. Anyone who keeps learning stays young.

HENRY FORD, 1863–1947

Most of the learning in use is of no great use.

BENJAMIN FRANKLIN; *Poor Richard's Almanac*, 1749

153

Learning hath gained most by those books by which the printers have lost.
THOMAS FULLER; *The Holy State and the Profane State*, 1642

Learning is not simply an event that happens naturally.
ROBERT M. GAGNÉ; *The Conditions of Learning*, 1985

We have not been cognizant of the ways in which basic inclinations of human learning turn out to be ill-matched to the agenda of the modern secular school.
HOWARD GARDNER; *The Unschooled Mind*, 1993

The trouble with most men of learning is that their learning goes to their head.
ISAAC GOLDBERG; *Reflex*, Dec. 1927

Learning ... happens all through life unless we block it.
CHARLES HANDY; *The Age of Unreason*, 1989

The world itself is a volume larger than all the libraries in it. Learning is a sacred deposit from the experience of ages; but it has not put all future experience on the shelf, or debarred the common herd of mankind from the use of their hands, tongues, eyes, ears, or understandings.
WILLIAM HAZLITT; *On the Conversation of Authors*, 1820

Learning is superior to beauty; learning is better than hidden treasure; learning is a companion on a journey to a strange country; learning is strength inexhaustible.
*The Hitopadesa, c.*500

The way to stay human is to keep on learning.
ROBERT M. HUTCHINS; *The Learning Society*, 1968

Without learning there is no knowing.
JAPANESE proverb

If education has been traditionally considered a function of teaching, today and even more in the future education means the permanent process of learning by every human being in society. Learning change has become one of the new prior objectives of education.
ALEXANDER KING & BERTRAND SCHNEIDER;
The First Global Revolution, 1991

[T]he physiological structures that govern learning allow for the emergence of unique individual adaptive processes that tend to emphasize some adaptive orientations over others.

DAVID A. KOLB; *Experiential Learning*, 1984

A great deal of learning can be packed into an empty head.

KARL KRAUS; *Aphorisms and More Aphorisms*, 1909

Abandon learning, and you will be free from trouble and distress.

LÂO-TZU (né LI URH), *c*.600–*c*.500

That is what learning is. You suddenly understand something you've understood all your life, but in a new way.

DORIS LESSING; *The Four-Gated City*, 1969

It is with concern, then frustration, then helplessness, that parents and educators of young children have noted that their curiosity, confidence and enthusiasm for learning evaporate.... Learning how to learn gives way to learning how to be taught.

JANET MEIGHAN;
in *Theory and Practice of Regressive Education*, 1993

I am still learning.

MICHELANGELO (BUONARROTI), 1474–1564

Change requires learning.

JEAN BAKER MILLER;
Toward a New Psychology of Women, 1976

Besides learning to see, there is another art to be learned – *not* to see what is not.

MARIA MITCHELL, 1818–1889

We need but little learning to live happily.

(MICHEL EYQUEM DE) MONTAIGNE, 1533–1592

The learning of things is better than the ignorance of them.

MOROCCAN proverb

Learning and seeing are more important than education.
                                 STEN NADLONY; *The Discovery of Slowness*, 1987

Learning is the life of the common wealth.
                                 GEORGE PETTIE; *Petite Pallace*, 1576

[A]ny significant learning involves a certain amount of pain, either pain connected with the learning itself or distress connected with giving up certain previous learnings.
                                 CARL ROGERS; *Freedom to Learn for the Eighties*, 1983

Learning is the weapon with which Satan is combatted.
                                 SA'DI, *c*.1184–1291

Wear your learning, like your watch, in a private pocket: and do not merely pull it out and strike it, merely to show that you have one.
                                 PHILIP DORMER STANHOPE, 1694–1773

Words are but wind; and learning is nothing but words; ergo, learning is nothing but wind.
                                 JONATHAN SWIFT, 1667–1745

To be fond of learning is to be near to knowledge.
                                 TZE-SZE, *c*.335–*c*.288

One can learn, at least. One can go on learning until the day one is cut off.
                                 FAY WELDON; *Down Among the Women*, 1971

Learning is remembering what you are interested in.
                                 RICHARD SAUL WURMAN; *Information Anxiety*, 1991

The excitement of learning separates youth from old age. As long as you're learning you're not old.
                                 ROSALYN S. YALOW, 1921–

Learning cannot be inherited.
                                 YIDDISH proverb

LECTURE

Lecturer, n[oun]. One with his hand in your pocket, his tongue in your ear and his faith in your patience.

> AMBROSE BIERCE; *The Devil's Dictionary*, 1911

Lecture – a period of uninterrupted talk.

> DONALD A. BLIGH; *What's the Use of Lectures*, 1971

Like musical composition and performance, lecturing is an art.

> DONALD A. BLIGH; *What's the Use of Lectures*, 1971

The lecturer can renounce the professional monologue only by abdicating a portion of his security.

> PIERRE BOURDIEU & JEAN-CLAUDE PASSERON;
> (*Rapport pédagogique et communication*, 1965) / *Academic Discourse*, 1994

The Lecture Method of Instruction is the single most commonly used teaching method in the world and by far the oldest existing method – and one of the least effective, if improperly used.

> MARTIN M. BROADWELL;
> *The Lecture Method of Instruction*, 1980

At present university lecturers normally receive no training in the techniques of lecturing. . . . It might be worth while to arrange short courses for newly appointed assistant lecturers.

> G(EORGE) LESLIE BROOK; *The Modern University*, 1965

We can observe the boredom, confusion and restlessness of students in many lecture classes.

> ROBERT CANNON; *Lecturing*, 1988

[A]lthough the lecturer may be employing an effective organization, there can be no certainty that the remarks are having the same effect on each and every student.

> ROBERT M. GAGNÉ; *The Conditions of Learning*, 1985

But I do believe that there is far more lecturing going on than can reasonably be justified by the evidence concerning the efficiency of lectures, especially bearing in mind the nature of the educational goals we claim to be striving for.

GRAHAM GIBBS; *Twenty Terrible Reasons for Lecturing*, 1982

Some experience of popular lecturing has convinced me that the necessity of making things plain to uninstructed people was one of the very best means of clearing up the obscure corners in one's own mind.

T(HOMAS) H(ENRY) HUXLEY, 1825–1895

The process of lecturing is often caricatured as the transferring of the lecturer's notes to the students' notepads without any intervening thinking.

GEOFF ISAACS; *Medical Teacher* (vol. 11), 1989

I cannot see that lectures can do so much good as reading the books from which the lectures are given.

SAMUEL JOHNSON, 1709–1784

I once lectured in a theatre newly decked out in nordic timber and sound baffles, the very latest thing. The students could hear me very well. But I could hear them too, especially the couple who throughout the lecture cuddled, fingered and kissed . . . it was a hard background to pontificate on rhetorical patterns in Chaucer's Nun's Priest's Tale.

STEPHEN KNIGHT; *The Selling of the Australian Mind*, 1991

Lecturing and demonstrating sometimes appeal to organizers on the grounds that they are "economical" ways of using a teacher's time: they do not involve elaborate technician or administrative support. However, no teaching method can be described as economical if it fails to meet the prime objective of helping students learn.

JENNIFER ROGERS; *Adults Learning*, 1971

LEFTHANDED

Teachers insisted I use my right hand for writing, but paid no attention to which hand I used when drawing.

an ARTIST; in *Enduring Schools*, 1992

For centuries, and in many countries today, left-handedness has been like the negative sign in electricity – an essential compensation, but the weaker side, the second best, indeed morally the evil side.

MICHAEL BARSLEY; *The Left-Handed Book*, 1966

[I]t is worth pointing out that no essential difference was apparent between left-handers and right-handers, except for the use of a different hand.

MARGARET M. CLARK; *Left-Handedness*, 1957

Other papers reveal the possibility of risks associated with routine [ultrasound] screening; more left-handed children, according to a Norwegian study.

MICHEL ODENT; *The European* (élan), 18–24 Mar. 1994

LEISURE

There can be no education without leisure, and without leisure education is worthless.

SARAH JOSEPHA HALE, 1788–1879

Leisure is the mother of philosophy.

THOMAS HOBBES, 1588–1679

LETTER

Letters are the instruments of learning.

YUKICHI FUKUZAWA; *An Encouragement of Learning*, 1969

LIBERAL EDUCATION

A liberal-arts education is supposed to provide you with a value system, a standard, a set of ideas, not a job.

CAROLINE BIRD; *The Case Against College*, 1975

A liberal education is at the heart of a civil society, and at the heart of a liberal education is the act of teaching.

A. BARTLETT GIAMATTI; *Harper's*, Jul. 1980

In the long run of history, the censor and the inquisitor have always lost. The only sure weapon against bad ideas is better ideas. The source of better ideas is wisdom. The surest path to wisdom is a liberal education.

ALFRED WHITNEY GRISWOLD, 1906–1963

A liberal education . . . frees a man from the prison-house of his class, race, time, place, background, family, and even his nation.

ROBERT M. HUTCHINS, 1899–1977

Bryn Mawr has done what a four-year dose of liberal education was designed to do: unfit her for eighty per cent of the useful work of the world.

TONI MORRISON; *Song of Solomon*, 1977

The basic meaning of liberal education lies in its capacity to deliver man from that which binds him and to set him free.

MICHIO NAGAI; *Higher Education in Japan*, 1971

It is the function of a liberal university not to give right answers, but to ask right questions.

CYNTHIA OZICK; *Motive*, 1969

Why "liberal studies" are so called is obvious, it is because they are the ones considered worthy of free men. But there is really only one liberal study that deserves that name – because it makes a person free – and that is the pursuit of wisdom.

(LUCIUS ANNAEUS) SENECA (the Younger), c.4BC–65

The arts or skills were "liberal" because they were liberating. That is, they freed their possessor from the ignorance that bound the uneducated.

CHARLES VAN DOREN; *A History of Knowledge*, 1991

The basic purpose of a liberal education is to liberate the human being to exercise his or her potential to the fullest.

BARBARA M. WHITE; *Christian Science Monitor*, 8 Sep. 1976

LIBERATION

[S]chooling is a two-edged social instrument. It is as much a tool of oppression as it is a lever of liberation.

DAVID HAMILTON; *Learning about Education*, 1990

Deschooling is, therefore, at the front of any movement for human liberation.

IVAN ILLICH; *Deschooling Society*, 1971

LIBRARY

There are times when I think that the ideal library is composed solely of reference books.

J. DONALD ADAMS; *The New York Times*, 1 Apr. 1956

A large university library could make good use of one or more members of its staff whose entire duties should be concerned with advising students how to use the library.

G(EORGE) LESLIE BROOK; *The Modern University*, 1965

They [students] have not been taught how to use a library. I sense that most of them have been conditioned and programmed to be conveniently pumped into the system of corporate America.

HELEN CALDICOTT; *If You Love This Planet*, 1992

These [libraries] are the tombs of such as cannot die.

GEORGE CRABBE; *The Library*, 1781

Th' first thing to have in a libry is a shelf. Fr'm time to time this can be decorated with lithrachure but th' shelf is th' main thing. [*sic*]

FINLEY PETER DUNNE; *Mr. Dooley Says*, 1910

Meek young men grow up in libraries, believing it their duty to accept views which Cicero, which Locke, which Bacon have given; forgetting that Cicero, Locke and Bacon were only young men in libraries when they wrote these books.

RALPH WALDO EMERSON;
an *oration* (Harvard University), 1837

A sanitorium for the mind.

an *inscription* (portal of the library), Alexandria,
Egypt, *c.*200BC

Let no profane person enter!

an *inscription* (old library), Berne, Switzerland

Libraries may well be reckoned among educational institutions, in the broadest sense.

PRESERVED SMITH;
A History of Modern Culture (vol. I), 1962

Nothing sickens me more than the closed door of a library.

BARBARA W. TUCHMAN; *The New Yorker*, 21 Apr. 1986

Shut not your doors to me, proud libraries.

WALT(ER) WHITMAN, 1819–92

LIFE

Great knowledge you have gained from books, 'tis true,
But don't forget that life can teach you something too.

(MARCUS PORCIUS) CATO, 234–149

A school is a place through which you have to pass before entering life, but where the teaching proper does not prepare you for life.

ERNEST DIMNET; *The Art of Thinking*, 1928

Life is a struggle for many and a puzzle for most.

CHARLES HANDY; *The Empty Raincoat*, 1994

The education explosion is producing a vast number of people who want to live significant, important lives but lack the ability to satisfy this craving for importance by individual achievement. The country is being swamped with nobodies who want to be somebodies.

ERIC HOFFER; *Wall Street Journal*, 23 Mar. 1978

School prepares for the alienating institutionalization of life by teaching the need to be taught.

IVAN ILLICH; *Deschooling Society*, 1971

The more the critical reason dominates, the more impoverished life becomes.

(CARL GUSTAV) JUNG, 1875–1961

Stake life upon truth.

(DECIMUS JUNIUS) JUVENAL(IS), *c.*60–140

A day spent without the sight and sound of beauty, the contemplation of mystery, or the search for truth and perfection, is a poverty stricken day; and a succession of such days is fatal to human life.

LEWIS MUMFORD; *The Condition of Man*, 1944

Theories and schools, like microbes, devour one another and by their warfare ensure the continuity of life.

(MARCEL) PROUST; *Remembrance of Things Past*, 1921

Teach him to live a life rather than to avoid death; life is not breath but action.

(JEAN JACQUES) ROUSSEAU; *Émile*, 1762

Life is a game boy. Life is a game that one plays according to the rules.

J(EROME) D(AVID) SALINGER; *The Catcher in the Rye*, 1951

We learn not in school but in life.

(LUCIUS ANNAEUS) SENECA (the Younger), *c.*4BC–65

The unexamined life is not worth living.

SOCRATES, 470?–399

In knowing nothing is the sweetest life.

SOPHOCLES, 496?–406

There is only one subject matter for education, and that is Life in all its manifestations.

ALFRED NORTH WHITEHEAD, 1861–1947

LITERACY

Literacy is by no means the blessing it is advertised to be.

ERICH FROMM; *To Have or To Be?*, 1976

The problem is that very few people believe academic literacy is superior, or equal, to real-world literacy.

JERRY HERRON;
Universities and the Myth of Cultural Decline, 1988

LITERATURE

The only test of a work of literature is that it shall please other ages than its own.

GERALD BRENAN; *Thoughts in a Dry Season*, 1978

Literature is the art of writing something that will be read twice; journalism what will be grasped at once.

CYRIL CONNOLLY; *Enemies of Promise*, 1938

[A]nd it must not be forgotten that during many centuries Greek thought and literature influenced European literatures through the medium of Latin.

NORBERT GUTERMAN;
The Anchor Book of Latin Quotations, 1990

It makes a great deal of history to produce a little literature.

HENRY JAMES, 1843–1916

Mediocrity is very strong all over the world. In totalitarian countries, it has the regime on its side. In democratic countries, mediocrity is promoted by the market. Very few people care about real literature.

ISMAIL KADARÉ; *Newsweek*, 20 Dec. 1993

Our American professors like their literature clear and cold and pure and very dead.

SINCLAIR LEWIS;
an *acceptance speech* (Nobel Prize), 12 Dec. 1930

An autobiography can distort; facts can be realigned. But fiction never lies, it reveals.

V(IDIADHAR) S(URAJPRASAD) NAIPAUL, 1932–

Literature is not like music: it isn't for the young; there are no prodigies in writing.

> V(IDIADHAR) S(URAJPRASAD) NAIPAUL;
> *New York Review of Books*, 23 Apr. 1987

Great literature is simply language charged with meaning to the utmost possible degree.

> EZRA POUND, 1885–1972

Literature changes more slowly than science.

> C(HARLES) P(ERCY) SNOW;
> *The Two Cultures and the Scientific Revolution*, 1961

I can say without affectation that I belong to the Russian convict world no less ... than I do to Russian literature. I got my education there, and it will last forever.

> (ALEXANDER) SOLZHENITSYN; *The Oak and the Calf*, 1980

Literature – creative literature – unconcerned with sex, is inconceivable.

> GERTRUDE STEIN, 1874–1946

Remarks are not literature.

> GERTRUDE STEIN; *The Autobiography of Alice B. Toklas*, 1993

I've never met a scientist who didn't believe that 80 percent of the scientific literature was nonsense.

> WALTER STEWART; *The Washington Monthly*, Mar. 1991

The inhabitants [Americans] have a sort of prejudice against anything really worthy of the name of literature.

> (ALEXIS CHARLES HENRI MAURICE CLÉREL DE) TOCQUEVILLE;
> *Democracy in America*, 1835

In China, literature is not viewed as a form of entertainment or simply as a source of aesthetic enjoyment, but as an effective means of education, of inspiring readers with high ideals and the belief that these can be obtained.

> GLADYS YANG;
> *Seven Contemporary Chinese Women Writers*, 1982

True literature can exist only where it is created not by diligent and trustworthy officials, but by madmen, hermits, heretics, dreamers, rebels, and skeptics.

YEVGENY ZAMYATIN; *A Soviet Heretic,* 1970

LOGIC

Men are so made that they can resist sound argument, and yet yield to a glance.

HONORÉ DE BALZAC, 1799–1850

Logic, n[oun]. The art of thinking and reasoning in strict accordance with the limitations and incapacities of the human misunderstanding.

AMBROSE BIERCE; *The Devil's Dictionary,* 1911

Logic is the study of ideal method in thought and research: observation and introspection, deduction and induction, hypothesis and experiment, analysis and synthesis. . . .

WILL(IAM) (JAMES) DURANT; *The Story of Philosophy,* 1926

LOVE

The teacher, professional or amateur, must teach the simple thing: live, and call it by its simple name.

ALFRED ADLER; *The Education of the Individual,* 1958

The truth is that I am enslaved . . . in one vast love affair with 70 children.

SYLVIA ASHTON-WARNER; *Spinster,* 1959

Significant learning is posited on a love of life and of living.

JEAN MARIE BENISKOS; *Person-Education,* 1980

Don't know much about history
Don't know much about biology
Don't know much about science book
Don't know much about French I took
But I do know that I love you
And I know that if you love me too
What a wonderful world this could be.

SAM COOKE; *Wonderful World* (pub. ABKCO-Music), 1959

Let no more gods or exploiters be served. Let us learn rather to love one another.

FRANCISCO FERRER, 1859–1909

In all things we learn only from those we love.

(JOHANN WOLFGANG VON) GOETHE, 1749–1832

We destroy the ... love of learning in children, which is so strong when they are small, by encouraging and compelling them to work for petty and contemptible rewards – gold stars, or papers marked 100 and tacked to the wall, or As on report cards, or honor rolls, or deans' lists, or Phi Beta Kappa keys – in short, for the ignoble satisfaction of feeling that they are better than someone else.

JOHN HOLT; *How Children Fail*, 1982

The teacher should love his children better than his State or his Church; otherwise he is not an ideal teacher.

BERTRAND RUSSELL; *Education and the Good Life*, 1926

Slaves and schoolboys often love their masters.

GEORGE BERNARD SHAW, 1856–1950

Beware you be not swallowed up in books! An ounce of love is worth a pound of knowledge.

JOHN WESLEY, 1703–1791

LYCÉE

"[L]ycées" were to be established in one or more cities of each *département*, with a curriculum combining the classic languages and literature with the sciences. To persuade French youths to enter this treadmill, Napoleon provided 6,400 scholarships, whose recipients pledged themselves to the teaching profession and promised to defer marriage at least to the age of twenty-five.

WILL(IAM) (JAMES) DURANT & ARIEL DURANT; *The Story of Civilization* (vol. XI), 1975

LYING

Painters and poets have leave to lie.

ENGLISH proverb

Without telling lies, do not yet tell at the truth; do not live by fixed principles, live by opportunity and circumstance.

BALTASAR GRACIÁN; *Gracian's Manuals*, 1653

In all my years of teaching I have never found myself in a school where children thought it was safe or reasonable to tell the truth to an adult. Children learn to lie because it is the only way to be safe and to protect their fellow pupils.

CHRIS SHUTE; *Compulsory Schooling Disease*, 1993

M

MANAGEMENT

By no stretch of the imagination are all, or even most, of America's colleges and universities suited to serve as management models for industry.

J. WADE GILLEY;
Thinking about American Higher Education, 1991

MASS EDUCATION

Mass-education cannot work to produce a fair society because its daily practice is rigged competition, suppression, and intimidation.

JOHN TAYLOR GATTO; *Dumbing Us Down*, 1992

Universal education is the most corroding and disintegrating poison that liberalism has ever invented for its own destruction.

(ADOLF) HITLER, 1889–1945

The mass education of our time is probably not the best education that any human beings have ever enjoyed.

CHARLES VAN DOREN; *A History of Knowledge*, 1991

MASTER

Most things are easy to learn, but hard to master.

CHINESE proverb

Practice is the best master.

LATIN proverb

In most schools the dominance of the master over his pupils is strongly and directly expressed, both socially and intellectually. He uses his greater experience to conquer their greater inventiveness. His brain has probably become more rigidified than theirs, but he masks this weakness by imparting large quantities of "hard" facts. There is no argument, only instruction.

DESMOND MORRIS; *The Human Zoo*, 1969

Few men make themselves masters of the things they write or speak.

JOHN SELDEN; *Table Talk, c.*1650

At Paris and later at Oxford, *master* was the prevailing rank although the term *professor* was frequently used. At Bologna, the common title was *doctor*, a usage that spread throughout Italy and into Germany.

STEPHEN H. SPURR; *Academic Degree Structures*, 1970

MASTER DEGREE

Gradually the master's degree became more common in the faculties of arts, while the doctor's degree became more common in the professional faculties of theology, law, and medicine which developed in most of the early European universities.

WALTER CROSBY EELLS; *Degrees in Higher Education*, 1963

The master's degree has been shaped by the traditional arts and sciences model as the first postbaccalaureate degree conferred upon candidates following one year of graduate study. It is the mid-point to the doctorate, the terminal degree for most professions and a source of enrichment in the chosen field of study.

JUDITH S. GLAZER; *The Master's Degree*, 1986

Although the master's degree dates back to the founding of the first universities, it has undergone more vicissitudes than the bachelor's degree.

STEPHEN H. SPURR; *Academic Degree Structures*, 1970

MATHEMATICIAN

It is easier to square the circle than to get around a mathematician.

AUGUSTUS DE MORGAN; *A Budget of Paradoxes*, 1872

Mathematicians who are only mathematicians have exact minds, provided all things are explained to them by means of definitions and axioms: otherwise they are inaccurate and insufferable, for they are only right when the principles are quite clear.

(BLAISE) PASCAL; *Pensées*, 1669

I have hardly ever known a mathematician who was capable of reasoning.
PLATO (né ARISTOCLES), c.428–c.348

MATHEMATICS

Mathematics, the non-empirical science par excellence ... the science of sciences, delivering the key to those laws of nature and the universe which are concealed by appearances.
HANNAH ARENDT, 1906–1975

Although I am not stupid, the mathematical side of my brain is like dumb notes upon a damaged piano.
MARGOT ASQUITH; *More or Less About Myself*, 1934

God forbid that Truth be confined to Mathematical Demonstration.
WILLIAM BLAKE, 1757–1827

He [A.S. Neill] believed that mathematics, his own favourite subject, should appeal to the imagination, that it was an art as much as a science. So he scrapped the rural arithmetic book he had inherited. "It's full of the sums of the How-much-will-it-take-to-paper-a-room? type", he wrote scornfully.
JONATHAN CROALL; *Neill of Summerhill*, 1983

When mathematics is applied, it can serve to describe, to predict, or to prescribe.
PHILIP J. DAVIS & REUBEN HERSH; *Descartes' Dream*, 1986

In a just, more rational world, mathematics would be used as a filter only for posts for which it is demonstrably required. Such a change would be gladly accepted by the mathematics professors. We do not really want to be gatekeepers and agents of exclusion.
PHILIP J. DAVIS & REUBEN HERSH; *Descartes' Dream*, 1986
[Commenting on educational institutions making unnecessary courses of mathematics (calculus is the example) prerequisites, to exclude and thus filter out students from certain programmes.]

As far as the laws of mathematics refer to reality, they are not certain, and as far as they are certain, they do not refer to reality.
ALBERT EINSTEIN, 1879–1955

MATHEMATICS   Desiccates the heart.
GUSTAVE FLAUBERT; *The Dictionary of Received Ideas*, 1913

Beauty is the first test: there is no permanent place in the world for ugly mathematics.
GODFREY HAROLD HARVEY;
A Mathematician's Apology, 1940

Math[ematics] occupies a place of honor in French business and industry in great part because it is seen as a useful means of selecting job applicants, being less subjective than literature or philosophy.
BARRY JAMES; *International Herald Tribune*, 12 Oct. 1994

Tradition has made certain courses [of mathematics] prerequisites for others – calculus before engineering, and so on. But few architects I know claim they've ever used the calculus that was prerequisite for the architecture they do use.
DEBORAH MEIER; *Dissent*, Winter 1994

The teaching of mathematics has always presented a somewhat paradoxical problem. There exists, in fact, a certain category of students, otherwise quite intelligent and even capable of demonstrating above average intelligence in other fields, who always fail, more or less systematically, in mathematics.
JEAN PIAGET;
Science of Education and the Psychology of the Child, 1970

In universities, mathematics is taught mainly to men who are going to teach mathematics to men who are going to teach mathematics to.... Sometimes, it is true, there is an escape from this treadmill. Archimedes used mathematics to kill Romans, Galileo to improve the Grand Duke of Tuscany's artillery, modern physics (grown more ambitious) to exterminate the human race. It is usually on this account that the study of mathematics is commended to the general public as worthy of State support.
BERTRAND RUSSELL;
Human Society in Ethics and Politics, 1954

I see a certain order in the universe and math[ematics] is one way of making it visible.
MAY SARTON; *As We Are Now*, 1973

MBA (Master of Business Administration)

The Master of Business Administration (MBA) has been one of the most successful marketing operations of the century. Much sought after – and in ample supply – it promises a golden ticket to top management jobs.

GEORGE BICKERSTAFFE;
International Management, Apr. 1994

The anti-MBA culture also flourishes in Britain, with its cult of the amateur, and France, where there is an obsession with the *écoles de commerce*.

The Economist, 4 Jun. 1994

The MBA degree has become an institution in Europe.... Varying greatly in content and quality, the programs range from homegrown European schools that rival the best in the United States to borderline diploma mills.

KIRSTEN GALLAGHER;
The Chronicle of Higher Education, 1 Dec. 1993

Germany ... with its already lengthy education process, has eschewed the MBA degree and the business school. As a result, the country is one of the biggest exporters of MBA students to other countries.

International Management, Apr. 1994

The MBA kids want to move up too fast, they don't understand politics and people and they aren't able to function as part of a team until their third year.

JAMES R. MARTIN; *International Herald Tribune*, 3 Jun. 1993

We must recognize that although the management school gives students MBA and MPA [Master of Public Administration] degrees, it does not in fact teach them how to manage. Hence, these degrees can hardly be considered prerequisites for managing, and the world is full of highly competent managers who have never spent a day in a management course.

HENRY MINTZBERG; *The Nature of Managerial Work*, 1973

MBA (Master of Brutal Action) management.

DEREK A. NEWTON; *Feed Your Eagles*, 1991

MEANING

The teacher's task is not to implant facts but to place the subject to be learned in front of the learner and, through sympathy, emotion, imagination, and patience, to awaken in the learner the restless drive for answers and insights which enlarge the personal life and give it meaning.

NATHAN M. PUSEY; *The New York Times*, 22 Mar. 1959

Be sure that you go to the author to get at *his* meaning, not to find yours.

JOHN RUSKIN; *Sesame and Lilies*, 1865

MEDIOCRITY

The educational foundations of our society are presently being eroded by a rising tide of mediocrity.

DAVID P. GARDNER; in *A Nation at Risk*, 1983

MEMORY

My memory, if slow, is a retentive one. I acquire deliberately both knowledge and liking: the acquisition grows into my brain, and the sentiment into my breast; and it is not as the rapid-springing produce which, having no root in itself, flourishes verdurous enough for a time, but too soon falls withered away.

CHARLOTTE BRONTË; *Shirley*, 1849

We all have forgotten more than we remember.

ENGLISH? proverb

Method is the mother of memory.

THOMAS FULLER, 1608–1661

The things we remember best are those better forgotten.

BALTASAR GRACIÁN; *The Art of Worldly Wisdom*, 1647

If you're in education just to make kids memorise so that you can make things easier for yourself, get out.

ROLAND MEIGHAN;
Theory and Practice of Regressive Education, 1993

MEN

Boys have much time and care and cost bestowed on their education; girls have little or none. The former are early initiated in the sciences, study books and men, have all imaginable encouragement: not only fame, but also authority, power and riches.

MARY ASTELL; *Reflections on Marriage*, 1706

Men have succeeded so well in brainwashing women to a belief in their own incapacities that a recent poll of college girls revealed that the majority of the girls downgraded the work of professionals of their own sex and believed that men were better at everything – even teaching and dietetics – than women were.

ELIZABETH GOULD DAVIS; *The First Sex*, 1973

A man who teaches women letters feeds poison to a frightful asp.

MENANDER, *c*.343–291

Violent television programs and films, war toys, and even some sports provide boys and men with detailed role models of violence, and help desensitize them to the suffering of others.

MYRIAM MIEDZIAN; *Boys Will Be Boys*, 1991

When students come to learn about economics or sociology (or language, literature, education, psychology, philosophy, political science, anthropology, science) they are taught about men, and men's view of the world, and this is a lesson in male supremacy.

DALE SPENDER; *Invisible Women*, 1982

Men hate learned women.

(ALFRED) TENNYSON; *The Princess*, 1847

Physically, these universities are ordered for men or unwomaned women. They are overhung with oil paintings of men; engraved with the rolling names of men; designed, like the Yale Club in New York, which for twenty years after women were admitted had no women's changing room, for men.

NAOMI WOLF; *The Beauty Myth*, 1990

MENS SANA IN CORPORE SANO

It was agreed that intercollegiate sports were a proper extension of physical education and the physical education was an important adjunct to moral education. Those whose knowledge of Latin had dwindled away to the amo-amas-amat level were nonetheless able to rise to their feet and quote Juvenal: mens sana in corpore sano.

ALLEN GUTTMANN; *A Whole New Ball Game*, 1988

We should pray for a sound mind in a sound body.

(DECIMUS JUNIUS) JUVENAL(IS), *c.*60–140

Mens sana in corpore sano is a foolish saying. The sound body is the product of the sound mind.

GEORGE BERNARD SHAW, 1856–1950
[Nowhere in the original Latin paragraph, found in Juvenal's
Satires X, is there a reference to sport or calisthenics, which
proponents wrongly attribute. Juvenal said a sound
body is best derived from hard labour.]

METAPHYSICS

Metaphysics is the science of proving what we don't understand.

JOSH BILLINGS (pseud. of HENRY WHEELER SHAW),
1818–1885

The attempt of the mind to rise above the mind.

THOMAS CARLYLE, 1795–1881

[M]etaphysics (which gets into so much trouble because it is not, like the other forms of philosophy, an attempt to coordinate the real in the light of the ideal) is the study of the "ultimate reality" of all things: of the real and final nature of "matter" (ontology), of "mind" (philosophical psychology), and of the interrelation of "mind" and "matter" in the processes of perception and knowledge (epistemology).

WILL(IAM) (JAMES) DURANT; *The Story of Philosophy*, 1926

Metaphysics is almost always an attempt to prove the incredible by an appeal to the unintelligible.

H(ENRY) L(OUIS) MENCKEN, 1880–1956

Education cannot help us as long as it accords no place to metaphysics. Whether the subjects taught are subjects of science or of the humanities, if the teaching does not lead to a clarification of metaphysics, that is to say, of our fundamental convictions, it cannot educate a man and, consequently, cannot be of real value to society.

E(RNST) F(RIEDRICH) SCHUMACHER; *Small is Beautiful*, 1973

MIND

The mind is an iceberg it floats with only one seventh of its bulk above water.

(SIGMUND) FREUD, 1856–1939

There is no monster more destructive than the inventive mind that has outstripped philosophy.

ELLEN GLASGOW; *Letters of Ellen Glasgow*, 1958

The remarkable thing about the human mind is its range of limitations.

CELIA GREEN; *The Decline and Fall of Science*, 1977

A man's mind stretched by a new idea can never go back to its original dimensions.

OLIVER WENDELL HOLMES, 1841–1935

[T]he mind is capable of erecting barriers far stronger than any physical fence.

SUSAN KAY; *Phantom*, 1990

Mind is ever the ruler of the universe.

PLATO (né ARISTOCLES), *c.*428–*c.*348

We must form our minds by reading deep rather than wide.

(MARCUS FABIUS) QUINTILIAN(US), *c.*35–*c.*95

The human mind is a magnificent force. When thought breaks open, even for a second, incredible power is released.

DARLENE L. STEWART; *Creating the Teachable Moment*, 1993

MINDLESS

What I'm concerned about is the people who don't dwell on the meaninglessness of their lives, or the meaningfulness of it – who just pursue mindless entertainment.

MICHAEL K. HOOKER; *Christian Science Monitor*, 1 Oct. 1986

The problem is that schools, as they are presently organized, breed mindlessness.

PHILLIP C. SCHLECHTY; *Schools for the 21st Century*, 1991

MINORITIES

Although minority activists dominate race relations on [the American] campus their original troubles began in the classroom, and it is to the classroom that their political energy ultimately returns.

DINESH D'SOUZA; *Illiberal Education*, 1992

Some of the most common institutional practices of schooling actually retard the development of children and act to handicap minorities and the poor further.

MARGARET DIANE LECOMPTE & ANTHONY GARY DWORKIN;
Giving Up on School, 1991

The research on the attitudes of the dominant group towards the visible minorities is quite clear, with increasing findings that negative attitudes towards the visible minorities are increasing and widespread.

SUBHAS RAMCHARAN; *Racism*, 1982

Tragically, the [test] scores and the educational establishment's real attitude toward minorities reinforces the lingering sense of inferiority that most minority students are afflicted with.

NATHAN RUTSTEIN; *Education on Trial*, 1992

MISFORTUNE

Of all the causes of misfortune in human life, there is nothing more pathetic than lack of knowledge and lack of reasoning power.

EIICHI KIYOOKA; *Fukuzawa Yukichi on Education,* 1985

MORALS

Everything's got a moral, if only you can find it.
LEWIS CARROLL (pseud. of CHARLES LUTWIDGE DODGSON),
1832–1898

Morality: walking like others upon the path.
CHAUANG-TZU, c.300–c.200

It can do truth no service to blink the fact, known to all who have the most ordinary acquaintance with literary history, that a large portion of the noblest and most valuable moral teachings has been the work, not only of men who did not know, but of men who knew and rejected the Christian faith.
JOHN STUART MILL; On Liberty, 1859

Vice is ignorance. Virtue is knowledge.
PLATO (né ARISTOCLES), c.428–c.348

To educate a man in mind and not in morals is to educate a menace to society.
THEODORE ROOSEVELT, 1858–1919

Nowadays it seems that moral education is no longer considered necessary. Attention is wholly centered on intelligence, while the heart life is ignored.
GEORGE SAND (pseud. of AMANDINE AURORE LUCIE DUPIN),
1804–1876

Schools discourage children from maturing socially by surrounding them with evidence that they are powerless and ignorant, and by enforcing on them a code of petty restrictions. These often have no value beyond the control which they enable teachers and other adults to exert over youngsters. Generally they have no moral content whatever.
CHRIS SHUTE; Compulsory Schooling Disease, 1993

Moral codes have suffered from the exaggerated claims made for them.
ALFRED NORTH WHITEHEAD; Adventures of Ideas, 1933

The defence of morals is the battle-cry which best rallies stupidity against change.
ALFRED NORTH WHITEHEAD; Adventures of Ideas, 1933

MOTHER

It is time for the voice of the mother to be heard in education.

NEL NODDINGS; *Caring*, 1984

I put the relation of a fine teacher to a student below the relation of a mother to a son, and I don't think I should say more than this.

T(H)OM(AS) (CLAYTON) WOLFE, 1900–1938

MOTIVATION

People pursue excellence and strive for improvement because they believe in what they are doing.

PHILLIP C. SCHLECHTY; *Schools for the 21st Century*, 1991

In order to understand why people do what they do, and certainly in order to change what people do, psychologists must turn away from the theory of the causal nature of the inner dynamic and look at the social context within which individuals live.

NAOMI WEISSTEIN;
an *address* (American Studies Association), 26 Oct. 1968

MULTICULTURALISM

Attitudes to multiculturalism in schools depend, in large measure, on attitudes in society in general.

ROBIN BARROW & GEOFFREY MILBURN;
A Critical Dictionary of Educational Concepts, 1986

MULTIVERSITY

What is the justification of the modern American multiversity?

DEREK BOK; *Beyond the Ivory Tower*, 1982

The "Idea of a University" was a village with its priests. The "Idea of a Modern University" was a town – a one-industry town – with its intellectual oligarchy. "The Idea of a Multiversity" is a city of infinite variety. Some get lost in the city; some rise to the top within it; most fashion their lives within one of its many subcultures. There is less sense of community than in the village but also less sense of confinement.

CLARK KERR; *The Uses of the University*, 1963

MUSES

Each of the Arts whose office it is to refine, purify, adorn, embellish and grace life is under the patronage of a Muse, no god being found worthy to preside over them.

ELIZA W. FARNHAM; *Woman and Her Era*, 1864

In later times each had her own special field. Clio was Muse of history, Urania of astronomy, Melpomene of tragedy, Thalia of comedy, Terpsichore of the dance, Calliope of epic poetry, Erato of love poetry, Polyhymnia of song to the gods, Euterpe of lyric poetry.

EDITH HAMILTON; *Mythology*, 1942

To the Greeks the Muse gave native wit, to the Greeks the gift of graceful eloquence.

(QUINTUS HORATIUS FLACCUS) HORACE, 65–8

MUSIC

Music is a higher revelation than philosophy.

(LUDWIG VAN) BEETHOVEN, 1770–1827

Music produces a kind of pleasure which human nature cannot do without.

CONFUCIUS (Latin for K'UNG FU-TZU), 551–479

After silence, that which comes nearest to expressing the inexpressible is music.

ALDOUS HUXLEY, *Music at Night*, 1931

Music is one family but the word is the thing. Words can teach the children something. It is something really serious, not entertainment.

BOB (ROBERT NESTA) MARLEY, 1945–1981

Without music life would be a mistake.
(FRIEDRICH WILHELM) NIETZSCHE, 1844–1900

MUSICOLOGIST

A musicologist is a man who can read music but cannot hear it.
THOMAS BEECHAM, 1879–1961

MYTH

In the nineteenth century universal education put an end to the myth of parental omniscience by making obvious the inability of some fathers to follow their children's studies, or even to explain their home world to them. The father had to confess that "he didn't know."
ELISABETH BADINTER; *The Myth of Motherhood*, 1981

You cannot really understand any myths till you have found out that one of them is not a myth.
G(ILBERT) K(EITH) CHESTERTON, 1874–1936

A myth is a fixed way of looking at the world which cannot be destroyed because, looked at through the myth, all evidence supports that myth.
EDWARD DE BONO, 1933–

Only the fortunate can take life without mythology.
WILL(IAM) (JAMES) DURANT & ARIEL DURANT;
The Story of Civilization (vol. VII), 1961

Myths are early science, the result of men's first trying to explain what they saw around them.
EDITH HAMILTON; *Mythology*, 1942

Unanswered questions are like open wounds. They demand our attention. A myth or a magic explanation is like a balm, a dressing that allows us to attend to other things.
ERICH HARTH; *Dawn of a Millennium*, 1990

The great enemy of truth is very often not the lie – deliberate, contrived, and dishonest – but the myth – persuasive and unrealistic.

JOHN F. KENNEDY, 1917–1963

When myth meets myth, the collision is very real.

STANISLAW LEC; *Unkempt Thoughts*, 1962

Schools are, in fact, operating on the basis of cultural myths, not real assessments of what students think and are like and how schools and society are linked.

MARGARET DIANE LECOMPTE & ANTHONY GARY DWORKIN;
Giving Up on School, 1991

Myths are fantasies shared by a whole culture.

ROBERT MAY; *Sex and Fantasy*, 1980

Contemporary man has rationalised the myths, but he has not been able to destroy them.

OCTAVIO PAZ, 1914–

[I]n many cultures the distinction between history and mythology has been acknowledged only with considerable hesitation.

ROBERT SOLOMON & JON SOLOMON;
Up the University, 1993

N

NATURAL SCIENCE

If, therefore, a man seeks education because he feels estranged and bewildered, because his life seems to him empty and meaningless, he cannot get what he is seeking by studying any of the natural sciences, i.e. by acquiring "know how". That study has its own value which I am not inclined to belittle; it tells him a great deal about how things work in nature or in engineering: but it tells him nothing about the meaning of life and can in no way cure his estrangement and secret despair.

E(RNST) F(RIEDRICH) SCHUMACHER; *Small is Beautiful*, 1973

NATURE

Nature gives the child no lines, she only gives him things, and lines must be given him only in order that he may perceive things rightly. The things must not be taken from him in order that he may see only lines.

(JOHANN HEINRICH) PESTALOZZI; *How Gertrude Teaches Her Children*, 1907

Nature without learning is blind, learning apart from nature is fractional, and practice in the absence of both is aimless.

(PLOUTARCHOS) PLUTARCH; *Of the Education of Children*, c.100

Nature is the raw material for education.

(MARCUS FABIUS) QUINTILIAN(US), c.35–c.95

We still have to learn how to live peacefully, not only with our fellow men but also with nature.

E(RNST) F(RIEDRICH) SCHUMACHER; *Small is Beautiful*, 1973

Come forth into the light of things, let Nature be your Teacher.

WILLIAM WORDSWORTH, 1770–1850

NEW

As I have emphasized more than once, the road of the new education is not an easier one to follow than the old road but a more strenuous and difficult one.

JOHN DEWEY; *Experience and Education*, 1938

I grow old learning something new every day.

SOLON, 636?–558?

NEW AGE

A candidate for a teaching position should have a new age view of the world.

NATHAN RUTSTEIN; *Education on Trial*, 1992

NOTHING

Man can learn nothing except by going from the known to the unknown.

CLAUDE BERNARD, 1813–1878

There is nothing so absurd but some philosopher has said it.

(MARCUS TULLIUS) CICERO, 106–43

Driven by our obsession to compete, we have embraced the electronic god with a frenzy. Soon, blessed with fax, voice- and E-mail, computer hook-ups and television sets with hundreds of channels, we won't have to leave our lonely rooms – not to write a check, work, visit, shop, exercise or make love. We will have raced at incredible speeds to reach our final destination – nothing.

BILL HENDERSON;
International Herald Tribune, 17 Mar. 1994

Do nothing you do not understand.

PYTHAGORAS, *c*.600–*c*.500BC

There is nothing either good or bad, but thinking makes it so.

WILLIAM SHAKESPEARE; *Hamlet*, 1600–01

They have learned nothing, and forgotten nothing.

(CHARLES MAURICE DE) TALLEYRAND(-PÉRIGORD), 1754–1838

Nothing ever comes to one, that is worth having, except as a result of hard work.

BOOKER T. WASHINGTON; *Up from Slavery*, 1901

NUMBER

We are in the grips of the symbol processors and the number crunchers.

PHILIP J. DAVIS & REUBEN HERSH; *Descartes' Dream*, 1986

The concept of number is the obvious distinction between the beast and man. Thanks to number, the cry becomes song, noise acquires rhythm, the spring is transformed into a dance, force becomes dynamic, and outlines figure.

JOSEPH MARIE DE MAISTRE, 1753–1821

Until the phenomena of any branch of knowledge have been submitted to measurement and number, it cannot assume the status and dignity of science.

FRANCIS GALTON, 1822–1911

Over the years the variety of ways children are numbered by schools has increased dramatically, until it is hard to see the human beings plainly under the weight of numbers they carry.

JOHN TAYLOR GATTO; *Dumbing Us Down*, 1992

The mystique of science proclaims that numbers are the ultimate test of objectivity.

STEPHEN JAY GOULD; *The Mismeasure of Man*, 1981

The zero is one of the most brilliant manifestations of human intelligence, almost as important as the discovery of fire.

GEORGES IFRAH; *International Herald Tribune*, 26 Sep. 1994

Tell me not, in mournful numbers,
Life is but an empty dream!
For the soul is dead that slumbers,
And things are not what they seem.

HENRY WADSWORTH LONGFELLOW; *A Psalm of Life*, 1839

[E]ducators find it quite impossible to do their work without numbers. They believe that without numbers they cannot acquire or express authentic knowledge.

NEIL POSTMAN; *Technopoly*, 1993

Numbers constitute the only universal language.

NATHANIEL WEST; *Miss Lonelyhearts*, 1933

Numbers are often not as important as they seem.

RICHARD SAUL WURMAN; *Information Anxiety*, 1991

O

OBEDIENCE

Despite our rich literature of freedom, a pervasive value instilled in our society is obedience to authority. Unquestioning obedience is perceived to be in the best interests of the schools, churches, families, and political institutions. Nationalism, patriotism, and religious ardor are its psychological vehicles.

SARAH J. McCARTHY, 1942–

I have thought about it a great deal, and the more I think the more certain I am that obedience is the gateway through which knowledge, yes, and love, too, enter the mind of the child.

ANNIE SULLIVAN, 1866–1936

OLD

Never too old to learn.

ENGLISH proverb

OPINION

The man who never alters his opinion is like standing water, and breeds reptiles of the mind.

WILLIAM BLAKE, 1757–1827

I never oppose the opinions of any; but I must own [admit] that I never adopt them to the prejudice of my own.

CHARLOTTE BREGY, 1619?–1693

New opinions are always suspected, and usually opposed, without any other reason but because they are not already common.

JOHN LOCKE;
An Essay Concerning Human Understanding, 1690

P

PAIN

We cannot learn without pain.

ARISTOTLE, 384–322

One of the greatest pains to human nature is the pain of a new idea.

WALTER BAGEHOT, 1826–1877

Learning is such a very painful business. It requires humility from people at an age where the natural habitat is arrogance.

MAY SARTON; *The Small Room*, 1961

The capacity for feeling pain increases with knowledge.

ARTHUR SCHOPENHAUER, 1788 1860

PARADOX

It's just impossible for education and schooling ever to be the same thing.

JOHN TAYLOR GATTO; *Dumbing Us Down*, 1992

All over the world the school has an anti-educational effect on society.

IVAN ILLICH; *Deschooling Society*, 1971

We are faced with the paradoxical fact that education has become one of the chief obstacles to intelligence and freedom of thought.

BERTRAND RUSSELL, 1872–1970

Yet, paradoxically, despite a failure to agree about what education should aim for, what it should actually *do*, everyone seems to be certain both that it should do *something*, and that it is not doing it.

MARY WARNOCK; *A Common Policy for Education*, 1988

PARENT

Parents will be well aware that mathematics and foreign languages have a tendency to arouse either an intense liking or an intense disliking.

R.R. DALE & S. GRIFFITHS; *Down Stream*, 1965

Parents give birth to children easily enough, but they do not know the principles of educating them.
YUKICHI FUKUZAWA; An Encouragement of Learning, 1969

For the first time in the history of the country, the educational skills of one generation will not surpass, will not equal, will not even approach those of their parents.
DAVID P. GARDNER; in A Nation at Risk, 1983

The only reason I always try to meet and know the parents is because it helps me to forgive their children.
ROBERT M. HUTCHINS; Life, 7 May 1965

Parents who expect gratitude from their children (there are even some who insist on it) are like usurers who gladly risk their capital if only they receive interest.
(FRANZ) KAFKA, 1883–1924

They fuck you up, your mum and dad
They may not mean to, but they do
They fill you with the faults they had
And add some extra, just for you.
PHILIP LARKIN, 1922–1985

Summerhill never turned any child against its parents; the turning took place long before the child came to school. Parents never realise that they lose the love of their children by their own wrong methods – punishment, nagging, prohibitions, sex suppression, yes, and lying to them.
A(LEXANDER) S(UTHERLAND) NEILL;
Talking on Summerhill, 1971

Parents in their turn desperately hope to be known as "good" parents. . . . "[G]ood" parents are generally assumed to be the ones who tolerate no dissent or disrespect from their children, and who have no difficulty in making them obey. . . . I am speaking of the truth that in our Western society child abuse is not an isolated aberration: it is normal.
CHRIS SHUTE; Compulsory Schooling Disease, 1993

Too many parents blindly demand careers for their children and view the university as a trade school and their children's education as an investment. . . . We teach too many students who should not be in school but feel coerced into being there because their parents are sure that sending their kids to college is the right thing to do.

ROBERT SOLOMON & JON SOLOMON;
Up the University, 1993

Parents learn a lot from children about coping with life.

MURIEL SPARK; *The Comforters*, 1957

PART-TIME

Part-timers have the disadvantage also that they usually do not become part of the academic community.

HOWARD R. BOWEN & JACK H. SCHUSTER;
American Professors, 1986

Part-time faculty operate under unfavorable conditions....

ERNEST L. BOYER; *College*, 1987

Part-timers ... have complicated schedules, they work and have family obligations – and yet, orientation activities and even college office hours often are not arranged conveniently for them.

ERNEST L. BOYER; *College*, 1987

Part-time study is not recognized as a distinguishable mode in some countries although students often work whilst studying, thus lengthening their course.

DEPARTMENT OF EDUCATION & SCIENCE;
International Statistical Comparisons in Higher Education, 1987

PASSION

Only the passions, only great passions, can elevate the mind to great things.

DENIS DIDEROT, 1713–1784

I have noticed that most of those who in school formulate the subtlest precepts of moderation and self-mastery themselves indulge in every kind of unbridled passion.

CORNELIUS NEPOS, *c*.99–25

The ruling passion, be it what it will,
The ruling passion conquers reason still.

ALEXANDER POPE; *Moral Essays*, 1735

PATIENCE

The educator must above all understand how to wait; to reckon all effects in the light of the future, not of the present.

ELLEN KEY (pseud. of KAROLINA SOFIA KEY);
The Morality of Women and Other Essays, 1911

[P]arents need not be in too great haste to see their children's talents forced into bloom. Let them watch and wait patiently, letting good example and quiet training do their work, and leave the rest to Providence.

SAMUEL SMILES, 1812–1904

Hateful is a teacher without patience.

WELSH proverb

PEDAGOGY

Nothing is more tiresome than a superannuated pedagogue.

HENRY (BROOKS) ADAMS;
The Education of Henry Adams, 1907

No pedagogy which is truly liberating can remain distant from the oppressed by treating them as unfortunates and by presenting for their emulation models from among the oppressors.

PAULO FREIRE; *Pedagogy of the Oppressed*, 1972

Pedagogy as a science is based on ethics and on psychology. The former points out the aim of culture, the latter the way, the means and the obstacles.

(JOHANN FRIEDRICH) HERBART, 1776–1841

PEN

Scholars are men of peace, they bear no arms, but their tongues are sharper than Actius and his razor, their pens carry farther and give a louder report than thunder; I had rather stand in the shock of a basilico* than in the fury of a merciless pen.

> THOMAS BROWNE; *Religio medici*, 1643
> [*a large cannon]

How much more cruel the pen may be than the sword.

> ROBERT BURTON; *The Anatomy of Melancholy*, 1621–1652

Clarity is the supreme politeness of him who wields a pen.

> JEAN HENRI FABRE, 1823–1915

My two fingers on a typewriter have never connected with my brain. My hand on a pen does. A fountain pen, of course.

> GRAHAM GREENE; *International Herald Tribune*, 7 Oct. 1977

When once the itch of literature comes over a man, nothing can cure it but the scratching of a pen.

> SAMUEL LOVER, 1797–1868

The pen is mightier than the sword.

> (EDWARD GEORGE BULWER-)LYTTON; *Richelieu*, 1839

To hold a pen is to be at war.

> VOLTAIRE (né FRANÇOIS MARIE AROUET), 1694–1778

PEOPLE

Most people acquire most of their knowledge outside school.

> IVAN ILLICH; *Deschooling Society*, 1971

The more heterogeneous people are, the more difficult it is for them to agree on educational issues. The more difficult it is to agree on educational issues, the stronger the pressure to move away from a system of majoritarian control of education.

MYRON LIEBERMAN; *Public Education*, 1993

[M]ost people prefer to carry out the kinds of experiments that allow the scientist to feel that he is in full control of the situation rather than surrendering himself to the situation, as one must in studying human beings as they actually live.

MARGARET MEAD; *Blackberry Winter*, 1972

For the crowd, the incredible has sometimes more power and is more credible than Truth.

MENANDER, *c.*343–291

Education makes a people easy to lead, but difficult to drive; easy to govern but impossible to enslave.

HENRY PETER; *The Present State of the Law*, 1828

People within schools (as elsewhere) are unwittingly victims of causal processes that *exercise power* over them.

JOHN SMYTH; *Teachers as Collaborative Learners*, 1991

PERFECTION

Let knowledge stop at the unknowable. That is perfection.

CHAUANG-TZU, *c.*300–*c.*200

The desire of perfection is the worst disease that ever afflicted the human mind.

(LOUIS MARQUIS DE) FONTANES, 1757–1821

To stand still on the summit of perfection is difficult, and in the natural course of things, what cannot go forward slips back.

(GAIS VELLEIUS) PATERCULUS, 20BC–AD30

PhD (Philosophiae Doctor)

Today there is a ritual abuse of Ph.D. students.

MARTIN ANDERSON; *Imposters in the Temple*, 1992

[A] drastic reform of the Ph.D. is called for.

CARROLL ATKINSON;
*True Confessions of a Ph.D. and Recommendations
for Reform*, 1939

The prominent American humanist Irving Babbitt argued that the Ph.D. degree led to a loss of balance. He complained about the "maiming and mutilation of the mind that comes from over absorption in one subject".

ERNEST L. BOYER; *Scholarship Revisited*, 1990

It is sometimes necessary to remind a Ph.D. candidate that the degree that he is seeking is in philosophy and that he is not a candidate for the degree of doctor of the development of the vowels of accented syllables in some little-known dialect, or whatever may be the subject of his thesis.

G(EORGE) LESLIE BROOK; *The Modern University*, 1965

I contend that the [Ph.D.] degree, now the pinnacle of university education in the major English-speaking nations, is a seriously flawed academic institution.

WILFRED CUDE; *The Ph.D. Trap*, 1987

[T]here are many negative views of the Ph.D [sic] as a training device to do original research or to become a skilled writer. The period of preparing a PhD is too long, it inhibits creativity, it is too specialized or tries to cover a too broad field.

PJOTR HESSELING; *Frontiers of Learning*, 1986

No answers have been found to the widespread and well-documented problems of failure, drop-out and low morale amongst PhD students.

PHILLIDA SALMON; *Achieving a PhD*, 1992

You are not yet aware of the excruciating self-tortures Ph.D. students go through. . . .

MAY SARTON; *The Small Room*, 1961

I will spare the reader further recounting of the inanities (and horrors) of the Ph.D. – the oral "qualifying exam," the rejected dissertation, the lost dissertation, the delayed dissertation. It is all too grim for words. In any event, that the Ph.D. is an incubus on higher education can, I assume, hardly be doubted.

PAGE SMITH; *Killing the Spirit*, 1990

Real severity enters with the PhD.

C(HARLES) P(ERCY) SNOW;
The Two Cultures and the Scientific Revolution, 1961

Ph.D. programs are not designed to prepare the holders for the profession of teaching that so many of them enter.

RICHARD F. STORR; *The Beginning of the Future*, 1973

[T]here is no real consensus on what a PhD is.

SIMEON UNDERWOOD;
The Times Higher Education Supplement, 15 Apr. 1994

PHILOSOPHER

The philosopher is the cartographer of human life.

RENÉ DAUMAL; *A Night of Serious Drinking*, 1980

Be a philosopher; but amidst all your philosophy, be still a man.

DAVID HUME;
An Enquiry Concerning Human Understanding, 1748

A philosopher is one who doubts.

(MICHEL EYQUEM DE) MONTAIGNE, 1533–1592

A great memory does not make a philosopher, anymore than a dictionary can be called grammar.

JOHN HENRY NEWMAN; *The Idea of a University*, 1853

Philosopher: a lover of wisdom, which is to say, truth.

VOLTAIRE (né FRANÇOIS MARIE AROUET), 1694–1778

PHILOSOPHIZE

To philosophize is to doubt.

(MICHEL EYQUEM DE) MONTAIGNE, 1533–1592

PHILOSOPHY

Philosophy means, first, doubt; and afterwards the consciousness of what knowledge means, the consciousness of uncertainty and of ignorance, the consciousness of limit, shade, degree, possibility. The ordinary man doubts nothing and suspects nothing.

HENRI FREDERIC AMIEL, 1821–1881

It is right also that philosophy should be called knowledge of the truth.

ARISTOTLE, 384–322

Philosophy, n[oun]. A route of many roads leading from nowhere to nothing.

AMBROSE BIERCE; *The Devil's Dictionary*, 1911

He is a fool that has nothing of philosophy in him, but not so much as he that has nothing but philosophy in him.

SAMUEL BUTLER; *Prose Observations*, 1660–1680

A little philosophy tends to despise learning; much philosophy leads men to esteem it.

(NICOLAS SÉBASTIAN ROCH) CHAMFORT;
Maximes et Pensées, 1796

Philosophy, like medicine, has many drugs, very few good remedies, and almost no specifics.

(NICOLAS SÉBASTIAN ROCH) CHAMFORT;
Maximes et Pensées, 1796

Philosophy is the best medicine for the mind.

(MARCUS TULLIUS) CICERO, 106–43

Philosophy removes from religion all reason for existing.

BENEDETTO CROCE, 1866–1952

The first step toward philosophy is doubt.

DENIS DIDEROT; *Last Conversation*, 1784

The prevailing philosophy of education tends to discredit hard work.

ABRAHAM FLEXNER; *Universities*, 1930

Philosophy is at once the most sublime and the most trivial of human pursuits.

WILLIAM JAMES; *Pragmatism*, 1907

Philosophy will clip an angel's wings.

JOHN KEATS; *Lamia*, 1820

A philosophy is characterized more by the formulation of its problems than by its solution of them.

SUSANNE K. LANGER; *Philosophy in a New Key*, 1942

Wonder is the foundation of all philosophy, inquiry its progress, ignorance its end.

(MICHEL EYQUEM DE) MONTAIGNE; *Essays*, 1580–1595

No matter how this may shock mankind, the duty of philosophy is to say everything.

(DONATIEN ALPHONSE FRANÇOIS COMTE DE) SADE;
Histoire de Juliette, ou les Prospérités du vice, 1797

There are more things in heaven and earth, Horatio,
Than are dreamt of in your philosophy.

WILLIAM SHAKESPEARE; *Hamlet*, 1600–01

I do not know how to teach philosophy without becoming a disturber of the peace.

(BARUCH) SPINOZA, 1632–1677

I think in no country in the civilized world is less attention paid to philosophy than in the United States.

(ALEXIS CHARLES HENRI MAURICE CLÉREL DE) TOCQUEVILLE;
Democracy in America, 1835

Philosophy asks the simple question, What is it all about?

ALFRED NORTH WHITEHEAD, 1861–1947

The object of philosophy is the logical clarification of thought.

(LUDWIG JOSEF JOHANN) WITTGENSTEIN;
Tractatus Logico-Philosophicus, 1922

PHYSICAL EDUCATION

Society feels that sport must be justified, and we have gotten away from the Greek concept of mind and body. That is a failure of the physical education process.

OLGA CONNOLLY; *Los Angeles Times*, 23 Apr. 1974

PHYSICIAN

Physician, heal thyself. . . .

The Bible (Luke: 4,23)

The essential principles of health are not understood by the people . . . and, alas! not by all our physicians, who as a rule have been educated to cure disease, not to prevent it. Too many have been taught to fight Nature's Laws, not stand by . . . as her adjutant.

ELLEN SWALLOW, 1850?–1911

PHYSICIST

The physicists have known sin; and this is a knowledge which they cannot lose.

J. ROBERT OPPENHEIMER, 1904–1967

PLAGIARISM

Plagiarize, v[erb]. To take the thought or style of another writer whom one has never, never read.

AMBROSE BIERCE; *The Devil's Dictionary*, 1911

If we steal thoughts from the moderns, it will be cried down as plagiarism; if from the ancients, it will be cried up as erudition.

C(HARLES) C(ALEB) COLTON; *Lacon*, 1825

[H]e [Pliny, 23–79] notes, in passing, that he found many authors transcribing their predecessors word for word without acknowledgement.

WILL(IAM) (JAMES) DURANT;
The Story of Civilization (vol. III), 1944

When a thing has been said and said well, have no scruple. Take it and copy it.

> ANATOLE FRANCE (pseud. of ANATOLE FRANÇOIS THIBAULT),
> 1844–1924

Plagiarism of students' work by professors has prompted the introduction of copyright protection laws in several Spanish universities.

> HARVEY McGAVIN;
> *The Times Higher Education Supplement*, 18 Mar. 1994

Plagiarism is dishonest, stupid and dangerous.

> CELIA MILLWARD & JANE FLICK;
> *Handbook for Writers*, 1985

When you take stuff from one writer, it's plagiarism; but when you take it from many writers, it's research.

> WILSON MIZNER, 1876–1933

Taking something from one man and making it worse is plagiarism.

> GEORGE MOORE, 1852–1933

Theft* from graduate students is the great unspoken scandal of academia.

> RICHARD W. MOORE; *Winning the Ph.D. Game*, 1985
> [* plagiarism by academics]

It is a mean thief, or a successful author that plunders the dead.

> AUSTIN O'MALLEY, 1858–1932

Most writers steal a good thing when they can.

> BRYAN WALLER PROCTOR, 1787–1874

Whatever is well said by another, is mine.

> (LUCIUS ANNAEUS) SENECA (the Younger), c.4BC–65

More than 40 percent of faculty in civil engineering and sociology have detected plagiarism among their graduate students. In civil engineering, 18 percent of faculty have noted plagiarism by their colleagues, a significantly higher proportion than in the other fields.

> JUDITH P. SWAZEY, MELISSA S. ANDERSON & SEASHORE LEWIS;
> *American Scientist*, vol. 81, 1993

Immature artists imitate. Mature artists steal.

LIONEL TRILLING; *Esquire*, Sep. 1962

PLATO

Plato is dear to me, but dearer is truth.

ARISTOTLE, 384–322

PLAY

You can do anything with children if you play with them.

(OTTO EDWARD LEOPOLD VON) BISMARCK, 1815–1898

[Play is] the highest phase of child-development – of human development at this period; for it is self-active representation of the inner – representation of the inner from inner necessity and impulse. Play is the purest, most spiritual activity of man at this stage, and, at the same time, typical of human life as a whole – of the inner hidden natural life in man and all things. It gives, therefore, joy, freedom, contentment, inner and outer rest, peace with the world. It holds the source of all that is good.

(FRIEDRICH) FROEBEL, 1782–1852

It should be noted that children's games are not merely games; one should regard them as their most serious activities.

(MICHEL EYQUEM DE) MONTAIGNE, 1533–1592

The idea that children's games are not the business of adults has clearly been rejected by Americans, who are insisting that even at age six, children play their games without spontaneity, under careful supervision, and at an intense competitive level.

NEIL POSTMAN; *The Disappearance of Childhood*, 1994

Work or play are all one to him; his games are his work; he knows no difference.

(JEAN JACQUES) ROUSSEAU, 1712–1778

PLEASURE

The pleasure and delight of knowledge and learning, it far surpasseth all other in nature.

FRANCIS BACON; *Advancement of Learning*, 1605

The test and the use of man's education is that he finds pleasure in the exercise of his mind.

JACQUES BARZUN; *Saturday Evening Post*, 3 May 1958

POEM

Verse is not written, it is bled;
Out of the poet's abstract head.
Words drip the poem on the page;
Out of grief, delight and rage.

PAUL ENGLE; *A Woman Unashamed and Other Poems*, 1965

No poems can please long, nor live, which are written by water drinkers.

(QUINTUS HORATIUS FLACCUS) HORACE, 65–8

Poem me no poems.

ROSE MACAULAY, 1881–1958

It is easier to write a mediocre poem than to understand a good one.

(MICHEL EYQUEM DE) MONTAIGNE, 1533–1592

The few bad poems which occasionally are created during abstinence are of no great interest.

WILHELM REICH, 1897–1957

POET

A taste of drawing-rooms has spoiled more poets than ever did a taste of gutters.

THOMAS BEER, 1889–1940

A famous poet is a discoverer, rather than an inventor.
JORGE LUIS BORGES, 1899–1986

Perhaps no person can be a poet, or can even enjoy poetry, without a certain unsoundness of mind.
THOMAS BABINGTON MACAULAY, 1800–1859

Poets utter great and wise things which they do not themselves understand.
PLATO (né ARISTOCLES), *c.*428–*c.*348

He who draws noble delights from the sentiments of poetry is a true poet, though he has never written a line in all his life.
GEORGE SAND (pseud. of AMANDINE AURORE LUCIE DUPIN),
1804–1876

Poets are the unacknowledged legislators of the world.
PERCY BYSSHE SHELLEY, 1792–1822

The poet is the priest of the invisible.
WALLACE STEVENS; *Opus Posthumous*, 1957

Who shall measure the heat and violence of the poet's heart when caught and tangled in a woman's body.
VIRGINIA WOOLF, 1882–1941

POETRY

Poetry is finer and more philosophical than history; for poetry expresses the universal and history only the particular.
ARISTOTLE, 384–322

It takes most men five years to recover from a college education, and to learn that poetry is as vital to thinking as knowledge.
BROOKS ATKINSON; *Once Around the Sun*, 1951

Being a professor of poetry is rather like being a Kentucky colonel. It's not really a subject you can profess – unless one hires oneself out to write pieces for funerals or the marriage of dons.
W(YSTAN) H(UGH) AUDEN, 1907–1973

This loss of self-consciousness is somehow connected with the banishment of poetry.

> ALLAN BLOOM; *The Closing of the American Mind*, 1987

Poetry is life distilled.

> GWENDOLYN BROOKS, 1917–

How poetry comes to the poet is a mystery.

> ELIZABETH DREW, 1887–1965

We read poetry because the poets, like ourselves, have been haunted by the inescapable tyranny of time and death; have suffered the pain of loss, and the more wearing, continuous pain of frustration and failure; and have had moods of unlooked-for release and peace.

> ELIZABETH DREW; *Poetry*, 1959

But the life of poetry lies in fresh relationships between words, in the spontaneous fusion of hitherto unrelated words.

> MARIE GILCHRIST; *Writing Poetry*, 1932

Poetry is what Milton saw when he went blind.

> DON MARQUIS, 1878–1937

[P]oetry, "The Cinderella of the Arts".

> HARRIET MONROE, 1860–1936

Poetry is what makes the invisible appear.

> NATHALIE SARRAUTE (née NATHALIE TCHERNIAK), 1900–

Poetry lifts the veil from the hidden beauty of the world, and makes familiar objects be as if they were not familiar.

> PERCY BYSSHE SHELLEY, 1792–1822

Poetry is the deification of reality.

> EDITH SITWELL, 1887–1964

Poetry is to prose as dancing is to walking.

> JOHN WAIN, 1925–

But the bias against poetry they had picked up, the view of it as a product of unsteady masculinity, was too much even for Yeats to overcome.

ROBERT JAMES WALLER;
The Bridges of Madison County, 1993

Poetry is the spontaneous overflow of powerful feelings: it takes its origin from emotion recollected in tranquillity.

WILLIAM WORDSWORTH, 1770–1850

POLICY

Until very recently, the study of educational policy was virtually monopolized by a tradition of 'administration and management' studies not especially renowned for their theoretical sophistication.

JOHN AHIER; in *Contemporary Education Policy*, 1983

Policy is the product, whether written (laws, reports, regulations), stated or enacted (for example, pedagogic practice), of the outcome of political states of play in various arenas.

GILLIAN FULCHER; *Disabling Policies?*, 1989

Letting a hundred flowers blossom and a hundred schools of thought contend is the policy. . . .

MAO ZEDONG, 1893–1976

Educational policy is a strategy or plan for achieving educational objectives.

NICK TAYLOR;
Democratising the Formation of Policies
for People's Education, 1990

The only nation in the world which, in the eighteenth century, did have a policy for education was Germany, though there was no German state.

HUGH THOMAS; *An Unfinished History of the World*, 1979

POLITICALLY CORRECT

American higher education has succumbed to a new politics of racial and sexual "sensitivity," which now dominates debate on all controversial questions involving race, gender, or sexual orientation.

DINESH D'SOUZA; *Illiberal Education*, 1992

Being "politically correct" is *not* simply a matter of holding certain opinions on various social or educational issues. Political correctness is *imposing those opinions on others* by harassment or punishment for expressing different views.

THOMAS SOWELL; *Inside American Education*, 1993

POSITIVE PHILOSOPHY

The positive philosophy has hitherto intervened to examine both (the theoretical and metaphysical philosophies), and both are abundantly discredited by the process. It is time now to be doing something more effective, without wasting our forces in needless controversy. It is time to complete the vast intellectual operation begun by Bacon, Descartes, and Galileo by constructing the system of general ideas which must henceforth prevail among the human race.

AUGUSTE COMTE; *Cours de philosophie positive*, 1840–2

POWER

Many intellectuals seem to have a barely concealed lust for power, a lust which is rarely sated, a constant source of longing and frustration.

MARTIN ANDERSON; *Imposters in the Temple*, 1992

Knowledge itself is power.

FRANCIS BACON, 1561–1626

He who has knowledge has power.

IRANIAN proverb

PREJUDICE

A great many people think they are thinking when they are rearranging their prejudices.

WILLIAM JAMES, 1842–1910

Prejudices are what fools use for reason.

VOLTAIRE (né FRANÇOIS MARIE AROUET);
Poème sur la vie naturelle, 1756

PRISON

[S]tudents stay inside school buildings in the same way prisoners remain in their cells. Like prisoners, they frequently increase their knowledge of ways to *subvert* the law, but not how to flourish *within* the law. High recidivism rates document former prisoners' difficulties in living within society's rules. Their jail experiences have not helped them deal with life out of jail. Similarly, students who are isolated in school buildings do not learn to live responsibly in society.

RITA S. BRAUSE; *Enduring Schools*, 1992

Education is a dull subject, for we remember it with pain, we do not care to hear about it, and we resist any further imposition of it after we have served our time at school.

WILL(IAM) (JAMES) DURANT & ARIEL DURANT;
The Story of Civilization (vol. X), 1967

The school imprisons children physically, intellectually, and morally, in order to direct the development of their faculties in the paths desired. It deprives them of contact with nature, in order to model them after its own patterns.

FRANCISCO FERRER; *The Modern School, c.*1909

School is a twelve-year jail sentence where bad habits are the only curriculum truly learned.

JOHN TAYLOR GATTO; *Dumbing Us Down*, 1992

It [an individual contract] would change the relationship between the student and the school making it more one of partnership under contract and less one of teacher and child or warder and prisoner.

CHARLES HANDY; *The Age of Unreason*, 1989

There is, on the whole, nothing on earth intended for innocent people so horrible as a school. To begin with, it is a prison. But it is in some respects more cruel than a prison. In a prison, for instance, you are not forced to read books written by the warders and the governor ... and beaten or otherwise tormented if you cannot remember their utterly unmemorable contents.

GEORGE BERNARD SHAW; *Parents and Children*, 1914

[T]hey were not being educated so much as sentenced to hard labour for the crime of being children.

CHRIS SHUTE; *Compulsory Schooling Disease*, 1993

Monday morning found Tom Sawyer miserable. Monday morning always found him so — because it began another week's slow suffering in school. He generally began that day wishing he had had no intervening holiday, it made the going into captivity and fetters again so much more odious.

MARK TWAIN (pseud. of SAMUEL LANGHORNE CLEMENS);
The Adventures of Tom Sawyer, 1876

The founding fathers in their wisdom decided that children were an unnatural strain on parents. So they provided jails called schools, equipped with tortures called education.

JOHN UPDIKE; *The Centaur*, 1963

PRIVATION

There is no education that can surpass privations.

JAPANESE proverb

PROBLEM

[E]xisting [educational] institutions cannot solve the problem, because they *are* the problem.

JOHN E. CHUBB & TERRY M. MOE;
Politics, Markets, and American Schools, 1990

Plasticine and self-expression will not solve the problems of education. Nor will technology and vocational guidance; nor the classics and the Hundred Best Books.

ALDOUS HUXLEY, 1894–1963

You are the problem.

(FRANZ) KAFKA, 1883–1924

A common error in analysis is the assumption that education is a relatively simple problem and that a simple solution, recognized by all sensible people, exists.

ROLAND MEIGHAN;
Theory and Practice of Regressive Education, 1993

For every problem there is an immediate and obvious solution that is wrong.

H(ENRY) L(OUIS) MENCKEN, 1880–1956

Fixing the school system is our most important problem.

JOHN R. OPEL, 1925–

Blaming social problems outside the school for academic shortcomings inside the school has become a common tactic of educators.

THOMAS SOWELL; *Inside American Education*, 1993

PROCESS

The result of the educative process is capacity for further education.

JOHN DEWEY, 1859–1952

Education, therefore, is primarily a process of living and not a preparation for future living.

JOHN DEWEY; *My Pedagogic Creed*, 1897

Our educational processes are in fact the upcoming major world industry.

R(ICHARD) BUCKMINSTER FULLER;
R. Buckminster Fuller on Education, 1979

Education is not a product: mark, diploma, job, money – in that order; it is a process, a never-ending one.

BEL KAUFMAN, *c.*1940–

There is now a good deal of research evidence to suggest that the more time and effort students invest in the learning process and the more intensely they engage in their own education, the greater will be their growth and achievement, their satisfaction with their educational experiences, and their persistence in college, and the more likely they are to continue their learning.

NATIONAL INSTITUTE OF EDUCATION;
Involvement in Learning, 1984

Process focuses on how something happens rather than on the outcome or results obtained.

MICHAEL QUINN PATTON;
Qualitative Evaluation and Research Methods, 1990

I am convinced that it is of primordial importance to learn more than the year before. After all, what is education but a process by which a person begins to learn how to learn.

PETER USTINOV, 1921–

PRODUCT

Schools see their students as their products.

CHARLES HANDY; *The Age of Unreason*, 1989

Modern industrial societies are obsessed with schooling. Children are processed en masse into standardized products of the education machine.

LIBERTARIAN EDUCATION; *Freedom in Education*, 1992

PROFESSION

The price one pays for pursuing any profession or calling is an intimate knowledge of its ugly side.

JAMES BALDWIN, 1924–1987

O young academic politician, my heart is full of pity for you, because you will not believe a word that I have said.... Your bread shall be bitterness, and your drink tears. I have done what I could to warn you.

F.M. CORNFORD; *Microcosmographia Academica*, 1908

All professions are conspiracies against the laity.

GEORGE BERNARD SHAW; *The Doctor's Dilemma*, 1906

As for doing good, that is one of the professions that are full.

H(ENRY) D(AVID) THOREAU, 1817–1862

PROFESSOR

They [universities and colleges] have little real authority over professors, particularly the tenured ones, who in effect run their own little fiefdoms.

MARTIN ANDERSON; *Imposters in the Temple*, 1992

A professor is one who talks in someone else's sleep.
W(YSTAN) H(UGH) AUDEN, 1907–1973

A good professor is a bastard perverse enough to think what *he* thinks is important, not what government thinks is important.
EDWARD C. BANFIELD; *Life*, 9 Jun. 1967

Professors simply can't discuss a thing. Habit compels them to deliver a lecture.
HAL BOYLE; *News Summaries*, 31 Dec. 1986

Professors in every branch of the sciences prefer their own theories to truth; the reason is that their theories are private property, but truth is common stock.
C(HARLES) C(ALEB) COLTON, 1780?–1832

They call themselves ignorant and say the "professor" is the one who has knowledge and to whom they should listen.
PAULO FREIRE; *Pedagogy of the Oppressed*, 1972

Every advance in education is made over the dead bodies of 10,000 resisting professors.
ROBERT M. HUTCHINS, 1899–1977

As a rule, professors tend to favor their own students and disciples. They instinctively tend to sidetrack talents and intellects superior to their own.
KARL JASPERS; *The Idea of the University*, 1959

People who have taken no intellectual food for ten years, except a few tiny crumbs from the journals, are found among professors; they aren't rare at all.
(GEORG CHRISTOPH) LICHTENBERG; *Aphorisms*, 1764–1799

Like so many aging college people, Pnin had long ceased to notice the existence of students on the campus.
VLADIMIR NABOKOV; *Pnin*, 1957

Professors complain about their lack of power, but the most horrifying fact about academic life is the abuse of academic power and the contempt so often evident for one's colleagues and students.

ROBERT SOLOMON & JON SOLOMON;
Up the University, 1993

PROGRAMME

It is necessary, therefore, that concepts of global development including issues of industrialization be integrated into *educational programmes*, to include instruction on environmental protection, energy and resource saving, the preservation of cultural values and many other aspects. We therefore call on UNESCO, Ministers of Education, parents' associations, television authorities and others to undertake this essential task.

ALEXANDER KING & BERTRAND SCHNEIDER;
The First Global Revolution, 1991

Books are, in one sense, the basis of all educational programmes.

KARL MARX, 1818–1893

In the pursuit of an educational program to suit the bright and the not-so-bright we have watered down a rigid training for the elite until we now have an educational diet in many of our public schools that nourishes neither the classes nor the masses.

AGNES MEYER; *Out of These Roots*, 1953

We have seen a great deal of activity involving new programs but little understanding of how to do it well.

DANIEL T. SEYMOUR; *Developing Academic Programs*, 1888

Many educational programs do not have clearly defined purposes.

RALPH W. TYLER;
Basic Principles of Curriculum and Instruction, 1949

PRONUNCIATION

Everyone knows that, in many ways and for many words, there is a poor match between English spelling and English pronunciation. The reason for this poor match is historical: English spelling was fixed in all but minor details when printing was introduced in England at the end of the fourteenth century. But English pronunciation has been changing continually during the past five centuries.

CELIA MILLWARD & JANE FLICK;
Handbook for Writers, 1985

They spell it Vinci and pronounce it Vinchy; foreigners always spell better than they pronounce.

MARK TWAIN (pseud. of SAMUEL LANGHORNE CLEMENS);
The Innocents Abroad, 1869

PROVERB

A proverb is much matter decorated into few words.

THOMAS FULLER, 1608–1661

A country can be judged by the quality of its proverbs.

GERMAN proverb

A proverb is the wisdom of many and the wit of one.

JOHN RUSSELL, 1792–1878

PSYCHOLOGY

Popular psychology is a mass of cant, of slush, and of superstition worthy of the most flourishing days of the medicine man.

JOHN DEWEY, 1859–1952

Psychology has a long past, but only a short history.

HERMANN EBBINGHAUS, 1850–1909

Psychology does not know what good and evil are in themselves; it knows them only as judgements about relationships.

(CARL GUSTAV) JUNG, 1875–1961

Psychology which explains everything explains nothing, and we are still in doubt.

MARIANNE MOORE, 1887–1972

The objective of psychology is to give us a totally different idea of the things we know best.

PAUL VALÉRY, 1871–1945

PUBLIC EDUCATION

It is in our public schools that the majority of our children are being formed. These schools must be guardians par excellence of our national character. They are the heart of our general education system. We must, therefore, focus our attention on them, and consequently on moral education as it is understood and practiced in them and as it should be understood and practiced.

(ÉMILE) DURKHEIM; *Moral Education*, 1961

Public education therefore is essentially a joint undertaking of parents and teachers designed to guarantee fulfillment of the child's rights to grow and learn. In the final reckoning it requires their mutual support and cooperation.

TERUHISA HORIO; *Educational Thought and Ideology in Modern Japan*, 1988

Public education is an industry in which the producers are dominant.

MYRON LIEBERMAN; *Public Education*, 1993

Free education for all children in public schools.

KARL MARX, 1818–1893

["Public education" does not have a consistent meaning. In the United Kingdom, public schools were established to educate those individuals destined to become public/civil servants; students from the perceived lower classes were not accepted. In other countries, public schools are egalitarian and accept people regardless of their future employment.]

PUBLISH OR PERISH

Jobs are scarce; outstanding letters of recommendation, 4.0 GPAs [Grade Point Averages], and good teaching records are not. As search committees wade through applications, candidates who have published stand out. Publication is a solid indication that you are capable of being a professional scholar. Thus, a publication class that might lead to vitae credits for you is a class worth petitioning for.

ALIDA ALLISON & TERRI FRONGIA;
The Grad Student's Guide to Getting Published, 1992

Published research emerges as the common currency of academic achievement, a currency that can be weighed and evaluated across institutional and even national boundaries.

DEREK BOK; *Higher Learning*, 1986

That non-tenured faculty on the tenure track were under great stress was evident not only from their own testimony but also from the comments of many senior faculty and administrators who observed their plight. The junior faculty...had become in a sense, "privatized"; that is, the overwhelming pressure to produce and publish had isolated them.

HOWARD R. BOWEN & JACK H. SCHUSTER;
American Professors, 1986

'Tis pleasant, sure, to see one's name in print;
A book's a book, although there's nothing in't.

(GEORGE GORDON) BYRON, 1788–1824

Even if you do publish a book that is well reviewed by some of your colleagues or if you publish articles in high-prestige, mainstream, refereed journals, members of the evaluating committee at your institution can argue that the work is actually of poor quality.

PAULA J. CAPLAN; *Lifting a Ton of Feathers*, 1993

The goal of scientific research is publication. Scientists, starting as graduate students, are measured primarily not by their dexterity in laboratory manipulations, not by their innate knowledge of either broad or narrow scientific subjects, and certainly not by their wit or charm: they are measured, and become known (or remain unknown), by their publications.

ROBERT A. DAY;
How to Write & Publish a Scientific Paper, 1989

But the old edict "publish or perish" has something rather comical about it. For the most part, professors don't publish a great deal, but they usually don't perish either.

GEORGE H. DOUGLAS; *Education Without Impact*, 1992

If there is one thing that the general public has heard about college professors, it is that they are somehow burdened with the necessity of publishing the results of their research. This notion has entered popular culture and folklore through the catch and memorable phrase, "publish or perish." If you don't publish, you can't get promoted, and if you don't get promoted you can't, in most cases, keep your job. Which is to say you perish.

GEORGE H. DOUGLAS; *Education Without Impact*, 1992

We all know that except for faculty members at a thin slice of elite institutions, the amount of research and publication is exaggerated. Few faculty members perish from failure to publish.

MILTON GREENBERG;
The Chronicle of Higher Education, 20 Oct. 1993

Publish or perish is the name of the game.

RALPH E. MATKIN & T.F. RIGGAR; *Persist and Publish*, 1991

[P]ublication had a salient position, for publication was the surest way for a rising young scholar or scientist to become known. . . .

TALCOTT PARSONS & GERALD M. PLATT;
The American University, 1973

For the scholarly record is ultimately a written one: this is the foundation for the principle, often maligned and sometimes abused, of "publish or perish."

JAROSLAV PELIKAN; *Scholarship and Its Survival*, 1983

We write, study, and publish not only selflessly to share our ideas with the international community of scholars, but also to advance from assistant to associate professor or to get a 7 percent salary increase when the average raise is 6 percent. No doubt these pressures can lead to adverse consequences usually associated with the slogan "publish or perish."

HENRY ROSOVSKY; *The University*, 1990

But publication, while one way to evaluate faculty members, is only one way, and the humanities have got to find other and more realistic means of evaluation if they are going to preserve their vitality. I do not mean to suggest that love of learning is enough. "Cherish or perish" is not a viable alternative.

WILLIAM D. SCHAEFER;
Education Without Compromise, 1990

Under the publish-or-perish standard, the university is perishing. Research *and* publication are not necessarily related.

PAGE SMITH; *Killing the Spirit*, 1990

The Commission is deeply concerned that a trend from the United States has been imported into Canada, namely a situation where the quantity of research publications is more important to the careers of university professors than is the excellence of their teaching.

STUART L. SMITH;
Report: Commission of Inquiry on Canadian University Education, 1991

"Publish or perish" is a misleading phrase. One can perish by publishing, if one's work is rejected time and again by all the leading scholarly journals, and can only emerge shamefacedly into print in some peripheral publication. Even those who make it into print in a respectable academic journal may find their article devastated by a cross fire of criticisms in later issues.

THOMAS SOWELL; *Inside American Education*, 1993

[I]t would be the greatest mistake to estimate the value of each member of a faculty by the printed work signed with his name ... there is at present some tendency to fall into this error; and an emphatic protest is necessary against an attitude ... which is damaging to efficiency and unjust to unselfish zeal.

ALFRED NORTH WHITEHEAD, 1861–1947

Given the production mania which sweeps the university, the power of publishing houses, as well as reviewing organs, is immense, nearly incredible, almost uncanny – as is clearly evident to those who live or die according to their fortunes here.

BRUCE WILSHIRE; *The Moral Collapse of the University*, 1990

PUNISHMENT

The question whether corporal punishment should be allowed in our schools is a difficult one, and is best approached in a practical manner. There is no doubt that in the past, in West Africa as well as elsewhere, corporal punishment was excessively used. Even today, in many teachers' minds, punishment means flogging.

S.A. BANJO; *A West African Teacher's Handbook*, 1953

He that spareth his rod hateth his son: but he that loveth him chasteneth him betimes.

The Bible (Proverbs: 13,24)

The bamboo stick produces obedient children.

CHINESE proverb

No corporal punishment shall be inflicted by elementary school [ages 6 to 14 years] directors or teachers on the children under their care.

DEPARTMENT OF EDUCATION;
Outlines of the Modern Education in Japan, 1893

We may think that petty power games have been banished along with the cane, and that *our* children will never be subject to ritual humiliation or unnecessary controls. But we would be wrong.

DEBORAH JACKSON;
The Guardian (International Edition), 23 Nov. 1993

Corporal punishment is as humiliating for him who gives it as for him who receives it; it is ineffective besides. Neither shame nor physical pain have any other effect than a hardening one....

ELLEN KEY (pseud. of KAROLINA SOFIA KEY), 1849–1926

Nothing would more effectively further the development of education than for all flogging pedagogues to learn to educate with the head instead of the hand.

ELLEN KEY (pseud. of KAROLINA SOFIA KEY);
The Century of the Child, 1909

Beating is the worst and therefore the last means to be used in the correction of children and that only in cases of extremity after all gentle ways have been tried and proved unsuccessful.

JOHN LOCKE, 1632–1704

No learning without beating.

MENANDER, *c.*343–291

So long as it is not shown that corporal punishment is in any way detrimental to its objects, what does it matter that it is self-perpetuating; that it frequently is used as a first response rather than a last resort; that its effectiveness as a deterrent is at best questionable; or finally, that it serves purposes of an extra-disciplinary nature? The boys mostly appear to hold up well in caning situations.

> JOSEPH A. MERCURIO; *Caning*, 1972

With the banning of caning from all its state schools in 1987, Britain is at least preparing to catch up with her friends and neighbours in America and Europe. . . .

> ROSALIND MILES; *The Rites of Man*, 1992

I have never seen any effect in rods but to make children's minds more base, or more maliciously headstrong.

> (MICHEL EYQUEM DE) MONTAIGNE, 1533–1592

I disapprove of flogging.

> (MARCUS FABIUS) QUINTILIAN(US), *c*.35–*c*.95

Learn or depart; a third alternative is to be flogged.

> H(ASTINGS) RASHDALL;
> *The Universities of Europe in the Middle Ages*, 1895
> [former greeting at Winchester School, UK; established *c*.1350]

Children should never receive punishment as such.

> (JEAN JACQUES) ROUSSEAU, 1712–1778

Physical punishment I believe to be never right.

> BERTRAND RUSSELL, 1872–1970

A boy is never the worse for a flogging.

> F(RANCIS) E(DWARD) SMEDLEY; *Frank Fairleigh*, 1850

Break their wills betimes: begin this great work before they can run alone, before they can speak plain, or perhaps speak at all. Let him have nothing he cries for, absolutely nothing, great or small. Make him do as he is bid, if you whip him ten times running to effect it. Break his will now and his soul will live, and he will bless you to all eternity.

> JOHN WESLEY, 1703–1791

PUPIL

The pupil is thereby "schooled" to confuse teaching with learning, grade advancement with education, a diploma with competence, and fluency with the ability to say something new.

IVAN ILLICH; *Deschooling Society*, 1971

"I am putting old heads on your young shoulders", Miss Brodie had told them at that time, "and all my pupils are the crème de la crème".

MURIEL SPARK; *The Prime of Miss Jean Brodie*, 1961

Q

QUALITY

The quality of university is measured more by the kind of student it turns out than the kind it takes in.

ROBERT J. KIBBEE; *The New York Times*, 27 Jul. 1971

Nowadays there is widespread dissatisfaction with the quality of schooling in the United States and most of what is spewed at us through our television sets.

ROBERT ORNSTEIN & PAUL EHRLICH; *New World New Mind*, 1989

More schools don't mean a higher quality of education.

RICHARD SAUL WURMAN; *Information Anxiety*, 1991

QUALITY OF LIFE

Children spend between a sixth and a quarter of their lives in schools. Teachers and administrators spend even more of their lives in schools. The quality of life in a school is therefore important, even if it has no effect whatever on students' chances of adult success.

CHRISTOPHER JENCKS; *Inequality*, 1972

QUESTION

Hypothetical questions get hypothetical answers.

JOAN BAEZ; *Daybreak*, 1966

The real questions are the ones that obtrude upon your consciousness whether you like it or not, the ones that make your mind start vibrating like a jackhammer, the ones that you "come to terms with" only to discover that they are still there. The real questions refuse to be placated.

INGRID BENGIS; *Ms*, Oct. 1973

He that nothing questions nothing learns.

ENGLISH proverb

There are two sides to every question.

ENGLISH proverb

The shy man will not learn; the impatient man should not teach. Ask and learn.

HILLEL (the Elder), c.60BC–?

Questioning is the door of knowledge.

IRISH proverb

Ask questions. Ask more questions.

HENRY ROSOVSKY; *The University*, 1990

What is the answer? . . . in that case, what is the question?

GERTRUDE STEIN, 1874–1946

If a question can be put at all, then it can also be answered.

(LUDWIG JOSEF JOHANN) WITTGENSTEIN, 1889–1951

QUOTATION

A quote is a personal possession and you have no right to change it.

RAY CAVE;
a *speech* (Northwestern University), 29 May 1985

It is a good thing for an uneducated man to read books of quotations. . . . The quotations when engraved upon the memory give you good insights. They also make you anxious to read the authors and look for more.

WINSTON (LEONARD SPENCER) CHURCHILL;
Roving Commission, 1930

I love them because it is a joy to find thoughts one might have, beautifully expressed with much authority by someone recognizedly wiser than oneself.

MARLENE DIETRICH; *Marlene Dietrich's ABC*, 1962

Sometimes it seems the only accomplishment my education ever bestowed on me, the ability to think in quotations.

MARGARET DRABBLE; *A Summer Bird-Cage*, 1962

Quotations (such as have point and lack triteness) from the great old authors are an act of filial reverence on the part of the quote, and a blessing to a public grown superficial and external.

LOUISE IMOGEN GUINEY, 1861–1920

Every quotation contributes something to the stability or enlargement of the language.

SAMUEL JOHNSON; *Dictionary*, 1755

Be careful – with quotations you can damn anything.

ANDRÉ MALRAUX, 1901–1976

A book that furnishes no quotations is, *me judice*, no book – it is a plaything.

T(HOMAS) L(OVE) PEACOCK, 1785–1866

The next best thing to being clever is being able to quote some one who is.

MARY PETTIBONE POOLE; *A Glass Eye at a Keyhole*, 1938

I always have a quotation for everything – it saves original thinking.

DOROTHY L. SAYERS; *Have His Carcase*, 1932

Famous remarks are very seldom quoted correctly.

SIMEON STRUNSKY; *No Mean City*, 1944

Some for renown, on scraps of learning dote,
And think they grow immortal as they quote.

EDWARD YOUNG, 1683–1765

R

RACE

Race involves the inheritance of similar physical variations by large groups of mankind, but its psychological and cultural connotations, if they exist, have not been ascertained by science.

AMERICAN ANTHROPOLOGICAL ASSOCIATION;
a *resolution*, Dec. 1938

No matter what learned scientists may say, race is, politically speaking, not the beginning of humanity but its end, not the origin of peoples but their decay, not the national birth of man but his unnatural death.

HANNAH ARENDT; *Origins of Totalitarianism*, 1951

Whoever controls the language, the images, controls the race.

ALLEN GINSBERG, 1926–

If you would study the ways of the human race, one household is enough.

(DECIMUS JUNIUS) JUVENAL(IS), *c*.60–140

No race can prosper till it learns that there is as much dignity in tilling the field as in writing a poem.

BOOKER T. WASHINGTON; *Up from Slavery*, 1901

RACISM

[B]antu education, does have a separate existence just as, for example, French education, Chinese education or even European education in South Africa, because it exists and can function only in and for a particular social setting, namely, Bantu society.

W.W.M. EISELEN;
Report of the Commission on Native Education 1945–51, 1952?

The whole purpose of education... an instinctive and comprehensive sense of race.

(ADOLF) HITLER, 1889–1945

Britain's black Africans are twice as educated as whites, but highly qualified black Africans are more than four times more likely to be unemployed than their white counterparts.

MORAG PRESTON;
The Times Higher Education Supplement, 15 Apr. 1994

Increasing hostility toward blacks and other racial minorities on college campuses has become so widespread that the term "the new racism" has been coined to describe it.

THOMAS SOWELL; *Inside American Education*, 1993

To separate [children] from others of similar age and qualifications solely because of their race generates a feeling of inferiority as to their status in the community that may affect their hearts and minds in a way unlikely ever to be undone.

EARL WARREN;
Brown vs. *Board of Education of Topeka*, 17 May 1954

We come then to the question presented: Does segregation of children in public schools solely on the basis of race, even though the physical facilities and other "tangible" factors may be equal, deprive the children of the minority group of equal education opportunities? We believe it does.

EARL WARREN;
Brown vs. *Board of Education of Topeka*, 17 May 1954

RADICALISM

What I mean by a radical is one who wants change that involves going to the root of the matter, as opposed to one who wants no change at all, or one who wants superficial change.

ROBIN BARROW; *Radical Education*, 1978

For many people, at least until recently, the hope has been that schooling on a national scale and well carried out would be the means for providing the freedom, justice, equality and happiness desired by the radicals too. The radicals represent one kind of reaction to the growing feeling that that hope was misplaced.

ROBIN BARROW; *Radical Education*, 1978

Only radical changes to reorient education toward the fundamentals and backed by a massive vocational system – which is how the Germans and Japanese organize their quite different systems – can slowly undo the damage wrought by a generation of foolish changes in Canada.

JEFFREY SIMPSON; *The Globe and Mail*, 30 Apr. 1992

Few radicals believed that the changes that they sought could be achieved by reasoned argument alone.

NIGEL WRIGHT; *Assessing Radical Education*, 1989

READ

Read not to contradict and confute; nor to believe and take for granted; nor to find talk and discourse; but to weigh and consider.

FRANCIS BACON, 1561–1626

When you don't read, you don't write.

HELEN BAROLINI; *The Dream Book*, 1985

The elementary school must assume as its sublime and most solemn responsibility the task of teaching every child in it to read. Any school that does not accomplish this has failed.

WILLIAM J. BENNETT; *The New York Times*, 3 Sep. 1986

Read, mark, learn, and inwardly digest.

Book of Common Prayer, 1650

Never read anything until not to have read it has bothered you for some time.

SAMUEL BUTLER, 1835–1902

We often read with as much talent as we write.

RALPH WALDO EMERSON, 1803–1882

Children who grow up in a reasonably articulate family with books and habitual reading going on are at an enormous advantage, because the important thing is not what you read, but the desire to read.

NORTHROP FRYE; *The Toronto Star*, 10 May 1987

Some people read only because they are too lazy to think.

(GEORG CHRISTOPH) LICHTENBERG, 1742–1799

Only if she wished to become a nun was there much chance of a girl learning to read.

HUGH THOMAS; *An Unfinished History of the World*, 1979

We are what we read. In both our professional and personal life, we are judged by the information we peruse. The information we ingest shapes our personalities, contributes to the ideas we formulate, and colors our view of the world.

RICHARD SAUL WURMAN; *Information Anxiety*, 1991

READER

Readers are of two sorts; one who carefully goes through a book, and the other who as carefully lets the book go through him.

DOUGLAS JERROLD, 1803–1857

READING

Reading a book is like re-writing it for yourself.... You bring to a novel anything you read, all your experience of the world. You bring your history and you read it in your own terms.

ANGELA CARTER, 1940–1992

Ignore those who suggest that children who are reading well have learnt to do so despite you, that many millions of children have learnt to read in the past with abysmal materials and negligible teaching. If you have competent readers in the class, they are demonstrating fluency solely as a result of your good teaching methods. And if you don't have competent readers in your class then it is almost certainly not your fault, but that of the teacher who had them before you, or the school that had them before you, or their parents who had them in the first place.

MARTIN COLES;
in *Theory and Practice of Regressive Education*, 1993

If you have a female child, set her to sewing and not reading, for it is not suitable for a female to know how to read unless she is going to be a nun.

PAOLA DA CERTALTO, *c.*1300–*c.*1370

The teaching of reading – all over the United States, in all schools, in all the textbooks – is totally wrong and flies in the face of all logic and common sense. Johnny couldn't read ... for the simple reason that nobody ever showed him how. Johnny's only problem was that he was unfortunately exposed to an ordinary American school.

RUDOLF FLESCH; *Why Johnny Can't Read*, 1956

The basis of education is the habit of reading, and it might be said that if young people were taught not simply how to read but taught the habit of reading so that it became continuous, perhaps nothing else would be necessary in our education.

NORTHROP FRYE; *On Education*, 1988

Reading is sometimes an ingenious device for avoiding thought.

ARTHUR HELPS, 1813–1875

No entertainment is so cheap as reading, nor any pleasure so lasting.

MARY WORTLEY MONTAGUE, 1689–1762

Reading is to the mind what exercise is to the body.

RICHARD STEELE; *The Tatler* (no. 147), 1709–1711

REASON

As far as you are able, join faith to reason.

(ANICIUS MANLIUS SEVERINUS) BOETHIUS, *c*.480–524

He who will not reason, is a bigot; he who cannot is a fool; and he who dares not is a slave.

WILLIAM DRUMMOND OF HAWTHORNDEN, 1585–1649

I'll not listen to reason . . . reason always means what someone else has got to say.

ELIZABETH GASKELL; *Cranford*, 1853

There is no method of reasoning more common, and yet none more blamable, than, in philosophical disputes, to endeavour the refutation of any hypothesis, by a pretense of its dangerous consequences to religion and morality.

DAVID HUME;
An Enquiry Concerning Human Understanding, 1748

All our knowledge begins with the senses, proceeds then to the understanding, and ends in reason. There is nothing higher than reason.

(IMMANUEL) KANT; *Critique of Pure Reason*, 1781

Reason is the greatest enemy that faith has....

MARTIN LUTHER; *Table Talk*, 1569

The sign of an intelligent people is their ability to control emotions by their application of reason.

MARYA MANNES; *More in Anger*, 1958

The soul of man is divided into three parts, intelligence, reason, and passion. Intelligence and passion are possessed by other animals, but reason by man alone.

PYTHAGORAS, *c.*600–*c.*500

Time heals what reason cannot.

(LUCIUS ANNAEUS) SENECA (the Younger), *c.*4BC–65

Make reason thy guide.

SOLON, 636? 558?

Reason deceives us more often than does nature.

(LUC DE CLAPIERS, MARQUIS DE) VAUVENARGUES, 1715–1747

REFORM

But what kind of educational responses do these world trends and looming global problems require? How can education help people perceive what is happening? What changes are needed in our schools? How can the needed change be brought about? What research, what knowledge, what experience can best serve these ends?

JAMES M. BECKER; *Schooling for a Global Age*, 1979

Together they [Maria Theresa and Joseph II] applied the confiscated property of the Jesuits to educational reform. In 1774 they issued an "Allgemeine Schulordnung" which effected a basic reorganization of both primary and secondary schools. Grade schools provided compulsory education for all children; they admitted Protestants and Jews as students and teachers, gave religious instruction in each faith to its adherents, but placed control in the hands of state officials; these *Volkschulen* soon came to be ranked as the best in Europe. Normal schools were established to train teachers; *Hauptschulen* specialized in science and technology, and *Gymnasien* taught Latin and the humanities.

WILL(IAM) (JAMES) DURANT & ARIEL DURANT;
The Story of Civilization (vol. X), 1967

Educational change is no substitute for social and political reform.

MICHAEL FULLAN; *The Meaning of Educational Change*, 1982

People do not understand the nature or ramifications of most educational changes.

MICHAEL FULLAN; *The Meaning of Educational Change*, 1982

The organs of education are, in every age, connected with the other institutions of the social body, with customs and belief, with the great currents of thought. But they also have a life of their own, an evolution which is relatively autonomous, in the course of which they conserve many features of their former structure. Sometimes they defend themselves against the influences exerted on them from outside, leaning on their past for support.

MAURICE HALBWACHS;
in *L'Évolution pédagogique en France*, 1977

Anyone who would attempt the task of felling a virgin forest with a penknife would probably feel the same paralysis of despair that the reformer feels when confronted with existing school systems.

ELLEN KEY (pseud. of KAROLINA SOFIA KEY);
The Century of the Child, 1909

The emergence of a priesthood of scientists, technologists and technocrats is hardly desirable and its prevention must be one of the objectives of educational reform.

ALEXANDER KING & BERTRAND SCHNEIDER;
The First Global Revolution, 1991

Most reform movements really are directed at and are most effective for middle-class students, not those most in need.

MARGARET DIANE LECOMPTE & ANTHONY GARY DWORKIN;
Giving Up on School, 1991

The problem of educational reform is not how to empower teachers; it is how to empower educational consumers to overcome the monopoly power of educational producers.

MYRON LIEBERMAN; *Public Education*, 1993

Unlike most academic disciplines, the origins of black, ethnic, and women's studies programs can be traced to oppositional social movements.

CHANDRA TALPADE MOHANTY; *Between Borders*, 1994

The first seeds of reformation in the education system of Japan were sown while the Dutch held the monopoly of trade at Nagasaki.

MOMBUSHO [Department of Education];
An Outline History of Japanese Education, Literature and Arts,
1877

Changing school curricula and teaching methods may be the most fundamental change that's needed, but, of course, that change will not bear fruit for twenty years or more, even if we can overcome all the serious barriers.

ROBERT ORNSTEIN & PAUL EHRLICH;
New World New Mind, 1989

Let us reform our schools, and we shall find little reform needed in our prisons.

JOHN RUSKIN; *Unto the Last*, 1862

While the reform movement of the 1980s elevated the mission of public education...in practice, it has meant tinkering with a fundamentally flawed machine.

THOMAS TOCH; *US News & World Report*, 11 Jan. 1993

As long as official reformers are primarily concerned with producing workers, making the school experience like life in a factory makes sense. Using the school to teach passivity, moving in crowds, taking orders, and following a preset agenda make great sense if your main agenda is to get kids ready to work in the growing service sectors of our economy.

GEORGE H. WOOD; *Schools That Work*, 1993

RELATIONS

Educational relations make the strongest tie.

CECIL RHODES, 1853–1902

RELIGION

The authentic test of a religion is not what you believe. It's what you do, and unless your religion expresses itself in compassion for all living things, it's not authentic.

KAREN ARMSTRONG; *A History of God*, 1993

If we look at our society, the glaring absurdity that we have is the existence of – indeed the strong support we give to – religious separation in schools. To have denominational schooling, to my mind, runs counter to a principal aim of education: to make people live together and work together in a society in which people differ in their beliefs.

HERMANN BONDI, 1919–

In the long run nothing can withstand reason and experience, and the contradiction religion offers to both is only too palpable.

(SIGMUND) FREUD; *The Future of an Illusion*, 1927

I am for religion against religions.

VICTOR HUGO; *Les Misérables*, 1862

For me the biggest problem is getting a professional job wearing a hejab ... I know that I am more than qualified, but a school official told me that there is a school policy against wearing hats. I told him it was a religious thing, and that I couldn't remove it, and that I would take it up with the board.

WANDA KHAN; *International Herald Tribune*, 9 Nov. 1993

There is only one religion, though there are a hundred versions of it.

GEORGE BERNARD SHAW, 1856–1950

Religion is love; in no other case is it logic.

BEATRICE POTTER WEBB; *My Apprenticeship*, 1926

[T]here will always be confusion about the role of religious education within the school curriculum when it is confused with faith. Religious education in school has, of course, nothing whatsoever to do with faith. . . .

KENNETH WILLIAMS;
The Times Educational Supplement, 25 Feb. 1994

REPORT

As we read the school reports on our children, we realize a sense of relief that can rise to delight that – thank heaven – nobody is reporting in this fashion on us.

J(OHN) B(OYNTON) PRIESTLEY; *Reader's Digest*, Jun. 1964

RESEARCH

Coupled with the role of science is the position of research, the activity that quickly became the raison d'être of graduate study and still is, despite decades of criticism from those concerned about the preparation of college teachers.

BERNARD BERELSON;
Graduate Education in the United States, 1960

Not many appreciate the ultimate power and potential usefulness of basic knowledge accumulated by obscure, unseen investigators who, in a lifetime of intensive study, may never see any practical use for their findings but who go on seeking answers to the unknown without thought of financial or practical gain.

EUGENIE CLARK; *The Lady and the Sharks*, 1969

After all, the ultimate goal of all research is not objectivity, but truth.

HELENE DEUTSCH; *The Psychology of Women*, 1944

[R]esearchers should not promise more than they can deliver and that consequently they should deliver what they have promised.

W.B. DOCKRELL;
in *Educational Research, Methodology, and Measurement*, 1988

I think that in discussion of natural problems we ought to begin not with the Scriptures, but with experiments and demonstrations.

GALILEO (GALILEI), 1564–1642

The way to do research is to attack the facts at the point of greatest astonishment.

CELIA GREEN; *The Decline and Fall of Science*, 1977

Research is formalized curiosity. It is poking and prying with a purpose.
ZORA NEALE HURSTON; *Dust Tracks on a Road*, 1942

[William Dilthey] published a classical treatise in which he made the distinction between *Verstehen* and *Erklären*. He maintained that the humanities had their own logic of research and pointed out that the difference between natural sciences and humanities was that the former tried to explain, whereas the latter tried to understand.
TORSTEN HUSÉN;
The International Encyclopedia of Education, 1985

Research! A mere excuse for idleness; it has never achieved, and will never achieve any results of the slightest value.
BENJAMIN JOWETT, 1817–1893

But let me state my position bluntly, for me research defines the university. Research is more basic to the university than even teaching, than even public service. Research lies at the university's core so that I feel that the very phrase, university research is a tautology.
LARKIN KERWIN; in *Hard Times in the Ivory Tower*
(Ideas – Canadian Broadcasting Corporation), 1983

The trouble with research is that it tells you what people were thinking about yesterday, not tomorrow. It's like driving a car using a rearview mirror.
BERNARD LOOMIS; *International Herald Tribune*, 9 Oct. 1985

The aim of research is the discovery of the equations which subsist between elements of phenomena.
ERNST MACH, 1838–1916

For God's sake, stop researching for a while and begin to think.
WALTER MOBERLY; *The Crisis in the University*, 1949

Research is an expression of faith in the possibility of progress.
HENRY ROSOVSKY; *The University*, 1990

The best research and the only research that should be expected of university professors is wide and informed reading in their fields and related fields.
PAGE SMITH; *Killing the Spirit*, 1990

It is that the vast majority of the so-called research turned out in the modern university is essentially worthless.

PAGE SMITH; *Killing the Spirit*, 1990

Authors have commented for years on the irony of universities recommending (and doing) research and development for the nation's industries while doing a disappearingly small amount of research into their own industry, namely higher education.

STUART L. SMITH;
Report: Commission of Inquiry on Canadian
University Education, 1991

The outcome of any serious research can only be to make two questions grow where only one grew before.

(THORSTEIN) VEBLEN, 1857–1929

[Animal Aid] has analysed more than 1,000 recent research papers which it says prove that animals continue to be burned, irradiated, poisoned, starved, turned into drug addicts and forced to suffer in a multitude of different ways for a bewildering number of reasons.

OLGA WOJTAS;
The Times Higher Education Supplement, 15 Oct. 1993

RESEARCHER

The true worth of a researcher lies in pursuing what he did not seek in his experiment as well as what he sought.

CLAUDE BERNARD, 1813–1878

None of the great discoveries was made by a "specialist" or a "researcher".

MARTIN H. FISCHER, 1879–1962

RITUAL

Much that passes for education ... is not at all but ritual ... the fact is that we are being educated when we know it least.

DAVID P. GARDNER; *Vital Speeches*, 15 Apr. 1975

The contemporary world civilization is also the first which has found it necessary to rationalize its fundamental initiation ritual in the name of education.

> IVAN ILLICH; *Deschooling Society*, 1971

ROUSSEAU

Like every meddler with children who ever lived, Rousseau wanted to educate poor Émile for a better world than this one.

> ALDOUS HUXLEY, 1894–1963

It* is the greatest book on education of children ever written. I do not say that all his ideas can be put into practice; but that is because he has too many of them, not because they are bad.

> AUBREY MENEN, 1912–1989
> [*Rousseau's *Émile*]

Rousseau understood. He was the first to view the child as a child, and to stop treating the child as an adult.

> J.H. VAN DEN BERG; *The Changing Nature of Man*, 1983

RULES

As a rule we believe all facts and theories for which we have no use.

> WILLIAM JAMES; *The Will to Believe*, 1897

Good citizens always obey rules, students are taught.

> JING LIN; *Education in Post-Mao China*, 1993

S

SCHOLAR

A scholar on whose clothes vermin is found is worthy of death.

*Babylonian Talmud, c.*450

A meer scholar a meer ass. [*sic*]

ROBERT BURTON, 1577–1640

The scholar teacheth his master.

ENGLISH? proverb

Every scholar is not a good schoolmaster.

ENGLISH proverb

A mere scholar, who knows nothing but books, must be ignorant even of them.

WILLIAM HAZLITT; *The Ignorance of the Learned,* 1821

When scholars vie, wisdom mounts.

HEBREW proverb

Much learning does not make a scholar.

HERACLITUS, *c.*540–*c.*470

The world's great men have not commonly been great scholars, nor great scholars great men.

OLIVER WENDELL HOLMES, 1809–1894

A scholar's ink lasts longer than a martyr's blood.

IRISH proverb

Learning is necessary and important to all citizens, but it does not mean that all men should be scholars.

EIICHI KIYOOKA; *Fukuzawa Yukichi on Education,* 1985

We live in a time of such rapid change and growth of knowledge that only he who is in a fundamental sense a scholar – that is, a person who continues to learn and inquire – can hope to keep pace, let alone play the role of guide.

NATHAN M. PUSEY; *The Age of the Scholar,* 1963

The ink of the scholar is more holy than the blood of the martyr.

Sunnah (sayings of Muhammad), *c.*630

Scholars are wont to sell their birthright for a mess of learning.

H(ENRY) D(AVID) THOREAU;
A Week on the Concord and Merrimack Rivers, 1849

SCHOLARSHIP

See in college how we thwart the natural love of learning by leaving the natural method of teaching what each wishes to learn. . . . Scholarship is to be created not by compulsion, but by awakening a pure interest in knowledge.

RALPH WALDO EMERSON, 1803–1882

Scholarship knows no national boundary.

KOREAN proverb

Scholarship is less than sense, therefore seek intelligence.

J. ROBERT OPPENHEIMER, 1904–1967

Scholarship is polite argument.

PHILIP RIEFF; *New York Herald Tribune*, 1 Jan. 1961

SCHOOL

Our population is generally school-conscious and school-dependent.

AMERICAN ASSOCIATION OF UNIVERSITIES;
Journal of Proceedings and Addresses, 1932

I and the public know
What all schoolchildren learn,
Those to whom evil is done
Do evil in return.

W(YSTAN) H(UGH) AUDEN; *Another Time*, 1940

[School] fails all children some of the time and most children all of the time.

WILLIAM AYERS; *Rethinking Schools*, Oct.–Nov. 1990

No one who has any sense has ever liked school.
ROBERT JOHN GRAHAM BOOTHBY, 1900–1986

Students are the *raison d'être* for establishing schools – yet few children would elect to go to school, given other options. They go because they are compelled.
RITA S. BRAUSE; *Enduring Schools*, 1992

Winning and losing are what our schools are all about, not education.
DAVID N. CAMPBELL; *Phi Delta Kappan*, Oct. 1974

America's schools are the least successful in the Western world.
MARVIN CETRON & OWEN DAVIES; *Crystal Globe*, 1991

It was then [late 19th century], and only then that primary schools and high schools emerged as distinct institutional units.
JOHN DEMOS; *Past, Present, and Personal*, 1986

Schools exploit you because they tap your power and use it to perpetuate society's trip, while they teach you not to respect your own.... Schools petrify society because their method, characterized by coercion from the top down, works against any substantial social change. Students are coerced by teachers, who take orders from administrators, who do the bidding of those stalwarts of the status quo on the board of education or the board of trustees. Schools petrify society because students, through them, learn to adjust unquestioningly to institutions.
JERRY FARBER; *The Student as Nigger*, 1971

We must destroy all which in the present school answers to the organization of constraint, the artificial surroundings by which children are separated from nature and life, the intellectual and moral discipline made use of to impose ready-made ideas upon them, beliefs which deprave and annihilate natural bent.
FRANCISCO FERRER, 1859–1909

And this goddamned school is antifemale, they look down on women, especially women my age. It's a goddamned monastery that's been invaded by people in skirts and the men who run it only hope that the people in skirts are pseudomen, so they won't disturb things, won't insist that feeling is as important as thinking and body as important as mind.
MARILYN FRENCH; *The Women's Room*, 1977

What are schools supposed to do?
> MICHAEL FULLAN; *The Meaning of Educational Change*, 1982

Schools need to be defended, as an important public service that educates students to be citizens who can think, challenge, take risks, and believe that their actions will make a difference in the larger society.
> HENRY GIROUX; *Schooling and the Struggle for Public Life*, 1988

Schools should be places where children learn what they most want to know, instead of what we think they ought to know.
> JOHN HOLT; *How Children Fail*, 1969

We think of schools as places where youth learns, but our schools also need to learn.
> LYNDON B. JOHNSON;
> a *message* (to Congress), 12 Jan. 1965

A kind of state-supported baby-sitting service.
> GERALD KENNEDY; *Time*, 11 Apr. 1960

We must assign to the schools what they can do best and surrender other functions to more specialized agencies outside the school system.
> MICHAEL W. KIRST; *Who Controls Our Schools?*, 1984

If every day in the life of a school could be the last day but one, there would be little fault to find with it.
> STEPHEN LEACOCK, 1869–1944

It is clear that schools have fallen out of touch with the lives of contemporary young people and the opportunity structure they face, and that school programs and educational policy are based upon obsolete conceptions of student characteristics, life experiences, family structure, labor market experience, and customary ways of learning.
> MARGARET DIANE LECOMPTE & ANTHONY GARY DWORKIN;
> *Giving Up on School*, 1991

What about your school? It's defective! It's a pack of useless lies.
> "MEAT LOAF" (pseud. of MARVIN LEE ADAY);
> *Bat Out of Hell II* (pub. Virgin Records), 1993

School days, I believe, are the unhappiest in the whole span of human existence. They are full of dull, unintelligible tasks, new and unpleasant ordinances, brutal violations of common sense and common decency.

H(ENRY) L(OUIS) MENCKEN, 1880–1956

Why assume that unsuccessful school performance means something is wrong with the children? Why should unsuccessful school performance, particularly when it is widespread, not suggest that something is wrong with the schools?

ELAINE MENSH & HARRY MENSH; *The IQ Mythology*, 1991

What are our schools for if not an indoctrination against communism?

RICHARD NIXON, 1913–1994

School was a worry to her. She was not glib or quick in a world where glibness and quickness were easily confused with ability to learn.

TILLIE OLSEN; *Tell Me a Riddle*, 1956

The ladder was there, "from the gutter to the university", and for those stalwart enough to ascend it, the schools were a boon and a path out of poverty.

DIANE RAVITCH; *The Great School Wars*, 1974

But for two centuries since the Industrial Revolution we have not questioned whether a school, in which large numbers of children are artificially herded together, is the right environment for education.

ROBERT VAN DE WEYER; *The Health of Nations*, 1991

Schools have been in a state of almost continuous revolution for the past two or three decades, as new methods and equipment are introduced. And whenever complaints are made, teachers and parents alike delude themselves that more money spent on computers, laboratories and videos will stop the rot.

ROBERT VAN DE WEYER; *The Health of Nations*, 1991

We try to keep constantly in mind the fact that the worth of the school is to be judged by its graduates.

BOOKER T. WASHINGTON; *Up from Slavery*, 1901

I . . . think schools, as they are now regulated, the hot-beds of vice and folly, and the knowledge of human nature supposedly attained there merely cunning selfishness.

MARY WOLLSTONECRAFT, 1759–1797

I went through sixteen years of education, just like everybody else. And just like everybody else, I kept asking myself the same thing the whole time. When do we get to the stuff I want to know about, as opposed to what somebody else thinks I should know about? We never did, even in college. School left me with a lot of unanswered questions.

ED ZOTTI; *Know It All!*, 1993

SCHOOL BOARD

We have strict orders on how to teach. There are certain methods that must be employed. Your way is easier to learn, but it hasn't been approved by the school board for use in the classroom.

VIÑA DELMAR; *The Becker Scandal*, 1968

School boards think that, if they offer the same printed information to all parents, they have made choice equally acceptable. That is not true, of course, because the printed information won't be read, or certainly will not be scrutinized aggressively, by parents who can't read or who read very poorly.

JONATHAN KOZOL; *Savage Inequalities*, 1991

In the first place God made idiots. This was for practice. Then he made school boards.

MARK TWAIN (pseud. of SAMUEL LANGHORNE CLEMENS), 1835–1910

Why is it that the thousands of independent school boards running our 15,000 school systems cannot turn out high-school graduates whose achievement scores match those of the Japanese?

MORTIMER B. ZUCKERMAN;
US News & World Report, 24 Aug. 1992

SCHOOLING

I believe, despite our rhetoric about the importance of schools, schooling currently is a waste of time for most students, inconsequential for some, while for a select few, it is highly beneficial.

RITA S. BRAUSE; *Enduring Schools*, 1992

Twenty years of schoolin'
And they put you on the day shift
Look out kid
They keep it all hid
Better jump down down a manhole
Light yourself a candle
Don't wear sandals
Try to avoid the scandals
Don't wanna be a bum
You better chew gum
The pump don't work
'Cause the vandals took the handles.

BOB DYLAN (né ROBERT ALLEN ZIMMERMAN);
Subterranean Homesick Blues (pub. Warner Brothers), 1965

Schooling emerged as the process of education became institutionalized.

DAVID HAMILTON; *Learning about Education*, 1990

Schooling, instead of encouraging the asking of questions, too often discourages it.

MADELEINE L'ENGLE; *Walking on Water*, 1980

Like many kids, I loved learning but not schooling.

IRA SHOR; *Empowering Education*, 1992

I think schooling is a waste of many pupils' time, and a cause of lifelong misery for some.

CHRIS SHUTE; *Compulsory Schooling Disease*, 1993

Public schooling's vast infrastructure – from those who change the light bulbs to the bureaucrats who push the paper – has grown so unwieldy and idiosyncratic that it is more often a hindrance than a support to education.

THOMAS TOCH; *US News & World Report*, 11 Jan. 1993

I have never let my schooling interfere with my education.
MARK TWAIN (pseud. of SAMUEL LANGHORNE CLEMENS),
1835–1910

SCHOOLMASTER

A schoolmaster should have an atmosphere of awe, and walk wonderingly, as if he was amazed at being himself.
WALTER BAGEHOT, 1826–1877

You sought the last resort of feeble minds with classical education. You became a schoolmaster.
ALDOUS HUXLEY, 1894–1963

The average schoolmaster is and always must be essentially an ass, for how can one imagine an intelligent man engaging in so puerile an avocation?
H(ENRY) L(OUIS) MENCKEN, 1880–1956

God forgive me for having thought it possible that a schoolmaster could be out and out a rational being.
WALTER SCOTT, 1771–1832

It is when the gods hate a man with uncommon abhorrence that they drive him into the profession of a schoolmaster.
(LUCIUS ANNAEUS) SENECA (the Younger), c.4BC–65

We schoolmasters must temper discretion with deceit.
EVELYN WAUGH, 1903–1966

SCIENCE

Science does not permit exceptions.
CLAUDE BERNARD, 1813–1878

Science knows only one commandment: contribute to science.
BERTOLT BRECHT, 1898–1956

I suspect that the truth is that far more students are likely to be put off science by the thought that they are expected to perform cruel and entirely pointless experiments on animals.

VERNON COLEMAN;
Why Animal Experiments Must Stop, 1991

After all, science is essentially international, and it is only through lack of the historical sense that national qualities have been attributed to it.

MARIE CURIE, 1867–1934

There is no certainty in science where one of the mathematical sciences cannot be applied.

(LEONARDO) DA VINCI, 1452–1519

Science tells how to heal and how to kill; it reduces the death rate in retail and then kills us wholesale in war....

WILL(IAM) (JAMES) DURANT; *The Story of Philosophy*, 1926

The eventual goal of science is to provide a single theory that describes the whole universe.

STEPHEN W. HAWKING; *A Brief History of Time*, 1988

The great tragedy of science – the slaying of a beautiful theory by an ugly fact.

T(HOMAS) H(ENRY) HUXLEY, 1825–1895

The phrase "popular science" has in itself a touch of absurdity, that knowledge which is popular is not scientific.

MARIA MITCHELL, 1818–1889

There are no such things as applied sciences, only application of science.

(LOUIS) PASTEUR, 1822–1895

Science is the search for truth – it is not a game in which one tries to beat his opponents, to do harm to others.

LINUS PAULING; *No More War*, 1958

Science is facts. Just as houses are made of stones so is science made of facts. But a pile of stones is not a house and a collection of facts is not necessarily science.

J(ULES) H(ENRI) POINCARÉ; *Value of Science*, 1904

Science may carry us to Mars, but it will leave the earth peopled as ever by the inept.

AGNES REPPLIER; *In Pursuit of Laughter*, 1936

All science is dominated by the idea of approximation.

BERTRAND RUSSELL, 1872–1970

The sciences have always been the disciplines considered most masculine, both in the way they are conceived and in the overwhelming predominance of male participants, particularly at the upper levels.

ANGELA SIMEONE; *Academic Women*, 1987

If mathematical measurement is the first principle of modern science, empirical observation is its second.

PRESERVED SMITH;
A History of Modern Culture (vol. 1), 1962

Science is organized knowledge.

HERBERT SPENCER, 1820–1903

Until scientists acknowledge and stress the ambiguities and uncertainties involved in interpreting data when they teach students – and the general public – about their work, the real essence of science will not be understood, and scientific literacy will continue to suffer.

JEFFREY H. SWARTZ;
The Chronicle of Higher Education, 8 Dec. 1993

True science teaches, above all, to doubt and to be ignorant.

(MIGUEL DE) UNAMUNO (Y JUGO);
The Tragic Sense of Life, 1913

One could count on one's fingers the number of scientists in the entire world who have a general idea of the history and development of their own particular science; there is not one who is really competent as regards sciences other than his own. As science forms an invisible whole, one may say that there are no longer, strictly speaking, any scientists, but only drudges doing scientific work.

SIMONE WEIL; *Oppression and Liberty*, 1955

Science is the record of dead religions.

OSCAR WILDE, 1854–1900

SCIENTIFIC

Alas! The scientific conscience has got into the debasing company of money, obligation and selfish respects.

GEORGE ELIOT (pseud. of MARY ANN EVANS);
Middlemarch, 1871

The man who discovers a new scientific truth has previously had to smash to atoms almost everything he had learnt and arrives at the new truth with hands bloodstained from the slaughter of a thousand platitudes.

(JOSÉ) ORTEGA Y GASSET; *The Revolt of the Masses*, 1930

A person can only be educated if he is able to be "critical" in a wide range of scientific knowledge.

CHARLES VAN DOREN; *A History of Knowledge*, 1991

SECRET

The secret of education lies in respecting the pupil.

RALPH WALDO EMERSON, 1802–1882

SELF-CONCEPT

How anybody dresses is indicative of his self-concept. If students are dirty and ragged, it indicates they are not interested in tidying up their intellects either.

S(AMUEL) I(CHIYÉ) HAYAKAWA;
Herald-Examiner, 8 Apr. 1973

SEMANTICS

Semantics teaches us to watch our prejudices.

STUART CHASE; *Guides to Straight Thinking*, 1956

SENSES

Education is our sixth sense.

CLIVE HOWARD BELL, 1881–1964

One might say that the American trend of education is to reduce the senses almost to nil.

ISADORA DUNCAN; *My Life*, 1942

SENTENCE

Some sentences release their poisons only after years.

ELIAS CANETTI; *The Human Province*, 1978

No complete son of a bitch ever wrote a good sentence.

MALCOLM COWLEY, 1898–1989

[T]he fool who knows nothing about writing and fills students with such patent absurdities as "You must never begin a sentence with and or but."

GEORGE H. DOUGLAS; *Education Without Impact*, 1992

In all pointed sentences, some degree of accuracy must be sacrificed to conciseness.

SAMUEL JOHNSON, 1709–1784

[B]y definition, a sentence is a group of words containing a subject and a predicate and expressing a complete thought. Yet various kinds of statements express a complete thought without a stated or implied subject or predicate.

HARRY SHAW; *Punctuate It Right!*, 1963

A perfectly healthy sentence is extremely rare.

H(ENRY) D(AVID) THOREAU; *Journal*, 1841

SERVICE

The aim of education is to cultivate people who can be of service to the State and nation.

ARINORI MORI; a *ministerial speech*, 1887

SEX EDUCATION

What my research has shown is that if you ask parents what they think, an overwhelming number want sex education to be taught in schools.
ISOBEL ALLEN; *The Guardian*, 25 Mar. 1994

Primary and secondary school systems in general are archaic in the dissemination of family life education, in particular sex education, which is only one small aspect of the entire program. School boards make judgements on the inclusion of sexual information in the curricula, often to the detriment of the student.
MARTHA U. BARNARD & BARBARA J. CLANCY;
in *Human Sexuality for Health Professionals*, 1978

Before the child ever gets to school it will have received crucial, almost irrevocable sex education and this will have been taught by the parents, who are not aware of what they are doing.
MARY S. CALDERONE; *The People*, 21 Jan. 1980

Yet there is still opposition to school sex education programs. . . .
KATHRYN CHRISTIANSEN;
in *Human Sexuality for Health Professionals*, 1978

So sex education has to be given *before* it is needed for practical purposes.
ALEX COMFORT & JANE COMFORT; *The Facts of Love*, 1979

The Netherlands has an enviable record on sex education and the lowest rate of teenage pregnancy in Europe.
The European (élan), 11–17 Mar. 1994

These kinds of [sex education] campaigners have made an industry out of ramming sex down young people's throats.
MICHAEL FALLON; *The Guardian*, 25 Mar. 1994

Discussion of sex in school has become like buying a cheap hamburger: where's the joy?
WARREN FARRELL; *The Myth of Male Power*, 1993

And of course there's sex education at school. Some people's experience of normal sex education isn't very encouraging. Sadly, even in a period of time in which the threat of HIV and AIDS makes ignorance about sexual matters potentially fatal, there's still a big problem with talking about sex in schools.

> NICK FISHER; *Your Pocket Guide to Sex*, 1994
> [Produced by the Health Education Authority, this book
> was censured and withdrawn by the UK government;
> it was later published commercially.]

The problem of teenage pregnancy I view as being tied up with the school system.... I believe that Family Education starts being taught at the secondary school level. It is too late. I suggest we again introduce this topic early in the students' learning process.

> M. GALETSHOGE; *Education for All in Botswana*, 1993

I regard this guide [*Your Pocket Guide to Sex*] as nothing more than state-funded official pornography.

> VICTORIA GILLICK; *The Guardian*, 25 Mar. 1994

There is today great agitation throughout the land to do something about sex education in schools and colleges.

> WARREN R. JOHNSON & EDWIN G. BELZER;
> *Human Sexual Behavior and Sex Education*, 1973

They [teachers] should be emotionally mature persons who have worked through their own feelings about sex to the point where they accept sex both emotionally and intellectually as a normal and natural part of human life to be discussed frankly without either prudishness or vulgarity.

> S(AMUEL) R. LAYCOCK; *Family Living and Sex Education*, 1967

Sex is a natural function. You can't make it happen, but you can teach people to let it happen.

> WILLIAM H. MASTERS; *The New York Times*, 29 Oct. 1984

For those enraged by the idea of sex education in schools, it is clear that honesty is not the best policy.... [H]ow can we tell our children sex is always a beautiful loving thing that occurs only within long-term relationships? We know different. They know different.

> SUZANNE MOORE; *The Guardian*, 25 Mar. 1994

Although many children now get some sex education in the classroom, typically teachers limit the discussion to the stark facts of reproduction – the "plumbing" of sex, rather than its emotional and social aspects.

CAROLE WADE OFFIR; *Human Sexuality*, 1982

A teachers' union has said it will support children who want to take legal action against their parents for preventing them receiving sex education in school.

FRANCES RAFFERTY;
The Times Educational Supplement, 11 Mar. 1994

In a recent World Health Organisation report on 19 countries, the overwhelming conclusion reached was that sex education does not encourage promiscuity but can actually delay a youngster's first sexual experience.

SANDRA SMITH; *The European*, 8–14 Apr. 1994

SEXISM

Governments are far from living up to their commitment to reduce gender disparity in education. While progress has been achieved in some countries, in too many cases women's position in society and their education is far from satisfactory. Their lower status is rooted in economic inequality, society's reluctance to change attitudes, and sexually discriminatory practices and habits.

MARCELA BALLARA;
International Herald Tribune, 8 Sep. 1993

The best educational training for a boy is not the best for a girl, nor that for a girl best for a boy.

EDWARD H. CLARKE; *Sex in Education*, 1873

The traditional belief in the inferiority of women is a doctrine that has been so thoroughly imposed in the past few centuries by the combined weight of law, religion, government, and education that its refutation by history, archeology, anthropology, and psychology will have little effect without extreme measures on the part of established authority.

ELIZABETH GOULD DAVIS; *The First Sex*, 1973

Most white students do not take gender and homosexuality very seriously as political issues.

DINESH D'SOUZA; *Illiberal Education*, 1992

Women were admitted to the student body, for Plato remained to this extent a radical, that he was an ardent feminist.

WILL(IAM) (JAMES) DURANT;
The Story of Civilization (vol. II), 1939

Overt and covert sexism stands in the way of equal education.

CECELIA H. FOXLEY; *Sex Equity in Education*, 1988

Research at all levels shows that a paper or thesis bearing a female name gets a lower grade than precisely the same paper or thesis delivered under a male name.

MARILYN FRENCH; *The War Against Women*, 1992

If the educational system is to change its traditional attitudes regarding gender roles and move toward increasing flexibility, individuals within the system have first to confront their own beliefs and attitudes about the limitations and potential of males and females.

ESTHER R. GREENGLASS; *A World of Difference*, 1982

With few exceptions girls have been educated to be drudges, or toys, beneath men; or a sort of angel above him. . . . The possibility that the ideal of womanhood lies neither in the fair saint nor in the fair sinner; that the female type of character is neither better nor worse than the male, but only weaker; that women are meant neither to be men's guardians nor their playthings, but their comrades, their fellows and their equals, so far as Nature puts no bar to the equality, does not seem to have entered into the minds of those who have had the conduct of the education of girls.

T(HOMAS) H(ENRY) HUXLEY;
Emancipation – Black and White, 1865

In those days, people did not think it was important for girls to read. Some people thought too much reading gave girls brain fever.

ANN McGOVERN; *The Secret Soldier*, 1975

If children go to single sex schools, they are likely to have their sexism reinforced.

ROLAND MEIGHAN;
Theory and Practice of Regressive Education, 1993

The split between the TV set and the school reflects the dichotomy between "masculine" and "feminine" values. On the one hand there are the powerful, wealthy broadcasters and advertisers – mostly male – who care primarily about making money and are rewarded with prestige and power. On the other hand there are the nice, caring teachers – mostly female – who look out for the welfare of children and enjoy low salaries and low prestige.

MYRIAM MIEDZIAN; *Boys Will Be Boys*, 1991

So the educational system which discriminates, in its early modes of teaching, against boys, turns at a later stage against girls.

ANNE MOIR & DAVID JESSEL; *Brain Sex*, 1989

In school books, the Dick and Jane Syndrome reinforced our emerging attitudes. The arithmetic books posed appropriate conundrums: "Ann has three pies . . . Dan has three rockets. . . ." We read the nuances between the lines: Ann keeps her eye on the oven; Dan sets his sights on the moon.

LETTY COTTIN POGREBIN; *The First Ms Reader*, 1972

When blatantly sexual or sexist remarks become an accepted part of classroom conversation, female students are degraded.

MYRA SADKER & DAVID SADKER; *Failing at Fairness*, 1994

Equality of the sexes must be recognized and reinforced through the proper use of terminology. An androgynous language will be balanced and complementary, and free of thoughts and concepts that are discriminatory and unfair. The changes to be made are not simple all the time, hence writers must use their discretion in making choices. Language has to reflect reality – women became "persons" a long time ago and should be acknowledged as such.

MANJU SAH & CATHERINE RANCY;
Guidelines for Non-sexist Writing, 1986
[pub. Canadian Advisory Council on the Status of Women]

We educate one another; and we cannot do this if half of us consider the other half not good enough to talk to.

GEORGE BERNARD SHAW, 1856–1950

Not the least original idea of Comenius was his demand for the equal education of girls and boys.

PRESERVED SMITH;
A History of Modern Culture (vol. I), 1962

If the men in the room would only think how they would feel graduating with a "spinster of arts" they would see how important this is.

GLORIA STEINEM; a *speech* (Yale University), Sep. 1981

[S]ome feminists say that campus sexism is simply an extension of discrimination that exists in Canadian society.

NORA UNDERWOOD; *Maclean's*, 15 Mar. 1990

Men, in general, employ their reason to justify their inherited prejudices against women, rather than to understand them and to root them out.

MARY WOLLSTONECRAFT, 1759–1797

SEXUALITY

The educability of a young person as a rule comes to an end when sexual desire breaks out in its final strength.

(SIGMUND) FREUD;
A General Introduction to Psychoanalysis, 1916–17

However liberal a teacher may be she early discovers that the rigid embargo imposed upon physical contact between teacher and pupil must be observed, because the last flame of sexual energy is only destructive and can only be corrupted, given the wider context and the socializing function of the school. It is an aching nerve in the education situation and will remain so, unless our whole sexual orientation is radically changed.

GERMAINE GREER; *The Female Eunuch*, 1971

SHAKESPEARE

I acknowledge Shakespeare to be the world's greatest dramatic poet, but regret that no parent could place the uncorrected book in the hands of his daughter, and therefore I have prepared the Family Shakespeare.... Many words and expressions occur which are of so indecent a nature as to render it highly desirable that they should be erased.... Expressions are omitted which can not with propriety be read aloud in the family.

THOMAS BOWDLER, 1754–1825

I have tried to read Shakespeare, and found it so intolerably dull that it nauseates me.

CHARLES DARWIN, 1809–1882

In the writing of other poets a character is too often an individual, in those of Shakespeare it is commonly a species.

SAMUEL JOHNSON; *The Preface to Shakespeare*, 1765

When I read Shakespeare I am struck with wonder
That such trivial people should muse and thunder
In such lovely language.

D(AVID) H(ERBERT) LAWRENCE, 1885–1930

We foreigners, born outside of the magic pale of the Anglo-Saxon race, place Shakespeare upon a much higher pedestal. We claim that, before being English, he was human, and that his creations are not bound either by local or ethnological limits, but belong to humanity in general.

HELENA MODJESKA; *Memories and Impressions*, 1910

Shakespeare seemed to have had the art of the Dervish in the Arabian tales who could throw his soul into the body of another man and be at once possessed of his sentiments, adopt his passions and rise to all the functions and feelings of his situation.

ELIZABETH MONTAGUE;
*An Essay on the Writing and Genius of Shakespeare Compared
with Greek and French Dramatic Poets (1769)*, 1785

Children are made to learn bits of Shakespeare by heart, with the result that after they associate him with pedantic boredom . . . Shakespeare did not write with a view to boring school-children; he wrote with a view of delighting audiences.

BERTRAND RUSSELL; *New Hopes for a Changing World*, 1951

Shakespeare, however, is remarkable among the great poets for being without a philosophy and without a religion. In his drama there is no fixed conception of any forces, natural or moral, dominating and transcending our moral energies.

(GEORGE) SANTAYANA;
Interpretation of Poetry and Religion, 1924

What do I miss, as a human being, if I have never heard of the Second Law of Thermodynamics? The answer is: nothing. And what do I miss by not knowing Shakespeare? Unless I get my understanding from another source, I simply miss my life.

E(RNST) F(RIEDRICH) SCHUMACHER; *Small is Beautiful*, 1973

Wonderful women! Have you ever thought how much we all, and women especially, owe to Shakespeare for his vindication of women in these fearless, high-spirited, resolute and intelligent heroines?

ELLEN TERRY, 1848–1928

Crude, immoral, vulgar and senseless.

(LEO NIKOLAYEVICH) TOLSTOY, 1828–1910

This enormous dunghill.

VOLTAIRE (né FRANÇOIS MARIE AROUET), 1694–1778

Each humbler muse at distance may admire,
But none to Shakespeare's fame e'er dare aspire.

MERCY OTIS WARREN, 1728–1814

SILENCE

He is nearest to the gods who knows how to be silent.

(MARCUS PORCIUS) CATO, 234–149

The non-social character of the traditional school is seen in the fact that it erected silence into one of its prime virtues.

JOHN DEWEY; *Education and Experience*, 1938

Silence is the essential condition of happiness.

HEINRICH HEINE, 1797–1856

A silent mouth is sweet to hear.

IRISH proverb

Even in elementary classrooms, going to school is a passive activity; children are expected to sit quietly.

MARGARET DIANE LECOMPTE & ANTHONY GARY DWORKIN;
Giving Up on School, 1991

Silence is man's chief learning.

PALLADAS, *c*.300–*c*.400

Whereof one cannot speak, thereof one must be silent.
(LUDWIG JOSEF JOHANN) WITTGENSTEIN, 1889–1951

SLANG

All slang is metaphor, and all metaphor is poetry.
G(ILBERT) K(EITH) CHESTERTON, 1874–1936

The one stream of poetry which is continually flowing is slang.
G(ILBERT) K(EITH) CHESTERTON, 1874–1936

Correct English is the slang of prigs who write history and essays. And the strongest slang of all is the slang of poets.
GEORGE ELIOT (pseud. of MARY ANN EVANS), 1819–1880

Slang is a language that rolls up its sleeves, spits on its hands and goes to work.
CARL SANDBURG; *The New York Times*, 13 Feb. 1959

SMILE

Schools are frequently perceived as exclusively serious places, where laughter and enjoyment are suspect. Suspicions are aroused when people smile.
RITA S. BRAUSE; *Enduring Schools*, 1992

A teacher should be sparing of his smile.
WILLIAM COWPER, 1731–1800

A reputation for humor is disastrous to statesmen and philosophers.
WILL(IAM) (JAMES) DURANT; *The Story of Philosophy*, 1926

Wipe that smile off your face.
in *Enduring Schools*, 1992

SOCIALIZATION

The most important thing children learn is not the three R's. It's socialization.
BRUNO BETTELHEIM, 1903–1990

The school is primarily a social institution.
JOHN DEWEY; *My Pedagogic Creed*, 1897

The educational system can be regarded as a significant socializing agent of gender roles. In fact, traditional attitudes about gender roles pervade the entire system.
ESTHER R. GREENGLASS; *A World of Difference*, 1982

Our schools have become vast factories for the manufacture of robots. We no longer send our young to them primarily to be taught and given the tools of thought, no longer primarily to be informed and to acquire knowledge; but to be "socialized."
ROBERT LINDER; *Must You Conform?*, 1956

[I]n daily life as well as in mass education, they [students] are exposed variously to racism, sexism, homophobia, fascination with the rich and powerful, excessive consumerism, the generation gap, heroic militarism, self-reliant individualism, and a dependent relationship to authority. In this totality of socializing experiences, students are developed into passive learners, unmotivated citizens and underperforming workers urged to buy things they don't need.
IRA SHOR; *Empowering Education*, 1992

SOCIAL RESEARCH

I will never know the experience of others, but I can know my own, and I can approximate theirs by entering their world. This approximation marks the tragic, perpetually inaccurate aspect of social research.
SHULAMIT REINHARZ; *On Becoming a Social Scientist*, 1984

SOCIOLOGIST

These terrible sociologists who are the astrologers and alchemists of our twentieth century.

(MIGUEL DE) UNAMUNO (Y JUGO), 1864–1936

SOCIOLOGY

[T]he sociology of education is a chapter, and not the least significant, in the sociology of knowledge and also the sociology of power....

PIERRE BOURDIEU; *la noblesse d'État*, 1989

The science with the greatest number of methods and the least results.

J(ULES) H(ENRI) POINCARÉ, 1854–1912

The study of people who do not need to be studied by people who do.

E(THEL) S(IBYL) TURNER, 1872–1958

SOCRATES

Socrates was condemned to death at Athens for teaching atheism to the young men, but in fact he had only criticized the myths about the Greek gods for being immoral.

GEOFFREY PARRINDER; *World Religions*, 1983

SOLITUDE

Learning, thinking, innovation, and maintaining contact with one's own inner world are all facilitated by solitude.

ANTHONY STORR; *Solitude*, 1989

SOPHISTRY

If we take in our hand any volume; of divinity or school metaphysics, for instances; let us ask, Does it contain any abstract reasoning concerning quantity or number? No. Does it contain any experimental reasoning, concerning matter of fact and existence? No. Commit it then to the flames: for it can contain nothing but sophistry and illusion.

DAVID HUME, 1711–1776

SPECIALIST

The specialist who is trained but uneducated, technically skilled but culturally incompetent, is a menace.

DAVID B. TUBMAN;
an *address* (Columbia University), 15 Apr. 1964

SPELLING

Spell well, if you can.

LUCY HAY, 1599–1660

English spelling is an affair of memory, not of reason.

GEORGINA GODDARD KING;
Bryn Mawr Spelling Book, 1909

[T]hey load their children with anxiety about the spelling system which English has developed. This is hard to learn, illogical and even downright silly sometimes, but children have to master it, suppressing the temptation to use their own phonetic alternative spellings, before anything they write can be taken seriously and appreciated for its content rather than its form.

CHRIS SHUTE; *Compulsory Schooling Disease*, 1993

SPIRIT

In order for teachers to satisfy the inherent requirements of a humanly meaningful form of education, it is absolutely imperative that they possess a free and magnanimous spirit.

TERUHISA HORIO;
Educational Thought and Ideology in Modern Japan, 1988

SPORT

Young women who make Stanford's [University sport] cheerleading team, called "Dollies," earn one unit of academic credit for their exertions.
MARTIN ANDERSON; *Imposters in the Temple*, 1992

Competitive sport in school is absolutely essential. Life's a competition, isn't it?
KEITH ANDREW; *The Independent*, 9 Apr. 1994

The traditional assumption that competitive sport builds character is still with us today in spite of overwhelming contrary evidence.
DORCAS SUSAN BUTT; *Psychology of Sport*, 1976

The last thing in the world a college or university should be concerned with is being number one in football or basketball if the price one pays for that is the corruption of character and the undermining of true student morale on campus.
HOWARD COSELL; *Like It Is*, 1974

The trouble is that games in our [UK] education system are based on the very Victorian idea that if you have girls and boys on the pitch you are stopping them thinking about other things.
BARRY CRIPPS;
The Times Educational Supplement, 11 Mar. 1994

I have yet to see the laboratory or library or dormitory built with football or basketball revenues.
A. BARTLETT GIAMATTI, 1938–1989

Sports have been institutionalized within the educational system.
ALLEN GUTTMANN; *A Whole New Ball Game*, 1988

In the German system, universities devote themselves to education . . . while private clubs provide for both participant and spectator sports. The corruption of the university is avoided by the elimination of temptation.
ALLEN GUTTMANN; *A Whole New Ball Game*, 1988

Should sport be forced on schoolchildren? . . . If sporting activities are educationally valuable, children can reasonably be forced to engage in them, just as they are forced to study mathematics for their own good. If sports are a substitute for war, if they glamorise or actually increase aggression, or if they are merely an outlet for primitive survival instincts, the case for compulsion is much weaker.

The Independent, 9 Apr. 1994

A school without football is in danger of deteriorating into a medieval study hall.

VINCE LOMBARDI; *The New York Times*, 10 Dec. 1967

Sports is an area of life in which it is permissible to suspend usual moral standards.

MYRIAM MIEDZIAN; *Boys Will Be Boys*, 1991

Sport must be counted as a primary rite of male deformation.

ROSALIND MILES; *The Rites of Man*, 1992

Athletic sports, save in the case of young boys, are designed for idiots.

GEORGE JEAN NATHAN, 1882–1958

It was like a heart transplant. We tried to implant college in him [a football player] but his head rejected it.

BARRY SWITZER; *Sports Illustrated*, 12 Nov. 1973

The addiction to sports, therefore, in a peculiar degree marks an arrested development of man's moral development.

(THORSTEIN) VEBLEN, 1857–1929

Big-time American football, for which the brittle human body is unsuited, flourishes on campuses, where it is inappropriate.

GEORGE F. WILL; *International Herald Tribune*, 6 Oct. 1993

STATE

[T]he state school sought to establish one uniform educational, if not social, experience for all by dispensing the same body of learning to all children. The child, who now spent the bulk of his time in school, was raised more by his teachers than his father.

ELISABETH BADINTER; *The Myth of Motherhood*, 1981

And if a person's curriculum of life was originally envisaged as a ladder leading to heavenly salvation, it was gradually recast as a branching tree or a journey that took each learner to a different location in the secular order of things.

DAVID HAMILTON; *Learning about Education*, 1990

In truth the teachers bear none of the blame for the problems of education; it is we, the voters, who are at fault for imagining that large institutions, managed by the state, can nurture young souls.

ROBERT VAN DE WEYER; *The Health of Nations*, 1991

STATISTICS

There are three kinds of lies: lies, damned lies, and statistics.

BENJAMIN DISRAELI, 1804–1881

I could prove God statistically.

GEORGE GALLUP, 1901–1984

Statistics don't bleed.

ARTHUR KOESTLER, 1905–1983

Statistics are like alienists – they will testify for either side.

FIORELLO LA GUARDIA, 1882–1947

He uses statistics as a drunken man uses lamp-posts – for support rather than illumination.

ANDREW LANG, 1844–1912

Statistics will prove anything, even the truth.

NOËL MOYNIHAN, 1916–

So here is yet another introductory book about statistics. Who needs it?

DEREK ROWNTREE; *Statistics Without Tears*, 1981

Statistics never prove anything.

E(RNST) F(RIEDRICH) SCHUMACHER; *Small is Beautiful*, 1973

Facts speak louder than statistics.
GEOFFREY STREATFIELD; *The Observer*, 19 Mar. 1950

We let information (especially in the form of statistics) push us around and make our decisions for us.
RICHARD SAUL WURMAN; *Information Anxiety*, 1991

STATUS QUO

[T]hey do their utmost to preserve the status quo.
SIMONE DE BEAUVOIR, 1908–1986

Citizens as conceived by governments are persons who admire the *status quo* and are prepared to exert themselves for its preservation.
BERTRAND RUSSELL; *Education and the Social Order*, 1932

Schools are organized to maintain and defend the status quo. . . .
PHILLIP C. SCHLECHTY; *Schools for the 21st Century*, 1991

Education is big business. As such, it has developed powerful institutions that fight all serious attempts to change the status quo.
WILLIAM TUCKER; *Forbes*, 2 Mar. 1992

STEINER

What Rudolf Steiner actually gave was an inexhaustible fund of fruitful suggestions. In fact his whole pedagogy can be looked upon as a path of self-education for the teacher. Whoever follows it patiently will gradually learn from the children the right way of teaching them.
FRANS CARLGREN; *Rudolf Steiner and Anthroposophy*, 1979

The name Rudolf Steiner is not a familiar one to mainstream American educators. Yet the visionary theories of this Austrian philosopher have provided the fundamental guidelines for the largest independent [Waldorf] school movement in the world.
WILLIAM A. REINSMITH; *Educational Forum*, vol. 54, 1989

STEREOTYPING

The perpetuating of gender-role stereotyping also characterizes the educational system from elementary school to university.

ESTHER R. GREENGLASS; *A World of Difference*, 1982

Educational institutions mirror the stereotypes of the larger society. The fact that education has become known as a "woman's field" stems at least in part from the identification of childcare and child rearing as woman's work. Men frequently view teaching as a stepping stone to educational administration while women look to careers as classroom teachers.

CAROL POLOWY; *Vital Speeches*, 1 Feb. 1975

After sitting through years and years of lessons that only rarely mention women (or only mention them in stereotyped contexts), it is no wonder that many students take with them from school a sex-stereotyped view of the world.

SHIRLEY WEITZ; *Sex Roles*, 1977

STOPOUT

Instead of regarding the *drop out* as a bad idea, why not have the *stop out* as a good idea.

CLARK KERR; *Higher Education for the Future*, 1971

Stopout students include the thinkers, the non-conformists, the innovators.

JUDI R. KESSELMAN; *Stopping Out*, 1976

STUDENT

Disciples do owe their master only a temporary belief, and a suspension of their own judgement till they be fully instructed; and not an absolute resignation nor perpetual captivity.

FRANCIS BACON, 1561–1626

I find most [US] college students to be almost totally ignorant about world geography, world history, English literature, the true history of America, or the history of the nuclear age. Most do not know about Hiroshima and Nagasaki or about Hitler, and do not have a true understanding of the etiology of environmental threats to earth.

HELEN CALDICOTT; *If You Love This Planet*, 1992

If you are dirty, promiscuous, idle and wear your hair long, you can always claim to be a student.

JOHN DUNNING; *Deadly Deviates*, 1986

In nearly every student there is a five-year-old "unschooled" mind struggling to get out and express itself.

HOWARD GARDNER; *The Unschooled Mind*, 1993

We have to stop being teacher-centered, and become student-centered. It's not what you think they need, but what they think they need.

MARY ANNE GUITAR; *Mademoiselle*, Feb. 1961

[Today's students] can put dope in their veins or hope in their brains. . . . If they can conceive it and believe it, they can achieve it. They must know it is not their aptitude but their attitude that will determine their altitude.

JESSE JACKSON; *Washington Post*, 21 May 1978

Often the school day is boring, humiliating, and unappealing to students. Students find that there is little connection between doing well in school and any real reward out of school.

MARGARET DIANE LECOMPTE & ANTHONY GARY DWORKIN; *Giving Up on School*, 1991

It is inevitable that bright young students will be seen as a threat by older academics, and it requires great self-control for teachers to overcome this.

DESMOND MORRIS; *The Human Zoo*, 1969

Students are asked to think for themselves but they don't know what to do. They're used to being told what to think and what to memorize.

MOTOI OMORI; *The Toronto Star*, 9 May 1987

Students from minority, female, and working-class groups face special challenges and sacrifices when trying to "make it" through education. Many face the painful choice between allegiance to their roots or to success.

IRA SHOR; *Empowering Education*, 1992

The student who, during the course of ten years in school, meets two or three outstanding and congenial teachers has had a fortunate experience. Many are not so lucky.

LAWRENCE STENHOUSE;
a *paper* (Simon Fraser University), 1980

Theories and goals of education don't matter a whit if you don't consider your students to be human beings.

LOU ANN WALKER; *A Loss of Words*, 1986

Much of what students produce is artificial. That is, it has no purpose, no audience, no reason for existence beyond satisfying a teacher, or, just as likely, satisfying whoever developed the dittos that go along with the prepackaged curriculum. Most kids get good at these exercises, figuring out that filling in the blanks with words or phrases copied from the text is all they need to do. As soon as these worksheets are handed back, they are wadded up and deposited in the trash, usually on the way out of the door in the afternoon.

GEORGE H. WOOD; *Schools That Work*, 1993

STUDY

Studies serve for delight, for ornament, and for ability.

FRANCIS BACON, 1561–1626

To spend too much time in studies is sloth; to use them too much for ornament is affectation; to take judgement wholly by their rules, is the humour of a scholar.

FRANCIS BACON, 1561–1626

Avoid studies of which the result dies with the worker.

(LEONARDO) DA VINCI, 1452–1519

Just as eating against one's will is injurious to health, so study without a liking for it spoils the memory, and it retains nothing it takes in.

(LEONARDO) DA VINCI, 1452–1519

Studying is a difficult task that requires a systematic critical attitude and intellectual discipline acquired only through practice.

PAULO FREIRE; *The Politics of Education*, 1985

The proper study of mankind is books.

ALDOUS HUXLEY; *Crome Yellow*, 1926

I am convinced that for the studies in question (literature, history, politics, science) the years after 18 are a better age, and those after 30 better still.

RICHARD LIVINGSTONE; *The Future in Education*, 1941

Study depends on the good will of the student, a quality that cannot be secured by compulsion.

(MARCUS FABIUS) QUINTILIAN(US), *c.*35–*c.*95

It's like the things you study in school: they are a pleasure to skim over, but when you apply yourself to them, go into them deeply, they are boring.

(LUCIUS ANNAEUS) SENECA (the Elder), *c.*54BC–AD39

If the study to which you apply yourself has a tendency to weaken your affections, and to destroy your taste for those simple pleasures in which no alloy can possibly mix, then that study is certainly unlawful, that is to say, not befitting the human mind.

MARY SHELLEY; *Frankenstein*, 1881

STUPIDITY

The University brings out all abilities, including stupidity.

(ANTON PAVLOVICH) CHEKOV; *Notebooks*, 1892–1904

The stupid people are an overwhelming majority all over the world.

(HENRIK) IBSEN, 1828–1906

Against stupidity the very gods fight in vain.

(JOHANN CHRISTOPH FRIEDRICH VON) SCHILLER, 1759–1805

There is no sin except stupidity.

OSCAR WILDE, 1854–1900

SUBJECT

[A]ny subject can be taught effectively in some intellectually honest form to any child at any stage of development.
JEROME S. BRUNER; *The Process of Education*, 1965

A teacher must believe in the value of his subject as a doctor believes in health.
GILBERT HIGHET; *The Art of Teaching*, 1950

Upon the subject of education, not presuming to dictate any plan or system respecting it, I can only say that I view it as the most important subject which we as a people may be engaged in.
ABRAHAM LINCOLN, 1809–1865

All subjects, no matter how specialized, are connected with a centre; they are like rays emanating from a sun.
E(RNST) F(RIEDRICH) SCHUMACHER; *Small is Beautiful*, 1973

Art and religion first; then philosophy; lastly science. That is the order of the great subjects of life, that's their order of importance.
MURIEL SPARK; *The Prime of Miss Jean Brodie*, 1961

SUCCESS

America is a country where one can achieve virtually unlimited success without formal education.
HOWARD GARDNER; *The Unschooled Mind*, 1993

Students who apparently succeed in school often have not understood in a deep sense the very concepts and principles around which their educational program has been designed.
HOWARD GARDNER; *The Unschooled Mind*, 1993

The only place where success comes before work is in the dictionary.
VIDAL SASSOON, 1928–

SUICIDE

If you kill imagination, that is a kind of long-term suicide.

PIERRE BOULEZ, 1925–

There is but one truly serious philosophical problem and that is suicide.

ALBERT CAMUS, 1913–1960

Science commits suicide when it adopts a creed.

T(HOMAS) H(ENRY) HUXLEY, 1825–1895

I take it that no man is educated who has never dallied with the thought of suicide.

WILLIAM JAMES, 1842–1910

To be, or not to be – that is the question. . . .

WILLIAM SHAKESPEARE; *Hamlet*, 1600–01

SYSTEM

Academics and students can walk away from the system, but at their own cost. Stay within the system, and their attitudes and behaviour will continue to express the particular logic of its operations.

PIERRE BOURDIEU & JEAN-CLAUDE PASSERON;
(*Rapport pédagogique et communication*, 1965)/*Academic Discourse*, 1994

As a student you're up against a SYSTEM.

TOM CARNEY & BARBARA CARNEY;
Liberation Learning, 1988

The great expansion of educational systems also inevitably increased their bureaucratization, which in turn led frequently to extreme centralization of decision making, to rigidities, delays and inefficiencies in execution, and to stifling new ideas and initiatives at lower echelons and in individual schools and classrooms.

PHILIP M. COOMBS;
Future Critical World Issues in Education, 1981

[W]e read about him in the newspaper: he had killed both his young sisters with a knife as they returned home from school.... Tim is a constant reminder to me of my failure to communicate and a reproach to an educational system that forced him into an environment so hostile to his needs.

NICK DISCOMBE; *Ottawa Citizen*, 16 Feb. 1988

In modern societies with universal elementary education so long established that compulsory attendance is no longer considered an infringement of individual liberty, it rarely occurs to anyone but lecturers in the philosophy of education to ask what the school system is intended to do.

R.P. DORE; *Education in Tokugawa Japan*, 1965

Britain has always been good at educating its elite, but its schools fail most of its children. The education systems ... are rooted still in a past of giant factories and semi-literate "hands", ignoring the present and future of high-tech firms and highly-skilled workers.... As jobs in manufacturing disappear – as they will, recession or no – many will find it even harder to get work. They will drift into welfare-dependency or law-breaking.

The Economist, 20 Nov. 1993

Computers can do all the left hemisphere processing better and faster than the human brain. So what's left for the human brain is global thinking, intuitive-problem solving, seeing the whole picture. All of that can not be done by the computer. And yet the school system goes on churning out reading, writing and arithmetic, spelling, grammar.

BETTY EDWARDS; in *Common Ground of Puget Sound*, 1989

We have inadvertently designed a system in which being good at what you do as a teacher is not formally regarded, while being poor at what you do is seldom corrected nor penalized.

ELLIOT EISNER; *The New York Times*, 3 Sep. 1985

Our system of education is a system of despair.

RALPH WALDO EMERSON; *Essays*, 1844

Schooling was invented to control and to redirect earlier educational practices, just as the factory system was devised to control and redirect the fortunes of domestic producers.

DAVID HAMILTON; *Learning about Education*, 1990

Education is delivered when, where, how and what the *system* decides.

> CHARLES HANDY & ROBERT AITKEN;
> *Understanding Schools as Organizations,* 1986

One of the things that is manifestly wrong with our school system is our thoughtless practice of hiring the youngest and the least experienced teachers for the lowest classes, when it should be quite the other way around.

> SYDNEY HARRIS; *Detroit Free Press,* 15 Jul. 1981

The school system is a modern phenomenon, as is the childhood it produces.

> IVAN ILLICH; *Deschooling Society,* 1971

The educational system in poor states is often largely irrelevant to their own needs; being too closely modelled on imported curricula which reflect other demands and priorities. The consequences are socially wasteful and explosive.

> MICHAEL KIDRON & RONALD SEGAL;
> *The New State of the World Atlas,* 1987

These westerners brought with them the concept of a new religion, their language (first English, then Afrikaans), their culture and their idea of progress. In transmitting all these to Blacks, education was an obvious tool. The whole system of education became White-oriented.

> P.C. LUTHULI;
> *An Introduction to Black-Oriented Education in South Africa,* 1982

Also in the process of decay is Africa's schooling system. Teachers are getting disprofessionalized in their commitment to teaching. They are often underpaid, and in some counties not paid at all for months on end. The teachers have to look for moonlighting opportunities, opportunities that give them an additional livelihood alongside teaching. In Africa, the sense of vocation in education is under severe strain.

> ALI A. MAZRUI; *Uganda Now,* 1988

The focus is now on perpetuating the system rather than remaining true to its original mission, educating children ... and the feeling among parents is that they are no longer in charge.

> PEGGY O'MARA; *The Globe and Mail,* 14 Aug. 1992

Our school system, as much under left-wing as under right-wing regimes, has been constructed by conservatives (from the pedagogic point of view) who were thinking much more in terms of fitting our rising generation into the molds of traditional learning than in terms of inventive and critical minds.

JEAN PIAGET;
Science of Education and the Psychology of the Child, 1970

Shorn of its role as a purveyor of national culture, the state system becomes vulnerable on one side to ethnic groups who complain that the system has not changed enough to meet their demands, and on the other to those who question whether the system has changed so much that it has lost its raison d'être.

DIANE RAVITCH; *The Economist,* 11 Sep. 1993

The US educational system overall is set up to package information and to process people to be plastic cogs in the economic engine.

STEPHEN H. SCHNEIDER; *World Monitor,* Apr. 1993

Our present education system enables some of us to become richer quicker, to travel further faster, and to establish ourselves more comfortably in the dark wood of meaningless existence.

E(RNST) F(RIEDRICH) SCHUMACHER; *Small is Beautiful,* 1973

We are still trapped in a public education system which is preparing our youth for jobs that no longer exist.

JOHN SCULLEY, 1939–

The brutal reality is that the American system of education is bankrupt.

THOMAS SOWELL; *Inside American Education,* 1993

The most American thing about America is the free common school system.

ADLAI EWING STEVENSON, 1900–1965

I am beginning to suspect all elaborate and special systems of education. They seem to me to be built upon the supposition that every child is a kind of idiot who must be taught to think.

ANNIE SULLIVAN; in *The Story of My Life,* 1903

[E]ducation since the late nineteenth century has become inextricably concerned with the history of schools and a national system.

HUGH THOMAS; *An Unfinished History of the World*, 1979

Many radical feminists see little point in attempting to change the educational system because women are trapped in a vicious circle in which men keep changing the rules if women show any sign of becoming as successful as them.

KIM THOMAS; *Gender and Subject in Higher Education*, 1990

But no other culture in history has ever herded hundreds, even thousands, of children into one place, day after day over fifteen years, as a preparation for adult life. We have become so accustomed to such a system that we rarely question it. . . .

ROBERT VAN DE WEYER; *The Health of Nations*, 1991

Theoretically, the goal of our educational system is bound by the limitations of any bureaucracy, in that the demands of administering the system often take precedence over the initial purpose of the system.

RICHARD SAUL WURMAN; *Information Anxiety*, 1991

T

TABULA RASA

The mind is at birth a clean sheet, a *tabula rasa*; and sense-experience writes upon it in a thousand ways, until sensation begets memory and memory begets ideas.

WILL(IAM) (JAMES) DURANT; *The Story of Philosophy*, 1926

[T]here is nothing in the mind except what was first in the senses.

JOHN LOCKE, 1632–1704

The mind that registers the impressions is conceived by Locke merely as a blank sheet or plain surface – a *tabula rasa*, the ideas being related only by the laws of association.

ROBERT R. RUSK; *Doctrines of the Great Educators*, 1918

When we think, we do not just think: we think with ideas. Our mind is not a blank, a *tabula rasa*. When we begin to think we can do so only because our mind is already filled with all sorts of ideas *with which* to think.

E(RNST) F(RIEDRICH) SCHUMACHER; *Small is Beautiful*, 1973

TALENT

It takes people a long time to learn the difference between talent and genius, especially ambitious young men and women.

LOUISA MAY ALCOTT; *Little Women*, 1868

Tremendous amounts of talent are being lost to our society just because that talent wears a skirt.

SHIRLEY CHISHOLM; *Unbought and Unbossed*, 1970

Mediocrity knows nothing higher than itself, but talent instantly recognizes genius.

ARTHUR CONAN DOYLE, 1859–1930

Nature is monstrously unjust. There is no substitute for talent. Industry and all the virtues are of no avail.

ALDOUS HUXLEY, 1894–1963

Genius does what it must, and Talent does what it can.

OWEN MEREDITH, 1831–1891

TAUGHT

The things taught in schools and colleges are not education, but the means of education.

RALPH WALDO EMERSON, 1803–1882

Nobody can be taught faster than he can learn.

SAMUEL JOHNSON, 1709–1784

Man is the only animal that knows nothing, and can learn nothing without being taught. He can neither speak nor walk nor eat, nor do anything at the prompting of nature, but only weep.

PLINY (the Elder), 23–79

The things we know best are things we haven't been taught.

(LUC DE CLAPIERS, MARQUIS DE) VAUVENARGUES; *Reflections and Maxims*, c.1747

TEACH

You cannot teach a man anything. You can only help him discover it himself.

GALILEO (GALILEI), 1564–1642

To teach one's self is to be forced to learn twice.

ELLEN GLASGOW; *The Woman Within*, 1954

He has learned to no purpose, that is not able to teach.

SAMUEL JOHNSON, 1709–1784

To teach is to learn twice.

JOSEPH JOUBERT; *Pensées*, 1842

I do not teach, I only tell.

(MICHEL EYQUEM DE) MONTAIGNE; *Essays*, 1595

For every person wishing to teach there are thirty not wanting to be taught.
W.C. SELLAR, 1898–1951

Men learn while they teach.
(LUCIUS ANNAEUS) SENECA (the Younger), *c.*4BC–65

I am glad to learn, in order that I may teach.
(LUCIUS ANNAEUS) SENECA (the Younger), *c.*4BC–65

He who can, does. He who cannot, teaches.
GEORGE BERNARD SHAW; *Maxims for Revolutions,* 1903
[In his *Dictionary of Quotations,* Bergen Evans points out that
most anti-intellectuals and so-called people of action have,
almost without exception, proved failures as teachers.]

A man willing to teach reading would wear one feather in his hat. One who would teach writing as well wore two feathers. One who could teach arithmetic wore three feathers.
HUGH THOMAS; *An Unfinished History of the World,* 1979

TEACHABLE MOMENT

A teachable moment occurs when a teacher in a positive state of mind interacts with learners who are in positive states of mind.
DARLENE L. STEWART; *Creating the Teachable Moment,* 1993

TEACHER

A teacher affects eternity.
HENRY (BROOKS) ADAMS;
The Education of Henry Adams, 1907

The true teacher defends his pupils against his own personal influence.
BRONSON ALCOTT, 1799–1888

A poor surgeon hurts 1 person at a time. A poor teacher hurts 130.
ERNEST L. BOYER; *People,* 17 Mar. 1986

Those who become long-term teachers frequently expect to be told what to do, while many of those who start with personal visions are disillusioned and leave dismayed. Thus, schools become havens for those who do not take teaching, or learning for that matter, as a serious, professional concern. They see teaching as a 9 to 3 job which frees them up for summer vacation and most evenings.

RITA S. BRAUSE; *Enduring Schools*, 1992

Teachers, I believe, are the most responsible and important members of society because their professional efforts affect the fate of the earth.

HELEN CALDICOTT; *If You Love This Planet*, 1992

Arrogance, pedantry, and dogmatism are the occupational diseases of those who spend their lives directing the intellects of the young.

HENRY S. CANBY, 1878–1961

Teachers must think for themselves if they are to help others think for themselves.

CARNEGIE CORPORATION OF NEW YORK;
The New York Times, 16 May 1986

A load of books does not equal one good teacher.

CHINESE proverb

Great teachers know that to provide an answer is to confuse ends with means.

LAURENT A. DALOZ; *Effective Teaching and Mentoring*, 1987

These worthy teachers were not overburdened with diplomas, but as far as devotion and morality were concerned, they were second to none.

SIMONE DE BEAUVOIR;
When Things of the Spirit Come First, 1982

We are all imperfect teachers, but we may be forgiven if we have advanced the matter a little, and have done our best.

WILL(IAM) (JAMES) DURANT; *The Story of Philosophy*, 1926

It is the supreme art of the teacher to awaken joy in creating expression and knowledge.

ALBERT EINSTEIN, 1879–1955

The teacher is no longer merely the-one-who-teaches, but one who is himself in dialogue with the students, who in turn while being taught also teaches.

PAULO FREIRE; *Pedagogy of the Oppressed*, 1972

It has been reported that the average schoolteacher reads a book a year.

HOWARD GARDNER; *The Unschooled Mind*, 1993

A teacher is better than two books.

GERMAN proverb

Teachers believe they have a gift for giving; it drives them with the same irrepressible drive that drives others to create a work of art or a market or a building.

A. BARTLETT GIAMATTI; *Harper's*, Jul. 1980

The profession of teacher requires ... as thorough and special training as that of any of the other intellectual professions. The great majority of our teachers are deficient in this training ... the complaint on this head is indeed universal, and it is coupled with another complaint of the inadequate salaries almost everywhere paid to teachers, but more especially in rural districts.

SARAH JOSEPHA HALE, 1788–1879

The members of the most responsible, the least advertised, the worst paid, and the most richly rewarded profession in the world.

IAN HAY, 1876–1952

The work of a teacher in helping students reapprehend the truths they have learned about nature and society within the context of their individualized thoughts and feelings is of primary importance.

TERUHISA HORIO;
Educational Thought and Ideology in Modern Japan, 1988

Schools are designed on the assumption that there is a secret to everything in life; that the quality of life depends on knowing that secret, that secrets can be known in orderly succession; and that only teachers can properly reveal those secrets.

IVAN ILLICH, 1926–

Better than a thousand days of diligent study is one day with a great teacher.

JAPANESE proverb

One looks back with appreciation to the brilliant teachers, but with gratitude to those who touched our human feelings. The curriculum is so much necessary raw material, but warmth is the vital element for the growing plant and for the soul of the child.

(CARL GUSTAV) JUNG, 1875–1961

Everywhere, teachers are facing difficulties with their pupils and students for they too are unprepared for teaching young people who are much more independent than they were at the same age, and considerably better informed and misinformed through the media.

ALEXANDER KING & BERTRAND SCHNEIDER;
The First Global Revolution, 1991

[T]eachers now work increasingly with alienated, uncooperative, and unsuccessful students.

MARGARET DIANE LECOMPTE & ANTHONY GARY DWORKIN;
Giving Up on School, 1991

A teacher is one who, in his youth, admired teachers.

H(ENRY) L(OUIS) MENCKEN, 1880–1956

We teachers can only help the work going on, as servants wait upon a master.

MARIA MONTESSORI, 1870–1952

What was the duty of the teacher if not to inspire.

BHARATI MUKHERJEE;
The Middleman and Other Stories, 1988

What a teacher doesn't say . . . is a telling part of what a student hears.

MAURICE NATANSON; *Time*, 6 Jan. 1985

We should honor our teachers more than our parents, because while our parents cause us to live, our teachers cause us to live well.

PHILOXENUS, *c.*435–380

Rather than serve as catalysts and facilitators for their students' search for knowledge, many teachers find themselves struggling desperately to extract a glint of responsiveness and involvement from large numbers of students who find little meaning from their classes, are frustrated or bored from a lack of challenge, or are committed to avoiding the discomfort of failure.

JAMES P. RAFFINI; *Winners Without Losers*, 1993

Teachers should unmask themselves, admit into consciousness the idea that one does not need to know everything there is to know and one does not have to pretend to know everything there is to know.

ESTER P. ROTHMAN; *Troubled Teachers*, 1977

The teachers of the younger classes, however, need to be more highly skilled than other teachers, and, according to Comenius, ought to receive higher salaries.

ROBERT R. RUSK; *Doctrines of the Great Educators*, 1918

To be an effective teacher, I believe, you have to be willing to take risks.

NATHAN RUTSTEIN; *Education on Trial*, 1992

A natural teacher is a loving, caring and giving person who likes people of all colors and backgrounds, who gains satisfaction from making others happy, who views everyone as fundamentally good, who possesses a positive personality and strong character, who communicates easily and effectively, who is a creative improvisational thinker, who is perceptive and empathetic, and has a genuine desire to help improve the social and economic quality of the community he or she serves.

NATHAN RUTSTEIN; *Education on Trial*, 1992

You don't have to think too hard when you talk to a teacher.

J(EROME) D(AVID) SALINGER, 1919–

Teachers teach children, not subjects. However, this cannot be taken for granted in the reality of today's schools.

MARIANNE SCHULTZ-HECTOR;
Frankfurter Allgemeine, 9 Feb. 1994

Today's educational world sacrifices respect for the conviction of the individual teacher in the beautiful name of school unity and reduces the teacher to a common laborer whose job it is to instruct children.

UNDO TSUZURIKATA SEIKATSU;
The Teaching of Reading, 1916

I'm not a teacher only a fellow traveller of whom you asked the way, I pointed ahead – ahead of myself as well as of you.

GEORGE BERNARD SHAW, 1856–1950

[T]eachers are not supposed to hold out some kind of final, correct worldview, personal philosophy, or set of cultural values to the student, but rather to equip that student better to choose his or her preferred combination of these.

NEIL J. SMELSER; *Daedalus*, vol. 122, 1993

In positive states of mind a teacher is in the mood to teach and to create a classroom atmosphere in which students are ready to learn.

DARLENE L. STEWART; *Creating the Teachable Moment*, 1993

A teacher should have maximal authority and minimal power.

THOMAS STEPHEN SZASZ, 1920–

Good teachers are costly, but bad teachers cost more.

BOB TALBERT; *Detroit Free Press*, 5 Apr. 1982

The only good teachers for you are those friends who love you, who think you are interesting, or very important, or wonderfully funny.

BRENDA UELAND; *If You Want to Write*, 1938

The teachers who bravely promote active pupil involvement are fighting their environment. . . .

ROBERT VAN DE WEYER; *The Health of Nations*, 1991

He is not necessarily the best teacher who performs the most labour; makes his pupils work the hardest, and bustle the most.

EMMA HART WILLARD, 1787–1870

Most of the teachers have but one object, viz. to draw their salary. I do not think that a teacher should have no salary. But I think they should earn it first and then think of it.

SARAH WINNEMUCCA, 1844–1891

One good teacher in a lifetime may sometimes change a delinquent into a solid citizen.

PHILIP WYLIE; *Generation of Vipers*, 1942

Teachers are greater benefactors than parents.

XYSTUS [SIXTUS] I, ?–c.AD125

TEACHER EDUCATION

Preference for stability and caution toward change, is rooted in the people recruited into the [teaching] profession.

LARRY CUBAN; *How Teachers Taught,* 1984

Teaching of others teaches the teacher.

ENGLISH proverb

The gap of contradiction between what perspective teachers are socialized to expect from their training in schools of education and what they experience in urban districts is a central element in the creation of burnout and alienation.

MARGARET DIANE LECOMPTE & ANTHONY GARY DWORKIN;
Giving Up on School, 1991

Teacher education is a huge industry.

MYRON LIEBERMAN; *Public Education,* 1993

Imposing high standards for teacher education programs would lower their enrollments and threaten their survival. Their incentive to keep standards low is very strong indeed.

MYRON LIEBERMAN: *Public Education,* 1993

The present crisis in education and the depressed condition of the teaching profession offer an unusual opportunity to reassess our present arrangements for preparing teachers.

DIANE RAVITCH; *The Schools We Deserve,* 1985

[O]ne of the greatest improvements in education is that teachers are now fitted for their duties by being taught the art of teaching.

MARY SOMERVILLE; *Physical Geography,* 1848

Education schools and education departments have been called "the intellectual slums" of the university.

THOMAS SOWELL; *Inside American Education,* 1993

TEACHING

Teaching is the highest form of understanding.

ARISTOTLE, 384–322

Teaching is not a lost art, but the regard for it is a lost tradition.

JACQUES BARZUN; *Newsweek*, 5 Dec. 1955

Teaching is at its most effective not when it succeeds in transmitting the greatest quality of information in the shortest time (and at least cost) but rather when most of the information conveyed by the teacher is actually received.

PIERRE BOURDIEU & JEAN-CLAUDE PASSERON;
(*Rapport pédagogique et communication*, 1965)/*Academic Discourse*, 1994

[G]ood teaching means that faculty, as scholars, are also learners.

ERNEST L. BOYER; *Scholarship Revisited*, 1990

Teaching is arguably one of the most important professions in our society because teachers are responsible for the most treasured of all resources, the human intellect.

TONY BUZAN; *The Mind Map Book*, 1993

Teaching itself has been handicapped by spurious educational thinkers, endemic politicking, untalented recruits, professional organizations more interested in work rules than in student achievement, poor support from parents, and all the structural ills of cancerous bureaucracy. If any problem could afflict American schools in theory, it probably does so in fact.

MARVIN CETRON & OWEN DAVIES; *Crystal Globe*, 1991

In teaching there should be no class distinctions.

CONFUCIUS (Latin for K'UNG FU-TZU), 551–479

The act of teaching presses toward preserving what is.

LARRY CUBAN; *How Teachers Taught*, 1984

Traditional teaching methods convince students that they are stupid and inferior because they can't do arithmetic, that they have no knowledge to share with others, and that they are cheating if they do their homework with others. Such methods effectively prepare students to compete for work at boring jobs over which they have no control.

MARILYN FRANKENSTEIN;
Critical Mathematics Education, 1987

Good teaching is one-fourth preparation and three-fourths theatre.

GAIL GODWIN; *The Odd Woman*, 1974

If the core-roles become those of learning-group managers not subject specialists (who could be confined to the staff roles or even pulled in from the contractual fringe), schools may look for people who have already practised such skills in other organizations. The end of the closed school may mean the end of the closed profession of teaching. That will be threatening to many, but liberating to others.

CHARLES HANDY & ROBERT AITKEN;
Understanding Schools as Organizations, 1986

The object of teaching a child is to enable him to get along without his teacher.

ELBERT HUBBARD, 1856–1915

Therefore for the love of God appoint teachers and schoolmasters, you that have the charge of youth; and give the teachers stipends worthy of their pains.

HUGH LATIMER, 1485–1555

Part of teaching is helping students learn how to tolerate ambiguity, consider possibilities, and ask questions that are unanswerable.

SARA LAWRENCE LIGHTFOOT; *In a World of Ideas*, 1989

Teaching is a product of the total personality of the teacher.

RICHARD MORTON;
in *Why Many College Teachers Cannot Lecture*, 1992

That rate of change is if anything, increasing; therefore *adapting to change must be the center of any new kind of teaching.*

ROBERT ORNSTEIN & PAUL EHRLICH;
New World New Mind, 1989

You are teaching the teacher.

(TITUS MACCIUS) PLAUTUS, 254–184

[Teaching] is a vastly over-rated function.
CARL ROGERS; *Freedom to Learn*, 1969

Another intellectual defect of almost all teaching, except the highest grade of university tuition, is that it encourages docility and the belief that definite answers are known on questions which are legitimate matters of debate.
BERTRAND RUSSELL; *Education and the Social Order*, 1932

The vanity of teaching often tempts a man to forget he is a blockhead.
GEORGE SAVILE, 1633–1695

To me the sole hope of human salvation lies in teaching.
GEORGE BERNARD SHAW, 1856–1950

Classroom teaching is the low-status work of education.... Yet despite their lesser pay, harder work, and fewer privileges the teachers who educate each generation are as important as researchers in university or institutions.
IRA SHOR; *Empowering Education*, 1992

Teaching is both one of the hardest and one of the easiest jobs in the world, depending on how conscientiously it is done. It is also one of the noblest and one of the most corrupt occupations – again, depending on how it is done. Because of the greater freedom of professors, compared to school teachers, the sweep of the variations tends to be even more extreme in higher education.... Cheap popularity, ego trips, and ideological indoctrination are just some of the pitfalls of teaching.
THOMAS SOWELL; *Inside American Education*, 1993

Yet the tests have made plain the depth of the crisis in teaching: many students selecting teaching as a career lack even the simplest of academic skills.
THOMAS TOCH; *In the Name of Academic Excellence*, 1991

Teaching has ruined more American novelists than drink.
GORE VIDAL (né EUGENE LUTHER VIDAL); *Oui*, Apr. 1975

Teaching is the royal road to learning.
JESSAMYN WEST; *The Life I Really Lived*, 1979

Everybody who is incapable of learning has taken to teaching – that is really what our enthusiasm for education has come to.

OSCAR WILDE; *The Decay of Lying*, 1889

TECHNOLOGY

Modern technology
Owes ecology
An apology.

ALAN M. EDDISON; *Worse Verse*, 1969

Education will no longer be an unpredictable and exciting adventure in human enlightenment, but an exercise in conformity and an apprenticeship to whatever gadgetry is useful in a technical world.

JACQUES ELLUL;
(*La Technique ou l'enjeu du siècle*, 1954)/*The Technological Society*, 1964

My own view is that a well-trained and effective teacher is still preferable to the most advanced technology, and that even excellent hardware and software are to little avail in the absence of appropriate curricula, pedagogy, and assessment.

HOWARD GARDNER; *The Unschooled Mind*, 1993

Technology dominates us all, diminishes our freedom.

DOROTHY MCCALL; *Los Angeles Times*, 14 Mar. 1974

TELEVISION

The purpose of television is to spare people with nothing on their minds the necessity of making conversation.

WILLIAM BAKER; *International Herald Tribune*, 1 Oct. 1993

Television is the first truly democratic culture – the first culture available to everybody and entirely governed by what the people want. The most terrifying thing is what the people do want.

CLIVE BARNES, 1927–

The bright gray blackboard.

HENRI DIEUZEIDE; *Réalités*, Jul. 1963

Television, because of its power of fascination and its capacity of visual and auditory penetration, is probably the technical instrument which is most destructive of personality and of human relations.

JACQUES ELLUL;
(*La Technique ou l'enjeu du siècle*, 1954)/*The Technological Society*, 1964

All television is educational. The only question is what is it teaching?

NICHOLAS JOHNSON; *Life*, 10 Sep. 1971

I am appalled by the canned rubbish we project by the hour on our television screens. We talk of trivia as entertainment, but it is more: it is a form of education, but a debilitating and bad one.

KENNETH KAUNDA; *Letters to My Children*, 1973

I find television very educational. Every time someone switches it on I go into another room and read a good book.

GROUCHO MARX, 1890–1977

American school children watch TV an average of twenty-four hours a week. This is more than they spend in schools.

MYRIAM MIEDZIAN; *Boys Will Be Boys*, 1991

The current generation of Americans are being raised on the most sadistic material ever conceived by humans.

NCTV (National Coalition on Television Violence);
News, Jun.–Oct. 1988

We are now well into a second generation of children for whom television has been their first and most accessible teacher and, for many, their most reliable companion and friend.

NEIL POSTMAN; *Amusing Ourselves to Death*, 1985

One is entirely justified in saying that the major educational enterprise now being undertaken in the United States is not happening in its classrooms but in the home, in front of the television set, and under the jurisdiction not of school administrators and teachers but of network executives and entertainers.

NEIL POSTMAN; *Amusing Ourselves to Death*, 1985

A spate of recent tales of death and destruction across Greece has spurred schoolchildren in Athens to seek an end to screen violence. In a letter to

Dimitris Fatouros, the education minister, a group of 11-year-olds has appealed for a clampdown on the "dreadful scenes" they are exposed to on television.

> HELENA SMITH; *The European*, 11–17 Feb. 1994

The television-educated child can spout words and ideas he does not comprehend and "facts" he doesn't have the experience or knowledge to judge the accuracy of.

> MARIE WINN; *The Plug-In Drug*, 1977

TENURE

There are in fact a large number of academic periodicals in existence that only exist in order to print articles that exist only in order that professors may get tenure or promotion.

> J.M. CAMERON; in *Hard Times in the Ivory Tower*
> (Ideas – Canadian Broadcasting Corporation), 1983

I do not have tenure. I hope its lack will not cost me my job when this book is published.

> ANNE INNIS DAGG; in *MisEducation*, 1988

The tenure process creates a need to win the approval of academic peers and tends to reinforce conventional wisdom in a field, stifling innovative research.

> DAVID P. HAMILTON, *The Washington Monthly*, Mar. 1991

Originally intended to protect the freedom of academics to study controversial topics, tenure has developed into a seven-year review of junior faculty that encourages useless publication....

> DAVID P. HAMILTON; *The Washington Monthly*, Mar. 1991

Marriages, among other things, are famous for biting the dust when one partner has to spend every night in the office. And if you don't get tenure when you become eligible for it, they often make you leave the university within a year. It's much worse in the States than it is in Europe, where the whole system is more merciful.

> a PROFESSOR; *International Herald Tribune*, 16 Feb. 1994

The process of achieving tenure is in the worst interests of students.

ROBERT SHUPP; *International Herald Tribune*, 16 Feb. 1994

The original universities can do little to stem the rising academic tide that threatens their perks except to demonstrate their higher status.... One way they can demonstrate their higher standards and greater rigor is by "terminating" – i.e., failing to give tenure to more assistant professors. That is why I call these dreadful terminations ritual murders.

PAGE SMITH; *Killing the Spirit*, 1990

Anyone who has been through this experience is likely to find it a horror not to be repeated. Those who must try two or three institutions before finally achieving tenure can spend the better part of a decade in limbo, without as much job security as a factory worker in a viable business.

THOMAS SOWELL; *Inside American Education*, 1993

Tenure corrupts, enervates, and dulls higher education.

CHARLES J. SYKES; *ProfScam*, 1988

The removal of tenure should improve the employment conditions of many academics, putting pressure on their institutions to grant them more competitive salaries and job packages.

MALCOLM TIGHT; in *Academic Freedom and Responsibility*, 1988

When I was denied tenure at another university my chairman explained that members of the tenure committee believed that my books did not make enough mistakes.

JAMES A. WINN; *The Chronicle of Higher Education*, 16 Sep. 1992

TEST

The test is the ultimate scholastic invention.

HOWARD GARDNER; *The Unschooled Mind*, 1993

The purpose of tests is to predict future performance in school, rather than outside of school.

HOWARD GARDNER; *The Unschooled Mind*, 1993

Some parents in Chicago are outraged over a "streetwise" math test administered to sixth-graders that included the following questions: "Hector knocked up six of the girls in his gang. There are 27 girls in the gang. What percentage of the girls in the gang has Hector knocked up?" and "Martin wants to cut his half-pound of heroin to make 20 percent more profit. How many ounces of cut will he need?"

MICHELLE MALKIN; *Sun-Sentinel*, 31 May 1994

In California, real estate prices are influenced by the school-by-school test scores that are widely reported in the media, and, for a time, Texas even based teachers' merit pay on the standardized achievement scores of their students.

JAMES P. RAFFINI; *Winners Without Losers*, 1993

The testing and evaluation procedures followed in most classrooms and schools are based either directly or indirectly on the practice of comparing one student's performance with that of another. Consequently, large numbers of students in any given class find it impossible to experience academic success, regardless of how hard they try.

JAMES P. RAFFINI; *Winners Without Losers*, 1993

THEOLOGY

Theology is anthropology.

LUDWIG FEUERBACH; *The Essence of Christianity*, 1841

In all systems of theology the devil figures as a male person. Yet it is women who keep the church going.

DON MARQUIS, 1878–1937

Theology is the effort to explain the unknowable in terms of the not worth knowing.

H(ENRY) L(OUIS) MENCKEN, 1880–1956

THEORY

Throw theory into the fire it only spoils life.

MIKHAIL A. BAKUNIN, 1814–1876

A thing may look specious in theory, and yet be ruinous in practice; a thing may look evil in theory, and yet be in practice excellent.

EDMUND BURKE, 1729–1797

Those who are enamoured of practice without science are like a pilot who goes into a ship without a rudder or compass and never has any certainty where he is going.

(LEONARDO) DA VINCI, 1452–1519

It is a capital mistake to theorize before one has data.

ARTHUR CONAN DOYLE, 1859–1930

A theory can be proved by experiment; but no path leads from experiment to the birth of a theory.

ALBERT EINSTEIN, 1879–1955

Don't confuse *hypothesis* and *theory*. The former is a possible explanation; the latter, the correct one. The establishment of theory is the very purpose of science.

MARTIN H. FISCHER, 1879–1962

There are also a number of confusions in the theory of education which are hangovers from a class-structured society.

NORTHROP FRYE; *On Education*, 1988

No theory is good except on condition that one use it to go beyond.

ANDRÉ GIDE; *Journal*, 1918

Dear friend, theory is all grey,
And the golden tree of life is green.

(JOHANN WOLFGANG VON) GOETHE, 1749–1832

Theories that go counter to the facts of human nature are foredoomed.

EDITH HAMILTON; *The Roman Way*, 1932

Theory without practice is empty, and practice without theory is blind.

J. ROBY KIDD, 1915–1982

The progress of science is strewn, like an ancient desert trail, with the skeleton of discarded theories which once seemed to possess eternal life.
ARTHUR KOESTLER, 1905–1983

This whole theory is good for nothing except disputing about.
(GEORG CHRISTOPH) LICHTENBERG; *Aphorisms*, 1764–1799

A professor must have a theory as a dog must have fleas.
H(ENRY) L(OUIS) MENCKEN, 1880–1956

A work of art that contains theories is like an object on which the price tag has been left.
(MARCEL) PROUST, 1871–1922

Theory helps us to bear our ignorance of facts.
(GEORGE) SANTAYANA; *The Sense of Beauty*, 1896

Very dangerous things, theories.
DOROTHY L. SAYERS;
The Unpleasantness at the Bellona Club, 1928

In making theories always keep a window open so that you can throw one out if necessary.
BÉLA SCHICK, 1877–1967

An ounce of practice is generally worth more than a ton of theory.
E(RNST) F(RIEDRICH) SCHUMACHER; *Small is Beautiful*, 1973

Let us work without theorizing . . . 'tis the only way to make life endurable.
VOLTAIRE (né FRANÇOIS MARIE AROUET);
Candide, 1759

THESIS

The average PhD thesis is nothing but a transference of bones from one graveyard to another.
J. FRANK DOBIE; *A Texan in England*, 1945

Research at all levels shows that a paper or thesis bearing a female name gets a lower grade than precisely the same paper or thesis delivered under a male name.

MARILYN FRENCH; *The War Against Women*, 1992

THINK

To live is to think.

(MARCUS TULLIUS) CICERO, 106–43

I think, therefore I am. [*Cogito, ergo sum*]

(RENÉ) DESCARTES, 1596–1650

Ye can lade a man up to th'university, but ye can't make him think. [*sic*]

FINLEY PETER DUNNE; *Mr. Dooley's Opinions*, 1900

What is the hardest task in the world? To think.

RALPH WALDO EMERSON, 1803–1882

Think today and speak tomorrow.

ENGLISH proverb

Think much, say little, write less.

FRENCH proverb

Never be afraid to sit awhile and think.

LORRAINE HANSBERRY; *A Raisin in the Sun*, 1959

Think before you think!

STANISLAW LEC; *Unkempt Thoughts*, 1962

Many people would sooner die than think. In fact they do.

BERTRAND RUSSELL, 1872–1970

It is difficult if not impossible, for most people to think otherwise than in the fashion of their own period.

GEORGE BERNARD SHAW, 1856–1950

First think, then speak.

TURKISH proverb

THINK!

THOMAS J. WATSON, 1914–

A man who does not think for himself does not think at all.

OSCAR WILDE; *Oscariana*, 1911

[O]nly that education deserves emphatically to be termed cultivation of mind which teaches young people how to begin to think.

MARY WOLLSTONECRAFT, 1759–1797

THINKER

Any positive thinker is compelled to see everything in the light of his own convictions.

ANTOINETTE BROWN BLACKWELL;
The Sexes Throughout Nature, 1875

Every thinker puts some portion of an apparently stable world in peril.

PETER DE VRIES, 1910–

The most fluent talkers or most plausible reasoners are not always the justest thinkers.

WILLIAM HAZLITT, 1778–1830

Readers are plentiful: thinkers are rare.

HARRIET MARTINEAU; *Society in America*, 1837

No Pestalozzian pedagogics can turn a born simpleton into a thinker: never!

ARTHUR SCHOPENHAUER; *Parerga and Paralipomena*, 1851

THINKING

Cram them full of noncombustible data, chock them so damned full of "facts" they feel stuffed, but absolutely "brilliant" with information. Then they'll feel they're thinking.

RAY BRADBURY; *Fahrenheit 451*, 1953

It is sometimes asserted that contemporary intellectual thought is dominated by five isms: scientism, relativism, materialism, evolutionism and
environmentalism. Scientism asserts that science is the final arbiter of truth
and values. Relativism asserts that no set of morals can be established
scientifically, and hence all are equally valid. Materialism asserts that
everything in the universe can be reduced to material objects and their
interactions. Evolutionism, that everything evolves and hence that people
have no special position in the universe. Environmentalism says that
people are what their environment makes them.

> PHILIP J. DAVIS & REUBEN HERSH; *Descartes' Dream*, 1986

Thinking is very far from knowing.

> ENGLISH proverb

The mania of thinking renders one unfit for every activity.

> ANATOLE FRANCE (pseud. of ANATOLE FRANÇOIS THIBAULT),
> 1844–1924

Thinking gets you nowhere. It may be a fine and noble aid in academic
studies, but you can't think your way out of emotional difficulties.

> ETTY HILLESUM; *An Interrupted Life*, 1983

Reading furnishes the mind only with material for knowledge; it is
thinking that makes what we read ours.

> JOHN LOCKE, 1632–1704

It is in and through education that a culture, and polity, not only tries to
perpetuate but enacts the kinds of thinking it welcomes, and discards
and/or discredits the kinds it fears.

> ELIZABETH KAMARCK MINNICK;
> *Transforming Knowledge*, 1990

Thinking is identical with being.

> PARMENIDES OF ELEA, *c*.600–*c*.500

Thinking is not knowing.

> PORTUGUESE proverb

There is no expedient to which man will not resort to avoid the real labour of thinking.

JOSHUA REYNOLDS, 1723–1792

One of the worst diseases to which the human creature is liable is its disease of thinking.

JOHN RUSKIN, 1819–1900

Sixty minutes of thinking of any kind is bound to lead to confusion and unhappiness.

JAMES THURBER, 1894–1961

It is not much good thinking of a thing unless you think it out.

H(ERBERT) G(EORGE) WELLS, 1866–1946

She had lost her way in a labyrinth of conjecture.

EDITH WHARTON; *The Angel at the Grave*, 1901

THIRD AGE EDUCATION

In the University of the Third Age (U3A) . . . every member is expected to learn, and, if he or she is in a position to do so, to teach as well.

PETER LASLETT; *A Fresh Map of Life*, 1991

The Third Age is a phrase of French origin, and was used in the title of Les Universités du Troisième Age when they began to be instituted in France in the 1970s. It seems to have entered Anglo-Saxon vocabulary when the first of the British universities of the Third Age was founded at Cambridge in the summer of 1981.

PETER LASLETT; *A Fresh Map of Life*, 1991

THOUGHT

Action and faith enslave thought, both of them in order not to be troubled or inconvenienced by reflection, criticism, and doubt.

HENRI FREDERIC AMIEL; *Amiel's Journal*, 1849–1872

[T]hought to some people is subversive. . . .

AUSTRALIAN BROADCASTING COMMISSION;
Thirty-seventh Annual Report (1968–69), 1969

Thought is free.

(MARCUS TULLIUS) CICERO, 106–43

There are no illegitimate thoughts.

THEODORE REIK; *The Need to be Loved*, 1963

THREE Cs

. . . communication, computation, and critical thinking. . . .

LYNNE HALL;
an *Executive in Residence comment* (Queen's University, Ontario), 1984

The skills involved are conceptualizing, co-ordinating and consolidating –
the three Cs. They are the "verbs" of education as opposed to the "nouns",
the doing words not the facts. We don't learn to use these verbs by sitting in
rows in a classroom, but by practice.

CHARLES HANDY; *The Empty Raincoat*, 1994

THREE Es

The big concerns for the future of America: Environment, Education, and
Ethics.

FAITH POPCORN; *The Popcorn Report*, 1992

THREE Rs – new

[H]ow are they doing in terms of such qualities as resilience, reliability, and
sense of responsibility – what some of us have started to call the other 3 Rs?

DEBORAH MEIER; *Dissent*, Winter 1994

THREE Rs – old (reading, writing, arithmetic)

Elementary education consisted mainly of the "three Rs", taught by private tutors who, early in the 4th century, were paid 50 denarii a month for each pupil – a poor wage.

KEITH BRANIGAN; *Roman Britain*, 1980

No candidates who fail to make proof of general attainments in respect of Reading, Writing, and Arithmetic shall be allowed to be examined for posts as special regular teachers.

DEPARTMENT OF EDUCATION;
Outlines of the Modern Education in Japan, 1893

It has been said that we have not had the three Rs in America, we had the six Rs: remedial readin', remedial 'ritin' and remedial 'rithmetic.

ROBERT M. HUTCHINS;
New York Herald Tribune, 22 Apr. 1963

Books are the least important apparatus in a school. All that any child needs is the three R's; the rest should be tools and clay and sports and theatre and paint and freedom.

A(LEXANDER) S(UTHERLAND) NEILL; *Summerhill*, 1969

Actually now one third of U.S. corporations are providing courses in reading, writing, and arithmetic to new employees who need them.

FAITH POPCORN; *The Popcorn Report*, 1992

THREE Ts

The three Rs of our school system must be supported by the three Ts – teachers who are superior, techniques of instruction that are modern, and thinking about education which places it first in all our plans and hopes.

LYNDON B. JOHNSON;
a *message* (to Congress), 12 Jan. 1965

TIME

Time is a great teacher, but unfortunately it kills all its pupils.

(HECTOR) BERLIOZ, 1803–1869

The stupid speak of the past, the wise of the present, fools of the future.
NAPOLÉON (BONAPARTE), 1769–1821

TOLERANCE

The highest result of education is tolerance.
HELEN KELLER; *Optimism*, 1903

TOTALITARIANISM

The aim of totalitarian education has never been to instill convictions but to destroy the capacity to form any.
HANNAH ARENDT, 1906–1975

TRAINING

I am convinced that we must train not only the head, but the heart and hands as well.
(Madam) CHIANG KAI-SHEK; (neé MAYLING SOONG);
This is Our China, 1940

With the revolution in technology and job function has come a staggering array of training designed to prepare workers to use the machines effectively and fearlessly. Computer-related courses are available from virtually *every* source of training and education.
NELL P. EURICH; *The Learning Industry*, 1990

The government first provides very poor schooling, and the harm is multiplied by the minimum wage law, which makes it difficult . . . to get on-the-job training.
MILTON FRIEDMAN; *US News & World Report*, 1 Mar. 1977

Training is everything. The peach was once a bitter almond;
cauliflower is nothing but cabbage with a college education.
MARK TWAIN (pseud. of SAMUEL LANGHORNE CLEMENS),
1835–1910

TRAVEL

Travel, in the younger sort, is a part of education; in the elder, a part of experience.

FRANCIS BACON, 1561–1626

The farther one goes, the more one learns.

CHRISTOPHER COLUMBUS (né CRISTOFORO COLOMBO),
1451–1506

Too often travel, instead of broadening the mind, merely lengthens the conversation.

ELIZABETH DREW; *The Literature of Gossip*, 1964

Travel broadens the mind.

ENGLISH? proverb

We travel to learn; and I have never been in any country where they did not do something better than we do it, think some thoughts better than we think, catch some inspiration from heights above our own.

MARIA MITCHELL, 1818–1889

TRIGONOMETRY

Trigonometry was very largely a Hindu invention. An amalgam of geometry and algebra, useful wherever lengths and angles have to be calculated, it was used first in Hindu astronomy, and became of prime importance in geometrical survey work and engineering drawing.

JOHN MCLEISH; *Number*, 1992

TRUANCY

Some teachers are not hostile to the fact that there are large levels of non-attendance. Some of these pupils they would not wish to see back in school.

ANDREW CANT;
The Times Educational Supplement, 11 Mar. 1994

A majority of the non-attendees had suggested that by truanting they had sought to avoid the hassle they had variously experienced during schooling.

PAT CARLEN, DENIS GLEESON & JULIA WARDHAUGH;
Truancy, 1992

Nineteenth- and early twentieth-century Western physicians taught that cutting out sexual organs improved women's health, curing masturbation, depression, melancholia, nymphomania, hysteria, insanity, epilepsy, kleptomania, and *truancy*!

MARILYN FRENCH; *The War Against Women*, 1992
[italics in original]

The village master taught his little school;
A man severe he was, and stern to view;
I knew him well, and every truant knew;
Well had the boding tremblers learned to trace
The day's disasters in his morning face. . . .

OLIVER GOLDSMITH, 1728–1774

Truancy has leapt to the top of the education agenda in Britain after an alarming report showing that nearly one-third of children are regularly "bunking off" school.

NAOMI MARKS;
The European (International Education), 4–10 Mar. 1994

At present the Government sees schools as a service to parents. They are not. They are a service to children and to no-one else. If children have to be dragged to them by so-called "welfare officers" the schools are clearly failing those children. Instead of branding absentees with the title of "truant" (originally a mediaeval French bandit!) schools ought to be asking why their clients don't want what they offer.

CHRIS SHUTE; *Compulsory Schooling Disease*, 1993

TRUTH

Simple are the words of truth.

AESCHYLUS, 525–456

A belief is not true because it is useful.

HENRI FREDERIC AMIEL, 1821–1881

We do not know a truth without knowing its cause.

ARISTOTLE, 384–322

There are in fact four very significant stumbling-blocks in the way of grasping truth, which hinder every man however learned, and scarcely allow anyone to win a clear title to wisdom, namely, the example of weak and unworthy authority, longstanding custom, the feeling of the ignorant crowd, and the hiding of our own ignorance while making a display of our apparent knowledge.

ROGER BACON; *Opus Majus*, 1266–7

You never find yourself until you face the truth.

PEARL BAILEY; *The Raw Pearl*, 1968

Between truth and the search for truth, I opt for the second.

BERNARD BERENSON; *Essays in Appreciation*, 1958

Truth breeds hatred.

BIAS OF PRIENE IN IONIA, *c.*600–*c.*500

We must prepare and study truth under every aspect, endeavoring to ignore nothing, if we do not wish to fall into the abyss of the unknown when the hour shall strike.

ELENA PETROVNA BLAVATSKY, 1831–1891

Again, there are four truths in this world – first, all living beings arise from ignorance; second, all objects of desire are impermanent, uncertain and suffering; third, all existing things are also impermanent, uncertain and suffering; fourth, there is nothing that can be called an "ego," and there is no such thing as "mine" in all the world.

BUKKYO DENDO KYOKAI; *The Teachings of Buddha*, 1966

Truth is like the use of words, it depends greatly on custom.

SAMUEL BUTLER, 1612–1680

But crushing truths perish from being acknowledged.

ALBERT CAMUS; *The Myth of Sisyphus*, 1955

Truth, like light, blinds. Falsehood, on the contrary, is a beautiful twilight that enhances every object.

ALBERT CAMUS; *The Fall*, 1957

There is absolutely no criterion for truth. For reason, senses, ideas, or whatever else may exist are all deceptive.

CARNEADES, *c.*214–129

The truth often does sound unconvincing.

AGATHA CHRISTIE; *Ordeal of Innocence,* 1959

Even in the most important subjects, I have never found anything more substantial to hold to or use in forming my opinions, than what seemed like the truth; the truth itself is hidden in obscurity.

(MARCUS TULLIUS) CICERO, 106–43

Truth is so impossible. Something has to be done for it.

IVY COMPTON-BURNETT; *Darkness and Day,* 1951

If you would be a real seeker after truth, it is necessary that at least once in your life you doubt, as far as possible, all things.

(RENÉ) DESCARTES; *Principles of Philosophy,* 1644

Truth is such a rare thing, it is delightful to tell it.

EMILY DICKINSON, 1830–1886

Since the knowledge of Truth is the sovereign good of human nature, it is natural that in every age she should have many seekers, and those who ventured in quest of her in the dark days of ignorance and superstition amidst the mists and tempests of the sixteenth century often ran counter to the opinions of dominant parties, and fell into the hands of foes who knew no pity.

P.H. DITCHFIELD; *Books Fatal to Their Authors,* 1895

The simplest and commonest truth seems new and wonderful when we experience it the first time in our own life.

MARIE VON EBNER-ESCHENBACH; *Aphorisms,* 1905

Truth is immortal; error is mortal.

MARY BAKER EDDY; *Science and Health,* 1875

A system-grinder hates the truth.

RALPH WALDO EMERSON, 1803–1882

For what appears to be truth to one, may appear to be error to the other.

(MOHANDAS KARAMCHAND) GANDHI; *Young India*, 6 Sep. 1922

Truth is the daughter of time.

AULUS GELLIUS, 130–175

The truth is generally seen, rarely heard.

BALTASAR GRACIÁN; *The Art of Worldly Wisdom*, 1647

What a word is truth. Slippery, tricky, unreliable.

LILLIAN HELLMAN; *Three*, 1979

Truth is a torch that gleams through the fog without dispelling it.

(CLAUD-ADRIEN) HELVÉTIUS; *De l'Esprit*, 1758

Speak then the truth, and the whole truth, and nothing but the truth.

BEN JONSON; *Tales of a Tub*, 1633

True words are not pleasant,
Pleasant words are not true.

LÂO-TZU (né LI URH), *c*.600–*c*.500

There are two kinds of truth; those of reason and those of fact. The truths of reasoning are necessary and their opposite is impossible; the truths of fact are contingent and their opposites are possible.

(GOTTFRIED WILHELM) LEIBNIZ; *The Monadology*, 1714

The fundamental thesis of dialectics is: there is no such thing as abstract truth, truth is always concrete.

(VLADIMIR ILYICH) LENIN (né VLADIMIR ILYICH ULYANOV);
One Step Forward, Two Steps Backward, 1904

There are no new truths, but only truths that have not been recognized by those who have perceived them without noticing.

MARY MCCARTHY; *On the Contrary*, 1962

You cannot have civilization and truth.

IRIS MURDOCH; *A Severed Head*, 1961

All truths that are kept silent become poisonous.

(FRIEDRICH WILHELM) NIETZSCHE;
Thus Spake Zarathustra, 1883–91

People think that if they avoid the truth, it might change to something better before they have to hear it.

MARSHA NORMAN; *The Fortune Teller*, 1987

Truth on this side of the Pyrenees may be heresy on the other!

(BLAISE) PASCAL; *Pensées*, 1669

Inquiry is human; blind obedience brutal. Truth never loses by the one but often suffers by the other.

WILLIAM PENN; *Some Fruits of Solitude*, 1693

Not only are there as many conflicting truths as there are people to claim them; there are equally multitudinous and conflicting truths within the individual.

VIRGILIA PETERSON; *A Matter of Life and Death*, 1961

Nothing is more sublime than love of truth.

(AURELIUS CLEMENS) PRUDENTIUS, 348–*c*.405

In the war between falsehood and truth, falsehood wins the first battle and truth the last.

MUJIBUR RAHMAN, 1920–1975

There are few nudities so objectionable as the naked truth.

AGNES REPPLIER; *Compromises*, 1904

I am the only real truth I know.

JEAN RHYS (pseud. of ELLA GWENDOLEN REES WILLIAMS),
1894–1979

Because if they continue to think that truth comes from the front of the room, and that learning is a product that can be standardized, we are going to end up with sheeplike, uninformed citizens who are not capable of conducting public debate on difficult issues.

STEPHEN H. SCHNEIDER; *World Monitor*, Apr. 1993

Truth has no special time of its own. Its hour is now – always.

ALBERT SCHWEITZER; *Out of My Life and Thought*, 1949

[T]his above all – to thine own self be true.

WILLIAM SHAKESPEARE; *Hamlet*, 1600–01

If you shut your door to all errors truth will be shut out.

RABINDRANATH TAGORE; *Stray Birds*, 1916

The first reaction to truth is hatred. The moment it appears, it is treated as an enemy.

(QUINTUS SEPTIMUS FLORENS) TERTULLIAN(US), *c.*160–223

Of course it's the same old story. Truth usually is the same old story.

MARGARET THATCHER, 1925–

It takes two to speak the truth – one to speak, and the other to hear.

H(ENRY) D(AVID) THOREAU, 1817–1862

Truth is more of a stranger than fiction.

MARK TWAIN (pseud. of SAMUEL LANGHORNE CLEMENS), 1835–1910

Truth is the beginning and end of material existence. Without truth there is no material existence.

TZE-SZE, *c.*335–*c.*288

There is nothing, nowhere, neither on earth nor in heaven, that can make the true untrue or the untrue true.

BARTOLOMEO VANZETTI, 1888–1927

Truth has as many coats as an onion . . . and each one of them hollow when you peel it off.

HELEN WADDELL; *Peter Abelard*, 1933

Much sheer effort goes into avoiding truth: left to itself, it sweeps in like the tide.

FAY WELDON; *The Riches of Life*, 1987

Truth is rarely pure, and never simple.

OSCAR WILDE; *The Importance of Being Earnest*, 1895

If you do not tell the truth about yourself you cannot tell it about other people.

VIRGINIA WOOLF; *The Monument and Other Essays*, 1947

Any truth creates a scandal.

MARGUERITE YOURCENAR; *The Memoirs of Hadrian*, 1954

TUNE-OUT

Even more important than the number of dropouts, and more difficult to portray statistically, is the number of students who give up on school. Tune-outs differ from dropouts because they actually are physically present in school. However, they are entrapped by truancy policies, parental expectations, personal aspirations, and child labor laws, and their consequent level of alienation prevents them from being deeply affected by what goes on in school.

MARGARET DIANE LECOMPTE & ANTHONY GARY DWORKIN;
Giving Up on School, 1991

TUTORING

To make ends meet, the tutor had to cram as many pupils as possible into each day, teaching each one for only an hour or two, and then not every day.

KEITH BRANIGAN; *Roman Britain*, 1980

A tutor is a teacher whose subject is the pupil herself.

ENGLISH? proverb

It is easier for a tutor to command than to teach.

JOHN LOCKE; *Some Thoughts Concerning Education*, 1693

Very few tutees speak warmly and gratefully of their tutors.

MICHAEL MARLAND; *The Tutor and the Tutor Group*, 1989

Whatever be the qualifications of your tutors, your improvement must chiefly depend on yourselves. They cannot think of labor for you. They can only put you in the best way of thinking and laboring for yourselves. If, therefore, you get knowledge you must acquire it by your own industry.

JOSEPH PRIESTLEY, 1733–1804

U

UNDERGRADUATE (Baccalaureate/Bachelor Degree Student)

[T]here is no more vulnerable human combination than an under-graduate.

> JOHN SLOAN DICKEY; *The Atlantic Monthly*, Apr. 1955

It is really the undergraduate who makes a university, gives it its lasting character, smell, feel, quality, tradition ... whose presence creates it and whose memories preserve it.

> SEÁN O'FAOLÁIN; *Harvard Alumni Bulletin*, 24 Oct. 1964

Academic prestige is usually research prestige, and it is often purchased by the neglect of undergraduate education.

> THOMAS SOWELL; *Inside American Education*, 1993

Generally young men are regarded as radicals. This is a popular misconception. The most conservative persons I ever met are college graduates.

> WOODROW WILSON, 1856–1924

UNDERSTAND

Everyone hears only what he understands.

> (JOHANN WOLFGANG VON) GOETHE, 1749–1832

Then my father organized for me a college in the east
But I went to California the sunshine and the beach
My parents and my lecturers could never understand
Why I gave it up for music and the free electric band.

> ALBERT HAMMOND & LEE HAZELWOOD;
> *The Free Electric Band* (pub. April Music), 1973

Much learning does not teach understanding.

> HERACLITUS, *c.*540–*c.*470

To understand via the heart is not to understand.

> (MICHEL EYQUEM DE) MONTAIGNE; *Essays*, 1580–1595

To be surprised, to wonder, is to begin to understand.
(JOSÉ) ORTEGA Y GASSET; *The Revolt of the Masses*, 1930

When we read too fast or too slowly we understand nothing.
(BLAISE) PASCAL, 1623–1662

Do nothing you do not understand.
PYTHAGORAS, *c*.600–*c*.500

To understand everything is to hate nothing.
ROMAIN ROLLAND, 1866–1944

I can never remember things I didn't understand in the first place.
AMY TAN; *The Joy Luck Club*, 1989

UNEDUCABLE

Children who are treated as if they are uneducable almost invariably become uneducable.
KENNETH B. CLARK; *Dark Ghetto*, 1965

UNEDUCATED

The danger of education, I have found, is that it so easily confuses means with ends. Worse than that, it quite easily forgets both and devotes itself merely to the mass production of uneducated graduates – people literally unfit for anything except to take part in an elaborate and completely artificial charade which they and their contemporaries have conspired to call "life".
THOMAS MERTON; *Love and Living*, 1980

A child educated only at school is an uneducated child.
(GEORGE) SANTAYANA, 1863–1952

UNION

Teacher unions exist to provide benefits for teachers; whether they achieve benefits for pupils, parents, or communities is secondary.

MYRON LIEBERMAN; *Public Education*, 1993

[T]he fundamental problem is a universal one, epitomizing as it does the deep cleft between the PhD degree as a "trade union card" and the PhD degree as a reward for scholarly research.

JAROSLAV PELIKAN; *Scholarship and Its Survival*, 1983

UNIVERSITY

Universities incline wits to sophistry and affectation.

FRANCIS BACON, 1561–1626

Today there is precious little thought about universities, and what there is does not unequivocally support the university's traditional role. In order to find out why we have fallen on such hard times, we must recognize that the foundations of the university have become extremely doubtful to the highest intelligences.

ALLAN BLOOM; *The Closing of the American Mind*, 1987

I have not had your advantages. What poor education I have received has been gained in the University of Life.

HORATIO BOTTOMLEY;
a *speech* (Oxford Union), 2 Dec. 1920

A *university* is only one of many different kinds of educational enterprise, and it may lose its distinctive value if attempts are made to enlarge its function unduly.

G(EORGE) LESLIE BROOK; *The Modern University*, 1965

The true University of these days is a collection of books.

THOMAS CARLYLE, 1795–1881

They wanted a great university without building a great university. They knew a lot about football, but not a lot about academia.

BRAD CARTER; *The New York Times*, 5 Mar. 1987

Life at a university with its technical discussions at the postgraduate level is on the whole a bad training for the real world. Only men of very strong character surmount this handicap.

PAUL CHAMBERS, 1904–1981

A university is what college becomes when the faculty loses interest in students.

JOHN CIARDI, 1916–1986

A university should be a place of light, of liberty, and of learning.

BENJAMIN DISRAELI, 1804–1881

The function of the university is not simply to teach bread-winning, or to furnish teachers for the public schools, or to be a centre of polite society; it is, above all, to be the organ of that fine adjustment between real life and the growing knowledge of life, an adjustment which forms the secret of civilization.

W(ILLIAM) E(DWARD) B(URGHARDT) DU BOIS;
The Souls of Black, 1903

The university must be a tributary to a larger society, not a sanctuary from it.

A. BARTLETT GIAMATTI, 1938–1989

If you feel you have both feet planted firmly on level ground, then the university has failed you.

ROBERT GOHEEN; *Time*, 23 Jun. 1961

The university becomes an essential site for the ideological meltdown of the middle class.

JERRY HERRON;
Universities and the Myth of Cultural Decline, 1988

There is only one justification for universities, as distinguished from trade schools. They must be centers of criticism.

ROBERT M. HUTCHINS; 1899–1977

The mediaeval university looked backwards: it professed to be a storehouse of old knowledge. . . . The modern university looks forward, and is a factory of knowledge: its professors have to be at the top of the wave of progress.

T(HOMAS) H(ENRY) HUXLEY, 1825–1895

Greek in origin, the idea of the university is part of the western tradition.

KARL JASPERS; *The Idea of the University*, 1959

[A university] is a series of separate schools and departments held together by a central heating system.

CLARK KERR; *The Uses of the University*, 1963

The university is so many things to so many different people that it must, of necessity, be partially at war with itself.

CLARK KERR; *Godkin Lectures*, 1963

University politics are vicious precisely because the stakes are so small.

HENRY (ALFRED) KISSINGER, 1923–

[T]he Australian [university] system has a good deal more body to it than the North American romp through matters like Tibetan myth or ice cream studies (theory and practice).

STEPHEN KNIGHT; *The Selling of the Australian Mind*, 1991

I enjoy learning things but a university is the last place in the world to learn anything.

CHARLES KOWAL; *Time*, 27 Oct. 1975

The term *University* does not of course mean a place where all forms of knowledge are taught.

CHARLES EDWARD MALLET;
A History of the University of Oxford, 1924

The modern Japanese university was born from translation.

MICHIO NAGAI; *Higher Education in Japan*, 1971

A university is an Alma Mater, knowing her children one by one, not a foundry, or a mint, or a treadmill.

JOHN HENRY NEWMAN, 1801–1890

What sort of university do we want?

JANICE NEWSON & HOWARD BUCHBINDER;
The University Means Business, 1988

The university has in its essential form demonstrated great capacity for survival.

OECD (ORGANIZATION FOR ECONOMIC COOPERATION AND DEVELOPMENT);
Universities under Scrutiny, 1987

A man who has never gone to school may steal from a freight car, but if he has a university education he may steal the whole railroad.

FRANKLIN D. ROOSEVELT, 1882–1945

If Newman was the household god of the liberal university, Clark Kerr occupied the same icon-like position for the modern university.

PETER SCOTT; *The Crisis of the University*, 1984

Both teachers and pupils at sixteenth-century universities had dressed and looked like clergymen even when they were not. Both professors and students at the seventeenth-century universities disguised themselves as gentlemen, even when they were not.

PRESERVED SMITH;
A History of Modern Culture (vol. I), 1962

It is possible to get an education at a university. It has been done; not often, but the fact that a proportion, however small, of college students do get a start in interested, methodical study proves my thesis.

LINCOLN STEFFENS; *Autobiography*, 1931

Although the university's formal structure is vertical, the real structure of academia is horizontal.

CHARLES J. SYKES; *ProfScam*, 1988

[T]he average American persists in thinking that the classroom is the centre of activity of a university.

CHARLES J. SYKES; *ProfScam*, 1988

Everyone who has contact with a university learns that men are more important than women, and that men's ideas are the ones that matter.

PATRICIA J. THOMPSON; in *MisEducation*, 1988

Graduates from Australia's universities are leaving their campuses with appalling verbal, writing and interpersonal skills, according to a survey of the nation's biggest employers. . . .

The Times Higher Education Supplement, 25 Feb. 1994

The "uni" in the university also became meaningless as the institution, possessing more and more power as government funds were pumped into it for research, turned into a loose confederation of dis-connected mini-states, instead of an organization devoted to the joint search for knowledge and truth.

CHARLES VAN DOREN; *A History of Knowledge*, 1991

Ignorance, arrogance, and racism have bloomed as Superior Knowledge in all too many universities.

ALICE WALKER; *In Search of Our Mothers' Gardens*, 1983

A university in the European sense could not come into being in the United States. Rather the American university had evolved, as had so many things American, from a combination of European and native forces.

EVERETT WALTERS; *Graduate Education Today*, 1965

They teach you anything in [US] universities today. You can major in mud pies.

ORSON WELLES, 1915–1985

UNKNOWN

Greatness is a road leading towards the unknown.

CHARLES DE GAULLE, 1890–1970

Everything unknown is taken for something great.

(PUBLIUS CORNELIUS) TACITUS, *c*.55–117

UNLEARN

The mind is slow in unlearning what it has been long in learning.

(LUCIUS ANNAEUS) SENECA (the Younger), *c*.4BC–65

The first problem for all of us, men and women, is not to learn, but to unlearn.

GLORIA STEINEM; *The New York Times*, 26 Aug. 1971

Education consists mainly in what we have unlearned.

MARK TWAIN (pseud. of SAMUEL LANGHORNE CLEMENS);
Notebook, 1935

V

VIDEO

Too violent [videos] for kids? Johnny Gage kills his victims with a bloody, decapitating uppercut. Rayden favors electrocution. Kano will punch through his opponent's chest and rip out a still-beating heart. Sub-Zero likes to tear his foe's head off and hold it up in victory, spinal cord twitching as it dangles from the neck.

PHILIP ELMER-DEWITT; *Time*, 27 Sep. 1993

The kids get it right away. Nobody has to explain to a 10-year-old boy what's so great about video games. Just sit him down in front of a Sega Genesis or Super Nintendo machine, shove a cartridge into the slot and he's gone – body, mind and soul – into a make-believe world that's better than sleep, better than supper and a heck of a lot better than school.

PHILIP ELMER-DEWITT; *Time*, 27 Sep. 1993

Even educators argue that the games release aggressions rather than create them. "I organize video-game activities for my students, especially the problem students," says Oliver Prezeau, 26, a high school teacher in St. Denis, a tough Paris suburb. "It helps channel their aggression. They never hit one another while playing video games."

JAMES O. JACKSON; *Time*, 27 Sep. 1993

VIOLENCE

At first, they viewed it as a prank, some kind of collegiate farce in keeping with the festive spirit that marked the second-last day of classes at the University of Montreal's Ecole polytechnique.... He [Marc Lépine, né Rachid Gharbi] entered the classroom slowly a few minutes past 5 on a bitterly cold afternoon. There was a shy smile on his face as he interrupted a dissertation on the mechanics of heat transfer.... He told the men to leave – they did so without protest – and, as one of the young women attempted to reason with him, the gun-toting man opened fire in earnest. Six of the women were shot dead. Over the course of the next 20 minutes, the young man methodically stalked the cafeteria, the classrooms and the corridors of the school, leaving a trail of death and injury in his wake. In four separate locations scattered around three floors of the six-storey structure, he gunned down a total of 27 people, leaving 14 of them dead. Finally, he turned his weapon against himself, blowing off the top of his skull.

BARRY CAME; *Maclean's*, 18 Dec. 1989

Institutionalized in sports, the military, acculturated sexuality, the history and mythology of heroism, it [violence] is taught to boys until they become its *advocates*.

ANDREA DWORKIN; *Photography*, 1981

Tell them the lessons are most boring. But the action that takes place here [Karl-Bröger-Oberschule, Berlin, Germany] is really cool. When the knives are pulled out . . . that's exciting.

ELVIRA [15-year-old student]; *Stern*, 18 Feb. 1993

Pakistani army commandos rescued five schoolboys and a teacher held hostage by Afghan gunmen for 36 hours after they stormed the city's Afghan embassy. . . . The hostage takers were armed with pistols and handgrenades and had been holding the boys and their teacher since seizing 73 children and staff when they hijacked a school bus the day before.

The European, 25 Feb.–3 Mar. 1994

Yet even today the violence against men in sports is still financed by our public education system; and by public subsidies of the stadiums in which sports teams play. Violence against men is not just called entertainment, it is also called education.

WARREN FARRELL; *The Myth of Male Power*, 1993

The bitter dispute inside the engineering faculty at Montreal's Concordia University grew worse by the day. Through the first half of 1992, professor Valery Fabrikant became increasingly angry over what he believed were attempts by the university to deny him a promotion and a sabbatical. At one point, Fabrikant became so belligerent that some faculty members installed panic buttons at their desks and doubled the locks on their office doors. Finally, on Aug. 24, 1992, Fabrikant, 53, entered the engineering building with three handguns and a briefcase full of ammunition. When the shooting ended, two professors were dead; two others would die later in hospital and a secretary was wounded.

TOM FENNELL; *Maclean's*, 23 Aug. 1993

[The new] school . . . has few windows facing the main street to make it less of a target for drive-by shootings.

ROBERT FRANK; *International Herald Tribune*, 16 Feb. 1994

Violence commands both literature and life, and violence is always crude and distorted.

ELLEN GLASGOW; *Letters of Ellen Glasgow*, 1958

[Jesse] Jackson told students at the Martin Luther King Jr. High School: "We lose more lives annually to the crime of blacks killing blacks than the sum total of lynchings in the entire history of the country."

BOB HERBERT; *International Herald Tribune*, 21 Oct. 1993

Three men opened fire on a crowd at a football game in the District of Columbia, killing a man and critically injuring a 4-year-old girl, the police said. The shooting at an elementary school was one of four within a four-hour period and within several blocks of each other. In all, three men were killed. Another girl, 12, also was wounded.

International Herald Tribune, 27 Sep. 1993

A 12-year-old girl was stabbed to death and two others were wounded Monday when a man burst into their [Middlesbrough, UK] classroom and ordered their teacher to leave. . . . [T]he police said the intruder stabbed the three students before he was overpowered by two teachers.

International Herald Tribune, 29 Mar. 1994

From Boston to Berlin, from Paris to Perth, from Jakarta to Djibouti, all the world's children are doing it: tearing off heads or ripping out hearts in Mortal Kombat, crashing race cars in Super Mario Kart, going to war in Battlesphere.

JAMES O. JACKSON; *Time*, 27 Sep. 1993

[W]hen you have violence in schools, you are not going to have education. . . .

LEE KUAN YEW, 1923–

In schools all over the world, little boys learn that their country is the greatest in the world, and the highest honor that can befall them would be to defend it heroically someday. The fact that empathy has traditionally been conditioned out of boys facilitates their obedience to leaders who order them to kill strangers.

MYRIAM MIEDZIAN; *Boys Will Be Boys*, 1991

Some commentators see child violence as an inevitable response to a society in which a [US] boy may have seen up to 200,000 acts of television violence by the age of 16, including 33,000 murders.

ROSALIND MILES; *The Rites of Man*, 1992

Classrooms are a wonderful place to start preventing violence.
DEBORAH PROTHROW-STITH;
The Globe and Mail, 27 Aug. 1993

The masked man entered a ground floor classroom at the Commandant-Charcot school [in France] and aimed a pistol at teacher Laurence Dreyfus. "There's a madman with a revolver in my classroom!" she screamed.
THOMAS SANCTON; *Time*, 24 May 1993

Violence suits those who have nothing to lose.
(JEAN-PAUL) SARTRE, 1905–1980

The little ones spit and bite, scratch and kick. The head of a Cologne day care centre complains that "it's not normal anymore, the way children behave today."
Der Spiegel, No. 3, 1994

Teachers will be able to react in a more relaxed manner to aggressive classroom moods.
official SPOKESPERSON (Schleswig-Holstein, Germany);
The European, 30 Sep. 1993
[Statement given with the introduction of judo
and aikido courses for teachers to help them
"fight violence" in their schools.]

They arm themselves with knives, pistols, and sticks, beat themselves into hospital, and demand protection money – horror and fear reign at many German schools.
Stern, 18 Feb. 1993

A schoolyard shooting has made this Atlantic seaport [Brest] apprehensive that the kind of crime usually dismissed as an American-only phenomenon may be coming to France. In the middle-class setting of Lycée Amiral Ronarc'h, David Van Laere, 16, was shot to death after a locker-room exchange of petty insults with a classmate.
Time, 11 Oct. 1993

Seventy percent of all educators [in Germany] are giving up their profession prematurely because they can no longer handle the increasingly aggressive behavior of children.
Welt am Sonntag, 6 Mar. 1994

VIVISECTION

We vivisect the nightingale
To probe the secret of his note.

T(HOMAS) B(AILEY) ALDRICH, 1836–1907

If you are a student and your teachers expect you to perform vivisection experiments, you have a right to protest and refuse to take part in animal experiments. Millions of animals are used in schools and colleges, but most good educational establishments now allow students to opt out of vivisection experiments without any penalties – although some rather outdated and unthinking lecturers still believe that students should be forced to chop up animals.

VERNON COLEMAN;
Why Animal Experiments Must Stop, 1991

Vivisection . . . is justifiable for real investigations on physiology; but not for mere damnable and detestable curiosity.

CHARLES DARWIN, 1809–1882

A teacher is paid to teach, not to sacrifice rats and hamsters.

EDWARD A. GALL;
Journal of Medical Education, vol. 36, 1961

VOUCHER

Diverting public money to private schools via vouchers will doom the public schools.

WILLIAM GREIDER; *Utne Reader*, Nov.–Dec. 1992

[T]he objection to vouchers is that if education is bought and sold on free market principles, we can expect a highly segregated and stratified educational system.

MYRON LIEBERMAN;
Privatization and Educational Choice, 1989

With vouchers, you have an unregulated private sector vs. a regulated public sector. It's a joke!

BELLA ROSENBERG; *Business Week*, 14 Sep. 1992

W

WAR

To be a teacher in Peru is a very dangerous way to live. To be a teacher in Peru is a very beautiful way to die.

R. DOLORIER;
The Chronicle of Higher Education, 30 Mar. 1994

Two mortar bombs hit an infant school killing seven people including three children and a teacher. Around 40 casualties, many of them small children, from the school and a nearby bread queue were taken to hospital in the Bosnian capital [Sarajevo] with serious injuries.

The European, 12–18 Nov. 1993

Sunday, 17 May 1992
Dear Mimmy,
It's now definite: there's no more school. The war has interrupted our lessons, closed down the schools, sent children to cellars instead of classrooms. They'll give us the grades we got at the end of last term. So I'll get a report card saying I've finished fifth grade.
Ciao!
Zlata

ZLATA FILIPOVIĆ; *Zlata's Diary*, 1994

Nations have recently been led to borrow for war; no nation has ever borrowed largely for education. Probably no nation is rich enough to pay for both war and education. We must make our choice; we cannot have both.

ABRAHAM FLEXNER; *Universities*, 1930

Suspected Muslim fundamentalists in Algeria killed two unveiled school-girls ... marking a bloody enforcement of a vow made last month that women that do not cover their heads in public would join a long list of targets that includes the Algerian Army, police, intellectuals, artists, journalists and foreigners.

International Herald Tribune, 31 Mar. 1994

Our education, politics, and economics lead to war.

A(LEXANDER) S(UTHERLAND) NEILL; *Summerhill*, 1969

WEALTH

The love of money and the love of learning rarely meet.

ENGLISH proverb

Better to have an empty purse than an empty head.

GERMAN proverb

The universities are tied to the military-industrial complex by financial bonds that I suspect can never be broken.

PAGE SMITH; *Killing the Spirit*, 1990

Learning is more substantial than accumulated riches.

TAMIL proverb

Intelligence is not sold for money.

TURKISH proverb

Better education than wealth.

WELSH proverb

WEAPON

Mostly we see .22 pistols, little .25 automatics or .38 revolvers, but we did have one kid bring a fully loaded .357 magnum to school.

LES BURTON; *The New York Times*, 25 May 1986

In Florida, students and professors can carry . . . weapons such as Chemical Mace, stun guns, and pepper poppers (a natural, pepper-based product used like Mace).

The Chronicle of Higher Education, 7 Apr. 1993

|G|ang related murders rose above 800 in Los Angeles county, and the Los Angeles school board recently decided to make carrying a gun an expellable offence.

The Economist, 6 Feb. 1993

A Harris poll of 2,508 school children, suggests that guns are startingly common in American schools. Almost a tenth of those interviewed admitted that they had shot at someone at some time in their lives, and 11% said that they had been shot at in the past year. Nearly 40% said they knew someone who had been killed or injured by a gun, and 15% that they had carried a gun within the past 30 days.

The Economist, 24 Jul. 1993

Nowadays, five-year-old children have to be taught at school what to do if they see a gun. Don't touch, tell a grown-up. When will the grown-ups, too, learn the obvious lesson?

The Economist, 16 Oct. 1993

An estimated 100,000 students carry a gun to school, according to the National Education Association.

JON D. HULL; *Time*, 2 Aug. 1993

A Denver pawnshop ad[vertisement] mistakenly announced pistols as a "back-to-school" special, and 400 people responded.

International Herald Tribune, 23 Aug. 1993

A nation-wide group of public school administrators is asking all American secondary-school students to sign a pledge not to bring guns to class any more. The administrators, the more than 40,000 members of the National Association of Secondary School Principals, declared that firearms and other weapons "are a hazard to a safe learning environment".

International Herald Tribune, 3 Mar. 1994

Entire classrooms are already armed.

JURGEN KLEMANN; *Stern*, 18 Feb. 1993

Nowadays one cannot leave the house without a weapon.

MEHMET [15-year-old student]; *Stern*, 18 Feb. 1993

I once knew a lady who had taught in a public school in Texas, and had found it necessary always to come armed with a revolver.

BERTRAND RUSSELL; *Education and the Social Order*, 1932

One third of the older students in Berlin come to the classroom with a knife or tear gas; some bring a murderous weapon such as Asian choking sticks or a throwing star knife. More and more teachers are prematurely quitting their jobs because they can no longer handle their students' aggression.

Der Spiegel, No. 3, 1994

Metal detectors in New York schools have reduced the number of students carrying weapons and handguns, the Centers for Disease Control and Prevention said. A survey of 1,399 New York high school students found 13.6% carried weapons to school without detectors; 7.8% brought them to schools with the devices. About 4% said they carried handguns to schools without detectors; 2.1% carried them to schools with detectors.

USA Today, 15 Oct. 1993

WISDOM

Wisdom is not acquired save as the result of investigation.

SANKARA ACHARYA, 769–820

Wisdom cometh by suffering.

AESCHYLUS, 525–456

To know how to grow old is the master-work of wisdom, and one of the most difficult chapters in the great art of living.

HENRI FREDERIC AMIEL, 1821–1881

For in much wisdom *is* much grief: and he that increaseth knowledge increaseth sorrow.

The Bible (Ecclesiastes: 1,18)

Wisdom *is* the principal thing; *therefore* get wisdom: and with all thy getting get understanding.

The Bible (Proverbs: 4,7)

The road to excess leads to the palace of wisdom.

WILLIAM BLAKE; *Notebook*, 1793

The beginning of wisdom is to call things by their proper names.

CONFUCIUS (Latin for K'UNG FU-TZU), 551–479

Wisdom begins where the fear of God ends.

ANDRÉ GIDE; *Journal*, 1947

With wisdom grows doubt.

(JOHANN WOLFGANG VON) GOETHE, 1749–1832

Knowledge can be communicated but not wisdom.

HERMANN HESSE, 1877–1962

Of all our possessions wisdom alone is immortal.

ISOCRATES, 436–338

It is the height of folly to want to be the only wise one.

(FRANÇOIS DE) LA ROCHEFOUCAULD, 1613–1680

The growth of wisdom may be gauged exactly by the diminution of ill-temper.

(FRIEDRICH WILHELM) NIETZSCHE;
The Wanderer and His Shadow, 1880

Behold, my son, with what little wisdom the world is ruled.

AXEL GUSTAFSSON OXENSTIERNA, 1583–1654

Nine-tenths of wisdom is being wise in time.

THEODORE ROOSEVELT; a *speech*, 14 Jun. 1917

Youth is the time to study wisdom; old age is the time to practise it.

(JEAN JACQUES) ROUSSEAU; *Reveries of a Solitary Walker*, 1782

Wisdom comes by disillusionment.

(GEORGE) SANTAYANA, 1863–1952

More education can help us only if it produces more wisdom.

E(RNST) F(RIEDRICH) SCHUMACHER; *Small is Beautiful*, 1973

No man ever became wise by chance.

(LUCIUS ANNAEUS) SENECA (the Younger), *c.*4BC–65

Wisdom is ever a blessing; education is sometimes a curse.

JOHN A. SHEDD; *Salt from My Attic*, 1928

A short saying oft contains much wisdom.

SOPHOCLES, 496?–406

Sciences may be learned by rote, but wisdom not.

LAURENCE STERNE; *Tristram Shandy*, 1759–1767

No wise man ever wished to be younger.

JONATHAN SWIFT, 1667–1745

Knowledge comes, but wisdom lingers.

(ALFRED) TENNYSON, 1809–1892

It is a characteristic of wisdom not to do desperate things.

H(ENRY) D(AVID) THOREAU; *Walden*, 1854

Knowledge shrinks as wisdom grows.

ALFRED NORTH WHITEHEAD;
Aims of Education and Other Essays, 1929

The chief aim of wisdom is to enable one to bear with the stupidity of the ignorant.

XYSTUS [SIXTUS] I, ?–*c.*AD125

WISE

The wise learn many things from their foes.

ARISTOPHANES: *The Birds.* 414BC

Abundance of knowledge does not teach men to be wise.

HERACLITUS, *c.*540–*c.*470

It is easier to be wise on behalf of others than to be so for ourselves.

(FRANÇOIS DE) LA ROCHEFOUCAULD, 1613–1680

A wise man hears one word and understands two.

YIDDISH proverb

WOMEN

The other sex, by means of a more expensive education to the knowledge of Greek and Roman languages, have a vaster field for their imaginations to rove in, and their capacities thereby enlarged.

APHRA BEHN; *Essay in Defense of the Female Sex*, 1696

Let the woman learn in silence with all subjection. But I suffer not a woman to teach, nor to usurp authority over the man, but to be in silence.

The Bible (I Timothy: 2,11&12)

Examples of anti-women language, "jokes," and remarks in academia are depressingly abundant.

PAULA J. CAPLAN; *Lifting a Ton of Feathers*, 1993

Women graduate students are at greater risk as targets for sexual harassment than are undergraduates.

PAULA J. CAPLAN; *Lifting a Ton of Feathers*, 1993

The acceptance of women as authority figures or as role models is an important step in female education. . . . It is this process of identification, respect, and then self-respect that promotes growth.

JUDY CHICAGO; *Through the Flower*, 1975

The amount India spent . . . on an order for 20 Mig-29 fighter aircraft from Russia could have given basic schooling to the 15m girls who currently get none.

The Economist, 4 Jun. 1994

Till of late, women were kept in Turkish ignorance; every means of acquiring knowledge was discountenanced by fashion, and impracticable even to those who despised fashion. . . . Many things which were thought to be above their comprehension or unsuited to their sex, have now been found to be perfectly within the compass of their abilities, and peculiarly suited to their situation.

MARIA EDGEWORTH; *Letters of Literary Ladies*, 1795

The idea of a girl's education is whatever qualifies her for going to Europe.

RALPH WALDO EMERSON; *Conduct of Life*, 1860

That we have not made any respectable attempt to meet the special educational needs of women in the past is the clearest possible evidence of the fact that our educational objectives have been geared exclusively to the vocational patterns of men.

BETTY FRIEDAN; *The Feminine Mystique*, 1963

Even if a woman has only the name of being educated she will be evilly spoken of.

MARIE DE JARS, 1566–1645

What are we educating women for? To raise this question is to face the whole problem of women's role in society. We are uncertain about the end of women's education precisely because the status of women in our society is fraught with contradiction and confusion.

MIRRA KOMAROVSKY; *Women in the Modern World*, 1953

The sum and substance of female education in America, as in England, is training women to consider marriage as the sole object of life, and to pretend that they do not think so.

HARRIET MARTINEAU; *Society in America* (vol. III), 1837

My sex is usually forbid studies of this nature, and folly reckoned so much our proper sphere, we are sooner pardoned any excesses of that, than the least pretensions to reading or good sense. We are permitted no books but such as tend to the weakening and effeminating of the mind.

MARY WORTLEY MONTAGUE, 1689–1762

When a woman inclines to learning there is usually something wrong with her sex apparatus.

(FRIEDRICH WILHELM) NIETZSCHE, 1844–1900

The more education a woman has, the wider the gap between men's and women's earnings for the same work.

SANDRA DAY O'CONNOR, 1930–

A better understanding of women's experience would permit, even force, a far-reaching revision of the broader fields of higher education and intellectual life in the United States.

PATRICIA PALMIERI;
Harvard Educational Review, vol. 49, 1979

To become truly educated and self-aware, against the current of patriarchal education, a woman must be able to discover and explore her root connection with all women.

ADRIENNE RICH, 1929–

The whole education of women should be relative to men.

(JEAN JACQUES) ROUSSEAU; *Émile*, 1762

A woman's thoughts, beyond the range of her immediate duties, should be directed to the study of men, or the acquirement of that agreeable learning whose sole end is the formation of taste; for the works of genius are beyond her reach, and she has neither the accuracy nor the attention for success in the exact science.

(JEAN JACQUES) ROUSSEAU; *Émile*, 1762

Because research on women is perceived as being outside of mainstream, biased, political, unimportant, and/or inaccurate, women whose interests and work lie in this area are at an obvious disadvantage in being published.

ANGELA SIMEONE; *Academic Women*, 1987

Give me a girl at an impressionable age, and she is mine for life.

MURIEL SPARK; *The Prime of Miss Jean Brodie*, 1961

While on the one hand women have achieved some success in gaining entry to education, it is entry to men's education and it serves to reinforce male supremacy and control in our society.

DALE SPENDER; *Invisible Women*, 1982

Women are wiser than men because they know less and understand more.

JAMES STEPHENS; *The Crock of Gold*, 1930

A female professor of mathematics is a pernicious and unpleasant phenomenon – even one might say, a monstrosity; and her invitation to a country where there are so many male mathematicians far superior in learning to her can be explained only by the gallantry of the Swedes toward the female sex.

AUGUST STRINDBERG, 1849–1912

Every effort has been made towards the encouragement . . . of independent work and independent thought. The time is fast coming when such qualities will be needed in our women, as they are called for in men, and education which only encourages reliance on teachers and dependence on others is the education which comes to an end as soon as the gates of the school are passed.

UME(KO) TSUDA, 1865–1929

Japan can never really progress so long as her growth is all on one side, and while one half of her people are pushed forward, the other half are kept back. I have felt that not until the women were elevated and educated, could Japan really take a high stand.

UME(KO) TSUDA, 1865–1929

Uneducated clever women, who have seen much of the world, are in middle life so much the most cultured part of the community. They have been saved from the horrible burden of inert ideas.

ALFRED NORTH WHITEHEAD, 1861–1947

Women's studies are kept on the margins of the curriculum, and fewer than 5 percent of professors are women; the worldview taught young women is male.

NAOMI WOLF; *The Beauty Myth*, 1990

The programs of schools, colleges, and vocational and professional training institutions ought to accommodate a plurality of women's life plans, combining childbearing and child-rearing with other activities. They should not assume that there is a single appropriate time to bear and rear children. No woman should be disadvantaged in her education and employment opportunities because she has children at age fifteen, twenty-five, thirty-five, or forty-five (for the most part, education and job structures are currently such that each of these ages is the "wrong time").

IRIS MARION YOUNG; *Dissent*, Winter, 1994
[italics in original]

WONDER

The chief wonder of education is that it does not ruin everybody concerned in it, teachers and taught.

HENRY (BROOKS) ADAMS;
The Education of Henry Adams, 1907

The longer the island of knowledge the longer the shoreline of wonder.
RALPH W. SOCKMAN, 1889–1970

Philosophy is the product of wonder.
ALFRED NORTH WHITEHEAD, 1861–1947

WORD

The investigation of the meaning of words is the beginning of education.
ANTISTHENES, *c*.445–*c*.360

Words are all we have.
SAMUEL BECKETT, 1906–89

Words are the clothes that thoughts wear – only the clothes.
SAMUEL BUTLER, 1835–1902

Be not the slave of words.
THOMAS CARLYLE; *Sartor Resartus*, 1831

We are students of words: we are shut up in schools and college recitation rooms for ten or fifteen years, and come out at last with a bag of wind, a memory of words, and do not know a thing.
RALPH WALDO EMERSON, 1803–1882

In fact, words are well adapted for description and arousing of emotions, but for many kinds of precise thought other symbols are much better.
J(OHN) B(URDON) S(ANDERSON) HALDANE, 1892–1964

Words are the only things that last forever.
WILLIAM HAZLITT; *Table Talk*, 1821–2

Words are, of course, the most powerful drug used by mankind.
RUDYARD KIPLING, 1865–1936

We think because we have words, not the other way around. The more words we have, the better able we are to think conceptually.
MADELEINE L'ENGLE; *Walking on Water*, 1980

Nothing is more common than for men to think that because they are familiar with words they understand the ideas they stand for.

JOHN HENRY NEWMAN, 1801–1890

Words are loaded pistols.

(JEAN-PAUL) SARTRE, 1905–1980

One forgets words as one forgets names. One's vocabulary needs constant fertilisation or it will die.

EVELYN WAUGH, 1903–1966

The meaning of a word is its usage.

(LUDWIG JOSEF JOHANN) WITTGENSTEIN, 1889–1951

WORLD

Give me a firm place to stand on, and I will move the earth.

ARCHIMEDES, *c.*287–212

What makes a company world class is its people. That's really what differentiates you from the other companies. What makes people world class is a world class education.

SANDRO CONTENTA; *The Toronto Star*, 9 May 1987

They go forth into it [the world] with well-developed bodies, fairly developed minds, and undeveloped hearts.

E(DWARD) M(ORGAN) FORSTER, 1879–1970

By reason only can we attain to a correct knowledge of the world and a solution of its great problems.

ERNST HEINRICH HAECKEL; *The Riddle of the Universe*, 1899

A man in this world without learning is as a beast in the field.

*The Hitopadesa, c.*500

Teenagers go to college to be with their boyfriends and girlfriends; they go because they can't think of anything else to do; they go because their parents want them to and sometimes because their parents don't want them to; they go to find themselves, or to find a husband, or to get away from home, and sometimes even to find out about the world in which they live.

HAROLD HOWE; *Newsweek*, 26 Apr. 1976

If we would have new knowledge, we must get a whole world of new questions.

SUSANNE K. LANGER; *Philosophy in a New Key*, 1942

We keep pretending we are sending students out into a world where things are logical and predictable, but the only time things are predictable are in the classroom.

NORAH MAIER; *The Toronto Star*, 10 May 1987

The philosophers have only interpreted the world in various ways; the point is to change it.

KARL MARX; *Theses on Feuerbach*, 1888

A truly valuable education helps children make sense of their world. Dividing schools into disciplines fails to prepare kids for the untidiness of life.

ROLAND MEIGHAN;
Theory and Practice of Regressive Education, 1993

Even at our best schools we are preparing young people for a world they won't live in.

JOHN SCULLEY, 1939–

WRITE

Who cannot limit himself can never be able to write.

NICOLAS BOILEAU-DESPÉREAUX; *L'Art poétique*, 1674

Write quickly and you will never write well, write well and you will soon write quickly.

(MARCUS FABIUS) QUINTILIAN(US), *c*.35–*c*.95

Charlemagne could not write.

HUGH THOMAS; *An Unfinished History of the World*, 1979

WRITER

It is by sitting down to write every morning that one becomes a writer.
GERALD BRENAN; *Thoughts in a Dry Season*, 1978

An original writer is not one who imitates no one, but whom no one can imitate.
(FRANÇOIS-RENÉ) CHATEAUBRIAND, 1768–1848

The world's writers are not in the academy, and they do not draw their values from it.
GEORGE H. DOUGLAS; *Education Without Impact*, 1992

Talent alone cannot make a writer. There must be a man behind the book.
RALPH WALDO EMERSON, 1803–1882

If you wish to be a writer, write.
EPICTETUS, *c.*50–120

Did you ever stop to think that a writer will spend three years, or many more, on a book that the average reader will skim through in a few hours.
ELLEN GLASGOW; *Letters of Ellen Glasgow*, 1958

Every great writer is a great reformer.
WALTER SAVAGE LANDOR;
Imaginary Conversations, 1824–9

Our principal writers have nearly all been fortunate in escaping regular education.
HUGH MACDIARMID; *The Observer*, 29 Mar. 1953

Only a mediocre writer is always at his best.
W(ILLIAM) SOMERSET MAUGHAM, 1874–1965

The writer is the Faust of modern society, the only surviving individualist in a mass age. To his orthodox contemporaries he seems a semi-madman.
(BORIS) PASTERNAK; *The Observer*, 20 Dec. 1959

For a country to have a great writer is like having a second government. That is why no regime has ever loved great writers, only minor ones.

(ALEXANDER) SOLZHENITSYN; *The First Circle*, 1964

American writers want to be not good but great; and so are neither.

GORE VIDAL (né EUGENE LUTHER VIDAL), 1925–

WRITING

The primary art is writing.

SAMUEL TAYLOR COLERIDGE; *On Posey and Art*, 1818

The best way to become acquainted with a subject is to write a book about it.

BENJAMIN DISRAELI, 1804–1881

Writing is busy idleness.

(JOHANN WOLFGANG VON) GOETHE, 1749–1832

Sound sense is the first principle and source of writing.

(QUINTUS HORATIUS FLACCUS) HORACE, 65–8

Writing is thinking.

ANNE MORROW LINDBERG; *Locked Rooms and Open Doors*, 1974

There are three basic rules about writing; unfortunately no one remembers what they are.

W(ILLIAM) SOMERSET MAUGHAM, 1874–1965

Whatever is clearly expressed is well wrote.

MARY WORTLEY MONTAGUE, 1689–1762

I suppose I have written novels to find out what I *thought* about something and poems to find out what I *felt* about something.

MAY SARTON; *Journal of a Solitude*, 1973

In composing, as a general rule, run your pen through every other word you have written; you have no idea what vigour it will give your style.

SYDNEY SMITH, 1771–1845

Writing is how we define ourselves for someone we don't get to meet.
RICHARD SAUL WURMAN; *Information Anxiety*, 1991

Writing organizes and clarifies our thoughts. Writing is how we think our way into a subject and make it our own. Writing enables us to find out what we know – and what we don't know – about whatever we're trying to learn.
WILLIAM ZINSSER; *Writing to Learn*, 1988

X

XENOCRATES

Xenocrates [c.395–314] would have no mistress but philosophy.

WILL(IAM) (JAMES) DURANT;
The Story of Civilization (vol. II), 1939

He [Xenocrates] wrote prolifically on natural science, astronomy and philosophy but only fragments of this output survive. He generally systematized and continued the Platonic tradition but seems to have had a particular devotion to threefold categories, perhaps reflecting a Pythagorean influence: philosophy is subdivided into logic, ethics and physics; reality is divided into the objects of sensation, belief and knowledge; he distinguished gods, men and demons; he also probably originated the classical distinction between mind, body and soul.

MAGNUS MAGNUSSON;
Chambers Biographical Dictionary, 1990

He [Xenocrates] is not a man but a statue.

PHYRNE;
Teachings, and Sayings of Famous Philosophers, c.300BC

XENOPHOBIA

Everyone's quick to blame the alien.

AESCHYLUS; *The Suppliant Maidens*, c.460BC

Modern man is educated to understand foreign languages and misunderstand foreigners.

G(ILBERT) K(EITH) CHESTERTON, 1874–1936

We must combat xenophobia and learn to appreciate our own culture without automatically disparaging other cultures and systems of values and creating enemy stereotypes.

MYRIAM MIEDZIAN; *Boys Will Be Boys*, 1991

Man is not man but a wolf, to those he does not know.

(TITUS MACCIUS) PLAUTUS, 254–184

He will deal harshly by a stranger who has not been himself a traveller and stranger.

SA'DI; *Rose Garden, c.*1258

XEROXING (Photocopying)

Copying has become a national disease.

DONALD G. ADAMS; *Newsweek,* 7 Sep. 1964

Today photocopying technology has given the public, both individuals and organizations which serve the public, facilities for making copies of published copyright material in vast quantities and at minimal cost.

BRITISH COPYRIGHT COUNCIL;
Reprographic Copying of Books and Journals, 1985

Y

YOKE

It is good for a man that he bear the yoke in his youth.

The Bible (Lamentations: 3,27)

The field of one's PhD – nay, not only the broader field, but the narrow area of emphasis – becomes the yoke the professor must wear for a lifetime.

GEORGE H. DOUGLAS; *Education Without Impact*, 1992

No process of humanity is possible unless it shakes off the yoke of authority and tradition.

ANDRÉ GIDE; *Journal*, 1947

[T]he Government seems to feel that schoolchildren should still experience learning to read and calculate as essentially functional disciplines which are important in the National Curriculum, not for the pleasures they bring but only for the yoke which they place on the pupils' shoulders.

CHRIS SHUTE; *Compulsory Schooling Disease*, 1993

YOUTH

Young people need confidence in the basics of the 21st century: extended literacy, a strong knowledge of all human endeavour, a global perspective, the ability to learn and re-learn, to think creatively as well as critically, and the self-esteem necessary to make use of all these. A society in which this does not happen will be economically weak, socially unstable and politically impoverished.

MICHAEL BARBER;
The Times Higher Education Supplement, 5 Nov. 1993

Youth is a disease that must be borne with patiently! Time, indeed, will cure it.

R(OBERT) H(UGH) BENSON, 1871–1914

Youth is something very new; twenty years ago no one mentioned it.

COCO CHANEL (née GABRIELLE BONHEUR CHANEL),
1883–1971

Youth is a period of missed opportunities.

CYRIL CONNOLLY, 1903–1974

In youth we learn; in age we understand.

MARIE VON EBNER-ESCHENBACH; *Aphorisms*, 1905

Youth and white paper take any impression.

ENGLISH proverb

A violently active, dominating, intrepid, brutal youth – that is what I am after . . . I will have no intellectual training.

(ADOLF) HITLER, 1889–1945

Young people are thoughtless as a rule.

HOMER, *c*.900–*c*.800

Youth easily grows old yet becomes learned with difficulty.

JAPANESE proverb

Youth is a continual intoxication; it is the fever of reason.

(FRANÇOIS DE) LA ROCHEFOUCAULD, 1613–1680

Youth is a malady of which one becomes cured a little every day.

(BENITO) MUSSOLINI, 1893–1945

Youth is a mortal wound.

KATHERINE PATERSON; *Jacob Have I Loved*, 1980

Leave thine home, O youth, and seek out alien shores; a larger range of life is ordained for thee.

(GAIUS) PETRONIUS (ARBITER), *c*.26–66

It takes a very long time to become young.

(PABLO RUIZ) PICASSO, 1881–1973

I would there were no age between ten and three-and-twenty, or that youth would sleep out the rest; for there is nothing in the between but getting wenches with child, wronging the ancientry, stealing, fighting.

WILLIAM SHAKESPEARE; *The Winter's Tale*, 1610–11

Youth is a wonderful thing; what a crime to waste it on children.

GEORGE BERNARD SHAW, 1856–1950

The right way to begin is to pay attention to the young, and make them just as good as possible.

SOCRATES, 470?–399

Youthful education will prove beneficial.

TAMIL proverb

Alas, poor youth! If only you could escape your harsh fate!

(PUBLIUS) VERGIL(IUS MARO), 70–19
[spelt Vergil or Virgil in English]

You are only young once. At the time it seems endless, and is gone in a flash; and then for a very long time you are old.

SYLVIA TOWNSEND WARNER;
Swans on an Autumn River, 1966

A young man is so strong, so mad, so certain, and so lost. He has everything and he is able to use nothing.

T(H)OM(AS) (CLAYTON) WOLFE; *Of Time and the River*, 1935

Z

(MISCELLANEOUS)

The highest aim of poetry and art is to integrate the individual into inner growth and outer adjustment.

MULK RAJ ANAND, 1905–

Eureka!

ARCHIMEDES, *c.*287–212
[Greek for "I have discovered it!"]

To perceive is to suffer.

ARISTOTLE, 384–322

Reading maketh a full man; conference a ready man; and writing an exact man.

FRANCIS BACON, 1561–1626

Histories make men wise; poets witty; the mathematics subtle; natural philosophy deep; moral grave; logic and rhetoric able to contend.

FRANCIS BACON, 1561–1626

Ignorance is content to stand still, with her back to the truth; but error is more presumptuous, and proceeds in the wrong direction. Ignorance has no light, but error follows a false one.

C(HARLES) C(ALEB) COLTON, 1780?–1832

I hear I forget, I see I remember, I do I understand.

CONFUCIUS (Latin for K'UNG FU-TZU), 551–479

[H]e who learns but does not think, is lost! He who thinks but does not learn is in great danger!

CONFUCIUS (Latin for K'UNG FU-TZU), 551–479

Whatever is, is right.

DEMOCRITUS, 460?–370?

[A] smattering of everything, and a knowledge of nothing.

CHARLES DICKENS, 1812–1870

The only good is knowledge, and the only evil is ignorance.

DIOGENES LÄERTIUS, c.100–c.200

It is the trained, living human soul, cultivated and strengthened by long study and thought that breathes the real breath of life into boys and girls and makes them human, whether they be black or white, Greek, Russian, or American.

W(ILLIAM) E(DWARD) B(URGHARDT) DU BOIS;
The Negro Problem, 1903

Zeal without knowledge is the sister of folly.

ENGLISH proverb

Zoology was formerly the handmaiden of ethics. Animals were studied not to observe their actual characteristics but to find moral examples in their nature or behavior.

BERGEN EVANS; *The Natural History of Nonsense,* 1946

Time is the father of truth, and experience is the mother of all things.

JOHN FLORIO; *First Flutes,* 1578

Life is short the art long [to learn], opportunity fugitive, experimenting dangerous, reasoning difficult.

HIPPOCRATES, *c.*460–*c.*370
[The quotation is usually abbreviated and
given in Latin as "*Ars longa, vita brevis*".]

I'm bilingual. I speak English and I speak educationese.

SHIRLEY M. HUFSTEDLER, 1926–

Once you have the cap and gown all you need do is, open your mouth. Whatever nonsense you talk becomes wisdom and all the rubbish, good sense.

MOLIÈRE (né JEAN-BAPTISTE POQUELIN), 1622–1673

We're drowning in information and starving for knowledge.

RUTHERFORD D. ROGERS; *The New York Times,* 25 Feb. 1985

You will more easily stamp out intelligence and learning than recall them.

(PUBLIUS CORNELIUS) TACITUS, *c.*55–117

The history of the race, and each individual's experience, are thick with evidence that a truth is not hard to kill and that a lie told well is immortal.

MARK TWAIN (pseud. of SAMUEL LANGHORNE CLEMENS),
1835–1910

Epilogue

After reading through this encyclopaedia it is anticipated that several quotations have spoken intensely to you, while others linger in the mind requiring further reflection. And if you have found quotations from the sublime to the ridiculous, or if you feel tension within yourself, then this work demonstrates its objectivity. Any compilation of quotations that only placates and panders to its readers cannot make a legitimate claim to being objective; at least in part. Because if a narrow and one-sided view is presented, readers are only given a subjective and biased perspective; not the big polychrome picture of reality.

Forgiveness is requested, however, if you have reached these final pages and found that a favoured author, work or quotation whom or which you consider relevant to education has not been included. There can be no definitive collection of quotations, just as Samuel Johnson stated: "No dictionary of a living tongue even can be perfect ...". Some old words and thoughts are slipping into obscurity, while other new ones are slowly becoming part of contemporary life and literature; and adopting an international perspective, as was done for this compilation, also means that a quotation that is well known in one country may be quite unknown in another.

You are no doubt aware of some of the challenges associated with the preparation of a work such as this. The flood of new publications that pour into the marketplace each day set limitations on any person's time; library shelves seem to be without end; time is constantly in short supply; and responsibilities are always abundant.

The subject of education itself is a deceptive thing that on analysis reveals a perplexing array of aspects, components, concepts, curricula, goals, meanings, objectives, politics, purposes, systems, values, et cetera. Education is not a simple subject, as the naive all too readily believe.

If there is some way this work can be improved, or if there is an author (please remember some authors are eminent but not eminently quotable), work or quotation you believe ought to be considered for inclusion in subsequent editions of this encyclopaedia, your advice would be gratefully received.

Many thanks

Keith Allan Noble
Neydhartinger Strasse 2b
61381 Friedrichsdorf
Germany

Author index

Compiler

A native of Australia, Keith Allan Noble now resides in Germany. For many years he lived in Canada where he completed a PhD at the University of Ottawa; the results of this international research were published by Open University Press (*Changing Doctoral Degrees*). His writing focuses primarily on business, education and health.